The Politics of Consultation

The
Politics of
Consultation

The
Consultation
Institute

Rhion Jones
Elizabeth Gammell

The Consultation Institute

The Consultation Institute is the global authority on best practice public consultation. A not-for-profit membership organisation based in the United Kingdom, the Institute brings together leading experts and skilled practitioners to formulate ideas and provide thought leadership. The Institute has been driving standards and providing solutions that give consultors confidence since 2003.

First published in Great Britain in 2018 by
The Consultation Institute
Station Road
Biggleswade
Bedfordshire
SG18 8AL

ISBN 978-1717016713

10 9 8 7 6 5 4 3 2 1

This book is dedicated to the Directors, Staff, Associates and Members of the Consultation Institute.

Contents

Preface   xi

Rationale   xiii

Part One: The Changing Landscape

Chapter 1:   Introduction: Vote for me!   3

Chapter 2:   Why politicians should consult   15

Chapter 3:   The legal framework   31

Part Two: The Role of Consultation in Politics

Chapter 4:   Introduction: Beyond tokenism?   59

Chapter 5:   Consultation and planning   69

Chapter 6:   Consultation and health   101

Chapter 7:   Consultation and government   143

Part Three: The Influence of Politics on Consultation

Chapter 8:   Introduction: Is anyone in charge?   173

Chapter 9:   How political timing affects consultation   193

Chapter 10:   The community's influence on   209
              consultation

Chapter 11:   The influence of business on consultation   223

Part Four: Where Next?
The Challenges Faced by Consultation

Chapter 12:   Introduction: Revisiting the rationale   247

Chapter 13:   What consultation must combat   259

Chapter 14:   Improving consultations: three duties for   271
              consultors

Chapter 15:   Improving dialogue: three rights for   291
              consultees

Chapter 16:   Is there a better way?   321

Chapter 17:   Dear Politician...   343

Last words   371

Index   377

Preface

This book is a commentary on aspects of democracy which are rarely considered. It illustrates current practice and explores important issues that will resonate with anyone interested in public affairs, policy-making and democratic institutions.

Our experience with the Consultation Institute has given us unique insights into the day-to-day activities of thousands of public servants who organise consultations in the UK. We have simultaneously been able to observe the machinery of government and the impact of politics on the process. We therefore hope to provide food for thought for anyone concerned with the health of our democracy. They may be academics and students of politics or public policy. They may be campaigners, or members of pressure groups or communities of interest. Or they may be active politicians in the council chamber or in Parliament. For all, there are stories and case studies which illuminate the fascinating world of political decision-making.

In Part One we describe the ever-changing landscape and the context within which public consultations take place. We also outline the legal framework which underpins this activity. In Part Two we illustrate the role of consultation by exploring its use in town planning and health, as well as in national and local government. In Part Three we recognise how politics affects the way in which consultation operates and Part Four explores the challenges faced by consultations.

Throughout this analysis we have drawn upon the experience of the Consultation Institute and its many Associates. We are indebted to their support and that of the individuals and organisations who are Members of the Institute. Collectively they have witnessed thousands of public consultations and contributed mightily to the specialist know-how that supports this work.

We are grateful to Quintin Oliver, John Underwood, Barry Creasy, Wendy Berliner and Penny Norton who patiently offered their thoughts and reflections on early drafts of chapters, sections, or the whole book.

Thank you to Jonathan Wadman for expertly editing our manuscript and to Siân Elmslie for her diligence and attention to detail in proofreading and indexing our work.

And we'd like to acknowledge the support Paul Parsons has given the Institute in producing and publishing this book.

Special thanks and love to Lesley Jones, Alistair Gammell and our growing families for their understanding and support during the writing of this book.

Rationale

Public consultation is a fact of modern life, as a wide variety of organisations purport to listen to the views of citizens, customers or other stakeholders.* In our first book, *The Art of Consultation*,† we explored the phenomenon, what goes right and, sadly, what all too often goes wrong. We even tried to chart the future of consultation, but looking back it strikes us as little short of amazing how quickly things are changing. Our own epiphany was the realisation that learning about the skills and techniques of consultation was comparatively straightforward compared to the complexities and challenges of getting to grips with the politics.

So, this book is about the relationship between the world of politics and the processes of consultation. Without delving into the philosophical bedrock of political science, we have taken the term to refer to the application of power in human affairs – particularly in determining and implementing public policies. We are conscious of the variety of political structures that are found across the globe, but our focus is on democratic countries, the role of elected representatives and the way in which they work with officials and with civic and civil society.

Politics in the UK and in other mature democracies is suffering a bad press. Disillusion and distrust have provoked a serious crisis of confidence in established institutions, and politicians have become the unpopular objects of many citizens' contempt.

---

* A stakeholder is anybody who has an interest in or will be affected by an organisation, strategy or project.

† Rhion Jones and Elizabeth Gammell, *The Art of Consultation* (London: Biteback, 2009).

Young people are believed to be pretty indifferent to traditional ways of expressing their views; visiting a polling station on Election Day is not seen as the accepted civic duty it once was.* It is in this context that we look at the various practices that constitute public consultation.

We are acutely aware that there are many descriptions of consultation and even governments have mistakenly characterised it just as the art of listening. The Consultation Institute,† which we founded in 2003, has defined consultation as 'the dynamic process of dialogue between individuals or groups, based upon a genuine exchange of views with the objective of influencing decisions, policies or programmes of action'. For the purposes of this book, that will remain our definition.

But in the same way that politics is to an extent discredited, so is consultation. Both seem to have been contaminated by sufficiently poor practice as to encourage detractors in droves. So our first task in this work is to explain why politics and consultation are, in fact, closely related and how the demands made upon contemporary public life drive us towards finding better and more meaningful ways to hold relevant dialogues. We hope to show that the role of consultation in politics is inevitable

---

* Contrary to the popular perception that youth turnout in the 2017 UK general election rose significantly, it is now known that the increase was marginal. The British Election Survey, in a research paper 'Tremors but no Youthquake', revealed the actual rise in turnout came from those in their late twenties and thirties.

† Founded in 2003, the Consultation Institute is a well-established not-for-profit *best practice* Institute, promoting high-quality public and stakeholder consultation in the public, private and voluntary sectors. It is a membership body, offering an innovative range of support services and training for any person or organisation with an interest in public dialogue, engagement and participation.

and poses fascinating challenges for so many who are active in political processes. Our second task is to try to understand the role of politics in consultation: how often the dynamics of political activity affects the integrity and the effectiveness of the consultative process.

These are two symbiotic perspectives on the same fundamental problem: namely, to what extent have politicians learnt how best to use the immense potential of a more consultative approach to governing advanced societies and taking decisions in the name of the people?

Our conclusions are uncomfortable. We see much confusion and a lot of uncertainty in the ways in which politicians and civil servants handle consultation; we see it at every level from the parish pump upwards. We see a dubious populace driven towards even greater scepticism when they suspect politicians and other public bodies of mass manipulation. This is despite the best of our body politic genuinely wishing to engage with citizens and despite millions of those same citizens being eager to participate in dialogue. If only the one group could learn to work successfully with the other...

An early critic of *The Art of Consultation* complained that we relied too much on anecdotes and stories, rather than theoretical analysis. We make no apology. Thousands of public consultations happen every year in the UK and in the absence of the academic research that is sorely needed on this subject, the best we can do is to observe the practice of politicians and public and seek to draw the most reasonable conclusions we can.

The truth is that the future is more, not less consultative. For reasons we advance in the final part of this book, unless governments, parliaments, councils and bureaucrats get better at engaging with the public, democratic values will be in jeopardy. Learning to listen will be the core skill for the next generation of leaders. For citizens, the concomitant attribute is learning to be heard.

Explanatory note:

Throughout this book we have used the term consultor to describe an organisation that undertakes a consultation. We use the term consultee to describe individuals or organisations who respond to, or participate in, such consultations.

Part One
The Changing Landscape

Chapter 1 – Introduction

Vote for me!

The politicians' dilemma | national, local and devolved politics | international perspective | is the UK the world leader in consultation?

Imagine the scene…

It may be the twenty-first century, but we still have a loudspeaker van touring the more marginal parts of a British constituency. True, this is a somewhat dated throwback to an ancient ritual. Pollsters tell us that minds were made up when the politicians strutted their stuff in the TV debates. But rumour has it that local candidates for the Mother of Parliaments still like to be heard in person. So on the eve of poll, your party hopeful, exhausted by weeks of door-knocking and hoarse from ceaseless campaigning, still has one more evening of exhortation.

'Vote for me,' they say.

Then follows the script: the same, barely changed version of the truth dictated from on high, repeated *ad nauseam*. All the reasons why their party knows best and will do best. All the jibes and barbs that remind the faithful why they hate the others.

What you would probably not have heard, until the general election of 2017, are the words 'Vote for me… and I will hold a public consultation.' We suddenly sat up, as Theresa May, finding herself embarrassed by an unpopular commitment on the ever-rising cost of providing social care for the elderly, sought to recover her position by declaring that *of course there would be consultation before this thorny issue was settled.*

Elections favour those with certainty in their souls. We expect our future leaders to know what they believe and to admit of few doubts. It's probably rather like religion. Worshipping in the church of the doubtful sounds a little tentative. One of the reasons for going there is to hear the clarion call of those whose lien on righteousness cannot be denied. The politician who admits of too many uncertainties is a bit of a rarity.

Paradoxically, many of our most impressive leaders have wavered and worried. The polls that regularly anoint Churchill as Britain's greatest ever prime minister seldom concede that his career was one of a turncoat and vacillator open to self-doubt and depression. The 2018 film *Darkest Hour* even, implausibly, showed him inexpertly facilitating a focus group on the District line. Others in high office have admitted to insecurities. Even Margaret Thatcher is known for hesitations that the popular press has kindly overlooked.

The traditional picture of a politician asking for votes is, therefore, one of a confident, dependable potential tribune of the people, who can be trusted to support the answers known to his or her party as being absolutely right for the country. 'Vote for me… we know the answers.'

Except it's all changing.

The public has moved on. Its lack of faith in politicians now extends to believing none of them. Its understanding of the ways of the world has also changed. It no longer believes that the issues of the moment are capable of answers – let alone by one political party. If any politician tries the phrase 'We know the answers', a hollow laugh can be confidently expected to follow.

Add to this the catastrophic loss of reputation arising from the furore that enveloped MPs over their expenses. Then also add the collateral damage suffered by all those in public office when lies and obfuscation surfaced in so many public scandals: Hillsborough, Mid-Staffordshire, Harold Shipman, Jimmy Savile, Grenfell Tower – even the Leveson and Chilcot inquiries.* All have served to undermine public confidence in what is frequently called the *body politic.* There is much debate as to the long-term consequences, but for our purposes what matters is that the once unquestioned authority of politicians has largely evaporated.

The malaise is not universal. There are popular politicians and much evidence that local MPs are often far more respected than either their parties or the system as a whole. What confidence is still held in those who stand for election is derived less from their status and more from their individual personalities, their prime-

---

* Hillsborough refers to the deaths at a Sheffield football stadium of ninety-six people in 1989. Mid-Staffordshire refers to an inquiry into failures at an NHS hospital in 2013. Harold Shipman was a doctor convicted in 2000 of killing large numbers of his patients, exposing failures in the NHS. Jimmy Savile was a popular entertainer posthumously exposed in 2012 as a serial paedophile. Grenfell Tower refers to the death in a fire of seventy-two residents of a London tower block in June 2017. The Leveson inquiry (2011–12) was a judicial public inquiry into the culture, practices and ethics of the British press. The Chilcot inquiry (2009–16) considered the role of the UK in the 2003 Iraq War.

time TV exposure or their track records on local issues. For every Farage, Sturgeon, Corbyn or Johnson* there are dozens of lower-key non-celebs whose public persona commands somewhat less attention.

All of this is terribly unfair. It reflects the vicious circle affecting the British Parliament whereby it no longer attracts the brightest and the best and they in turn no longer have the arrogance and self-belief that once was the politician's hallmark. Taken together all these developments paint a picture of a system that lacks the self-confidence it once possessed. In short, one of the established pillars of British democracy is creaking and we are at that point where smart people realise that it is time to stop pretending that they can ask for endorsement by saying 'Vote for me… we know the answers.'

Local government is hardly healthier. Oppositions at Westminster regularly promise that they will reverse the long-term British penchant for centralisation. But when they reach government, they rarely do much to change things. The 2010 coalition spoke lovingly of localism but delivered less than it promised. Few councillors admit to having been re-empowered, even though new laws gave them a clutch of fresh powers. The average age of English councillors is over sixty and the turnout statistics for local elections make quite depressing reading.

Councils have faced massive expenditure cuts since the banking crisis of 2008 and are squeezed by the need to maintain funding for social care, schools and children's services, leaving historic

---

* Nigel Farage was the Leader of UKIP (United Kingdom Independence Party) from 2006 to 2009 and from 2010 to 2016. Nicola Sturgeon has served as First Minister of Scotland since 2014. Jeremy Corbyn became leader of the Labour Party in 2015. Boris Johnson was Mayor of London from 2008 to 2016 and has been Foreign Secretary since 2016.

shortfalls elsewhere. It is hardly surprising that candidates for council wards are scarcely queuing up to stand for election. Councillors' most visible role has become taking difficult financial decisions and having to justify to their voters why once-cherished services, like libraries, are facing the axe.

Unlike national politicians, however, the local variety have never claimed much omnipotence and their style has consistently been more consultative. Our major cities have a long tradition of municipal pride and although the nineteenth-century model has long disappeared, it is notable that the sporadic debate about regional devolution in England has sparked a degree of interest in city-regions. The idea of there being a local identity and that policies and activities could be given a local flavour comes naturally to some parts of the country. To make this happen councillors have for generations taken to consult and engage with local people. Size makes it easier. A city such as Leeds is over half a million people in a larger conurbation of about 1.8 million – big enough to be a viable socio-economic and political unit but small enough for stakeholders to be known and for dialogues to be manageable.

In a pattern we will see repeated again and again, one of the 2010– 15 coalition government's less endearing characteristics was to demand of local government somewhat better public consultation than it undertook itself. The best example is the transfer to local authorities in England of responsibility for council tax benefit in 2012. Instead of a single national scheme, the administration that committed itself to reduce the burden of bureaucracy contrived to replace it with no fewer than 300 local schemes, each to be run by the local top-tier council. Before being too critical, we should acknowledge that this was indeed devolution from the centre and no doubt ministers would have claimed to be responding to demands for more power in local hands. It was, however, a poisoned chalice. The amount of money available for those who qualified for reductions in council tax was cut by 10 per cent. Legislation demanded that local schemes were barred from penalising pensioners and had to promote working for a living. In practice most councils had 18 per cent less cash with which to subsidise the least well off in their areas.

Now it is firmly outside the scope of this book to pass comment on the rights and wrongs of government policies; our focus lies elsewhere. What makes this tale of welfare woe interesting is the role played by consultation. In this case Parliament required each and every council to conduct a full-scale public consultation exercise as part of agreeing its local scheme. MPs and peers effectively threw down the gauntlet to local leaders, suggesting, in effect, that 'this is going to be a difficult decision whatever you do', and urging them to secure as much consensus as possible behind the new arrangements.

To their great credit, most local authority members and their officers undertook this thankless task with commendable grace and many made the best they could of a bad job. In one important respect, it led to a key legal judgment when the London Borough of Haringey failed to defend a legal challenge alleging that its consultation had been unfair. After a closely fought contest in the High Court, the case went to the Court of Appeal with local residents arguing that the council had failed to place before them the full range of options it had available when defining the local scheme. They lost. But in the Supreme Court,* the judgment was reversed and the law took a substantial step forward towards requiring public bodies to consult in a particular way.

---

* R (*ex parte* Moseley) *v* Haringey LB [2014] UKSC 56.

This turn of events illustrates perfectly what has been happening to our national politicians when they seek to reform public services as they are delivered on the ground. They saw a great opportunity to appeal to people's sense of local identity. By requiring councillors and managers to engage and consult at every turn, they sought to align these services with local preferences.

We see this across the board. The National Health Service, well before Andrew Lansley's 2011 reorganisation, imposed demanding consultative processes on its managers. Duties to consult local people that were part of the regime of police authorities were carried forward to police and crime commissioners. Educational policy has for years called for the proper consultation of parents and governors before changes are made to schools.

None of this is wrong; indeed much is to be warmly commended. But it also betrays more than a whiff of 'do as I say, not as I do'. Fundamentally, politicians are better at telling other people to consult than they are at doing it themselves. It is as well that the honourable tradition of local government in the UK finds it possible to engage quite effectively with local communities, no matter what deprivations it suffers at the hands of our centralist tendencies.

Might we find more coherence in the political system if we look beyond Westminster?

The devolved administrations in Edinburgh, Belfast and Cardiff all set out to be better at public consultation. When they began, they had a long list of new policies to adopt and an eagerness to strike out in different directions. They all adopted rather more comprehensive guidelines than the UK government and were quicker off the mark in publishing consultation documents on the internet.

There were impressive numbers of public consultations, especially in Scotland, but as in England, civil servants mostly ran them as part of a bureaucratic policy-making process. We will examine these in some detail, as they play an important role in our politics. But, once again we seldom witness a genuine dialogue between politicians themselves and stakeholder communities. What we see are interactions of variable quality between the political machine and the rest of society. It is not an easy interface and no one in Scotland, Northern Ireland or Wales can claim to have made a significant breakthrough in understanding how to make it work better.

So can we see anything better elsewhere? We met some Eurocrats, part of the Brussels machinery, responsible for organising the vast numbers of consultative papers that circulate around the countries of the *ever-closer union*! In theory the EU is an overwhelming vortex of policy proposals, consultations, amendments and a range of dialogues that would baffle a boffin, but in practice it is a largely closed system feeding on itself more than engaging external bodies and interest groups, save in the time-honoured style of pork-barrel lobbying and counter-lobbying.

Our friendly Eurocrats came to the UK, as do others from overseas because, in spite of our national self-deprecating sense of occasional inadequacy, there is evidence that we have the most developed consultative culture in the world. Apparently, we contrive to involve and engage people more successfully here than anywhere else on the planet. We cannot be sure this is true.

There is little or no academic research and our own insights are largely anecdotal.

A few years ago, a well-known pundit, working for a top market research firm, undertook a round-the-world trip. The aim was to gauge the state of the art in this and related disciplines. He returned and confirmed what others had said – that the UK was far more committed than other nations to the principle of public consultation. We might not be particularly good at it, but at least we give it a go. It sparked off an interesting review of global political cultures: how the Europeans profess to consult as an article of their *communautaire* faith; how it is a particular challenge to the ex-Eastern bloc, where people still hold public bodies and those in authority with suspicion; why the USA has in general failed to embrace the consultative culture at federal level; how politics in the Land of the Free is so influenced by big money and big lobby.

Our worldwide horizon scan notes how California, other American states and countries such as Switzerland allow the public to vote on propositions, and the use of referendums is certainly a topic we will cover. Town meetings are certainly a feature of community dialogues across the Atlantic, and the use of social media has transformed the conduct of public debate. However, the British will certainly struggle to recognise too many comparable examples of political consultation in the USA.

Elsewhere we find consultation best developed in Commonwealth countries such as Canada, Australia, New Zealand and South Africa. Much of Africa has officials educated in Europe and lawyers who have been schooled in the tenets of English law. They are showing increasing interest in participative structures – as are those in the Indian sub-continent. There, the

11

ex-colonial legacy plays alongside local cultural pre-dispositions in the world's largest democracy and creates all the pre-conditions for a consultative culture.

Towards the end of 2012, we were invited to Washington, DC, to meet colleagues from the World Bank. Under the leadership of Jim Yong Kim, a fresh approach had been agreed whereby recipients of World Bank-sourced funding had to consult their populations before significant projects were given the go-ahead. To our knowledge this is the first time a major world body has established such a policy and it is, of course, absolutely right. 'What about countries that are not democracies?' we asked in discussion with the Bank's then Director of community development, a genial Cameroon national called Cyprian Fisiy. He had just returned from China and painstakingly explained that where citizens are denied a meaningful vote at the ballot box, the nearest they get to exerting influence on what happens to their local communities or their particular interest is through some form of consultation.

In 2014, his words were confirmed when the offices of the Consultation Institute in Bedfordshire hosted a delegation from the Legislative Affairs office in Beijing. We had been advised not to use the word 'democracy' very much, or at least without too much overt enthusiasm. In they came, claiming to have been thoroughly confused in Brussels. Within minutes they were explaining to us how importantly they regarded their quest for a better understanding of _pre-legislative consultation_... as part of their _democracy_! It so happens that this is one form of engagement that our own Parliament has for the most part abjectly failed to organise, but they were not to know this. For them, as for so many others around the world, the UK is where it happens.

Whether we like it or not, we are world leaders in public consultation.

That is not to say we in Britain do it consistently well. But we most certainly *do* it. And in general we know *how* to do it. When we wrote *The Art of Consultation* in 2009, we were able to chronicle an impressive learning curve that public agencies, as well as government departments, had followed over a decade and more. We claimed that collectively the home nations spent a billion pounds, or more, per annum on seeking the public's views on everything from doctors' surgeries to wind farms. We pinpointed a variety of visible successes, but we also pored over the known problems.

In the event, technical shortcomings can be addressed, though some of our institutions continue to make heavy weather of them. The more intractable challenges centre on the motives for ✱ organising a public consultation, the scope and context of the dialogues and the willingness of the organisers to take proper account of what emerges in the exercise. In short, they concern the ways in which power is exercised, affecting the decisions, policies or programmes that the consultation is intended to influence.

If politics equates to how power is distributed and exercised, then many of the concerns we identified in 2009 can be collectively grouped as the 'politics' of consultation.

Hence this book.

Chapter 2

Why politicians should consult

decisions | unpopular choices | stakeholder support | public education | previous promises | blunders and mistakes | public relations spin | an impression of activity | decision avoidance | legislative obligations | best and worst motives

Actually, politicians *do* consult. It is just that the reasons why they do so aren't always the same as the reasons why they *should* be doing so.

It may be a trifle unjust, but numerous observers would insist that many politicians consult because they feel it makes them look good. Just spin and public relations. Whether this is true or not we can examine later, but for the record there are ample reasons why this need not be the case. Here are six reasons why they should consult.

Firstly, and most obviously, there is the search for sounder decisions. All the textbooks tell us, and common sense suggests, that decisions should be better if a proper process of research and consideration has preceded them. It is not for nothing that the phrase *evidence-based policy-making* became popular in the last twenty years. It was a great way of capturing a logical approach that went well with an independent civil service and a pragmatic outlook to public administration.

Great theory, but did this go much beyond the slogan? There are several difficulties. Obtaining good evidence is seldom cheap and almost always time-consuming. Answers are not always clear cut or politically acceptable and it is little wonder that sceptics have inverted the phrase and talked about 'policy-based evidence-making.'

Nevertheless, the fact remains that across a range of decisions, it is helpful to have gathered what evidence there might be about the likely implications of various choices. A good example might be the way in which local authorities are meant to consult local people about their annual budgets. This is a complex question. There are literally hundreds of local services, with few people aware of those beyond a very basic list, at the top of which is collecting waste. With ever-shrinking budgets, councils will take sounder decisions if they seek to engage with various stakeholders before re-casting their budgets. There is no parallel process for Whitehall departments. Maybe there should be.

✕ Secondly, consultation helps politicians make unpopular choices. Few politicians like the odium of unpopular decisions, though those sitting on large immovable majorities are of course in a stronger position to weather any electoral backlash. Neither should we suggest that taking unpopular decisions necessarily alienates voters. There are ways of persuading people that tough choices are inevitable and securing their support in making sure they are the right ones.

We were much minded of this when visiting the Channel Islands. Since the Second World War, the States of Jersey has benignly presided over a successful island economy with a flourishing financial services industry and prosperous tourism and agricultural sectors that kept taxation to levels low enough to be the envy of the UK and other EU countries. It now faces a cocktail of *wicked issues* – decisions that have been gradually emerging for years, but a little too difficult to tackle and easy to postpone. So now it has to confront its ageing population and the difficulty of having no NHS. It is under pressure from the banks and other financiers to admit a greater number of foreign nationals, to strengthen and replenish its skills-base. But it fears the social consequences of further immigration. In any case, there is finite space on the small island to build more houses – the place is already full.

There are many Jerseys to be found – places with multiple interacting issues, threatening to change forever a society where people are quite content, thank you very much. Leaders who challenge such a status quo are inevitably going to disturb the political peace and tranquillity. What's that phrase about making omelettes without breaking eggs?

Wise politicians have learnt that the smart way to approach such a scenario is to share the analysis and effectively to challenge local communities to devise the solutions together. It's a painful task, for many will be in denial and the process of education does not guarantee success. Jersey's politicians, like others in comparable positions, may or may not bring dissident residents with them. The case for conscientious consultation is that it is one way of securing sufficient support to take action. Impose decisions with little or no constructive engagement and you may be voted out of office. Taking difficult decisions is easier when you have consulted.

Thirdly, politicians need stakeholder support. They may not like it, but the truth is that on any given subject there are people who know more than they do. If in doubt, watch the proceedings of parliamentary select committees. Occasionally they present a hapless civil servant called to account for a piece of obvious bungling, but more frequently what is on show is a true expert on a specific subject courteously explaining to MPs how something really works. Some of the questioning betrays scant understanding by committee members, but the exchange is usually productive in helping our legislators obtain the best possible advice.

Stakeholders come in many shapes and sizes and not all are expert witnesses. In general they are the individuals and organisations that are affected by government or other formal proposals. They are the ones that are expert on the implications of government or public policies in practice. Nothing upsets them more than for changes to be proposed or implemented without an opportunity to discuss them. In short, they crave consultation.

For much of the post-war period the UK's world-class voluntary and community sector, what we call civil society, pestered government to be given a more formal role in public policy-making; other legislatures had such processes. But it took until the 1997 Blair government for agreement to be reached and even then it was pretty flimsy, taking the form of a national agreement known as the Compact – later devolved to local compacts through local authorities. Among the Compact's provisions was an undertaking that the sector would be consulted when anything affecting it was being considered. The Compact also committed to a twelve-week timescale when consultation became necessary. Despite fears that the coalition government would row back from this agreement, it remained in force* and probably reflects a Whitehall view that obtaining a degree of understanding and support from key stakeholders can be useful. For certain, ignoring them arouses their hostility.

There are issues and proposals where implementation might be difficult or impossible without a degree of co-operation from key stakeholders. Imagine trying to change the school curriculum if teachers are not on side. Or trying to change primary care in the NHS if doctors are wholly hostile. Very few groups have anything close to a veto on change, but they claim a right to be consulted and politicians wishing to advance the cause of change are well advised to hold a dialogue with stakeholders if they want their ideas to be realised.

Fourthly, there is a need to inform the public. This is not the main role of consultation, but there is no denying that one of the most valuable contributions it can make is as a means to educate citizens about important issues and especially about difficult decisions.

Take an emotive subject like climate change, where much of the public's view is, in fact, influenced by mass media generalisations; where scientific facts play a secondary role to wishful thinking and some vague green ideas. Politicians have found it troublesome to propose policies that address such issues, especially if they require sacrifice. Regrettably, they have sometimes found it easier to pass

---

* The 2010 version of the Compact commits the government to 'give early notice of forthcoming consultations, where possible, allowing enough time for CSOs to involve their service users, beneficiaries, members, volunteers and trustees in preparing responses. Where it is appropriate, and enables meaningful engagement, conduct 12-week formal written consultations, with clear explanations and rationale for shorter time frames or a more informal approach.'

contentious legislation by inserting the critical clauses into parliamentary bills late in the process and without too much scrutiny. Years later, as in the case of some of the UK's so-called green taxes, we wonder if a more visible public debate and consultation might not have been better and perhaps have built a more sustainable body of support for the policy.

It is often only when proposals are spelt out in proper detail that the strength of an argument can be assessed. Indeed one of the most persuasive reasons to consult formally is to see if a proposal can withstand the scrutiny that follows. Maybe this is why politicians hesitate. If there is any suggestion that stakeholders or the public may not quite understand what's afoot, this surely is a solid reason to consult.

Fifthly, there are occasions when overt commitments to consult have been made; such promises have to be kept. Typically these occur when a decision of principle has already been taken but where its advocates recognise the value of letting a range of opinions influence some of the detail. One of the best examples is when Ken Livingstone won the London mayoral election in 2000 on a promise to introduce a congestion charge. This he took as a binding decision based on a manifesto commitment. But he had also promised to consider the views of Londoners on some important issues of detail. What area should the charge cover? How much should be charged? How should the charge be collected? Who should be exempt? And so forth.

On a more strategic level, when political parties promise to hold a referendum, they are effectively making a commitment to consult. The 2011 vote on new electoral arrangements was implementing a commitment made by the Liberal Democrats, and honoured by the coalition. The Scottish independence referendum was similarly an agreement between David Cameron and Alex Salmond. David Cameron's Conservative Party manifesto in 2015 also contained the commitment to hold an in/out referendum on the UK's membership of the EU – leading to the vote for Brexit in 2016.

Politicians are certainly conscious of the potential penalties for breaking promises. Just ask Nick Clegg.* Whether they can explain away *procedural* promises to consult as being inherently different from overtly *substantive* policy promises is an interesting question. It may depend how clear the commitment was. Promising to consult can be somewhat vague, especially if clothed in the language of involvement, participation or engagement. For Tony Blair's government in 2003, however, there was no ambiguity. In a passage of an energy White Paper that was later to become rather more significant than might have been anticipated, the Secretary of State wrote:

> However ... at some point in the future new nuclear build might be necessary if we are to meet our carbon targets. Before any decision to proceed with the building of new nuclear power stations, there will need to be the fullest public consultation and the publication of a further White Paper setting out our proposals.

When the White Paper was finally published, Greenpeace successfully persuaded the High Court that it had not met the

---

* Clegg, as leader of the Liberal Democrats, became deputy Prime Minister of the coalition government (2010–15), which among other things increased university fees substantially, in breach of his party's election manifesto. Political observers cite it as the main reason why his party lost 80 per cent of its parliamentary seats in 2015.

requirements for a lawful consultation.* But that's another story. For now, a promise to consult has to be kept.

Finally, consultation helps to avoid blunders and mistakes. If any politician or civil servant remains unconvinced, we suggest they read Anthony King and Ivor Crewe's seminal book *The Blunders of Our Governments*.† In it they have dissected a large number of acknowledged horror stories from the period up to 2010 and they make the point that there has been no shortage since. They include mis-sold pensions, the Child Support Agency, the Millennium Dome, individual learning accounts, ID cards, tax credits and many others. It is a long list and what is surprising is that relatively few of these mistakes can be blamed upon party political policies – the one exception probably being the poll tax.

Their fascinating analysis rewards study, for they isolate a number of relatively well-known pitfalls for policy-makers, from *groupthink* to *operational disconnect*. They see rather too much emphasis on symbols and spin and not enough on the practicalities of making things work. Speed is often quoted as the enemy of good administration and they certainly find plenty of examples of haste, to which we will return later.

But their two biggest conclusions should resonate with every serious politician in the land and possibly even more so with civil servants. They have noticed two phenomena which, in classic academic language, they call *asymmetries of expertise* and a *deficit of deliberation*.

---

* R (*ex parte* Greenpeace) *v* Secretary of State for Trade & Industry [2007] ECHC 311.

† Anthony King and Ivor Crewe, *The Blunders of Our Governments* (London: Oneworld, 2013).

The first of these we can describe better as governments or public bodies knowing less than their suppliers or stakeholders and being unable to work alongside them satisfactorily as a result. Sometimes manufacturers sell products that don't work well enough; this has certainly happened in defence procurement and also in information technology. More frequently, ministers and their officials are just outgunned in negotiations by consultancies or suppliers who know the issues better.

The *deficit of deliberation* is even more to the point. The distinguished authors do not use the word 'consultation' especially often, but their overall conclusion seems clear enough. In their own words, 'a decision emanating from a process of due deliberation seems likely to be a better decision than one taken off the cuff, in haste or in isolation.'

So here is the message to all political activists. Your reputation is at risk from mistakes that are easy to make and almost impossible to rectify, once they have gone wrong. So many of them are avoidable and one of the best defence-mechanisms is to consult widely and wisely when good advice can be heeded.

What is interesting about this list is that few politicians or civil servants would disagree with a single word we have written. They would probably concede everything, with the proviso that it sounds too much like the fabled motherhood and apple pie and maybe takes insufficient account of the constraints of the job. In this they have some of our sympathy, for the *realpolitik* within which many legislators and administrators work is full of complexities and disconnects, affecting their abilities to consult properly every time they should. Many of these feature in subsequent chapters, but can be summarised as based on the expectations of others – including the media. And also their expectations of themselves.

As a result, we have a wealth of political or policy-based consultations, arguably too many. There is no real shortage of consultations, but they stem from a different set of motivations. So here – maybe a little unfairly, are some reasons why politicians *actually* consult.

Firstly, it looks and sounds good. Anyone who listens to the *Today* programme* on a consistent basis will have heard many a minister proudly announce across the airwaves that he or she is launching a consultation. It can be great public relations, especially if there is an agenda of being seen to be listening in one way or another. Equally, of course, there are many government policies which are all about being more responsive to the public. Think consumer protection, or broadcasting standards. In fact, virtually any public service is now compared with private provision amid references to customer satisfaction, product choice and individual preference.

Take the National Health Service. All recent governments have used the language of patient choice as a way of explaining how the twenty-first-century NHS differs from what went before. The jargon of customer service is undoubtedly well meant but comes across to people as management-speak. So when a minister, or a senior clinician, intones over the airwaves how keen they are to 'hear your views so we can shape our services to better meet your needs', what Joe Public often understands is, 'We want to close your walk-in centre and wish to make it sound more palatable for you by holding a consultation.'

---

* BBC Radio 4's flagship news and current affairs programme.

24

Millions of people probably regard all consultations as a complete con trick. Nothing but spin, and insofar as they cost public money, a waste of resources as well. Over the years, when arriving in a British town or city, we have taken to informally asking our taxi-driver what he or she thinks of the local council and how it consults them. The range of invective that can follow such an innocent enquiry could, if repeated, make this an X-rated publication. Councillors throughout the land might well worry if they realised that such dialogues as they have sought to organise are held in such low esteem.

The most prevalent prejudice seems to be that politicians are only going through the motions. Sadly, it is often true. A northern county council leader we met was open about it. We were discussing the authority's *duty to consult* on the budget; he was disarmingly frank in claiming that his reason for consulting was so that he could be *seen* to be listening. Great! At least we know where *he* stands.

Secondly, consultation can give the impression of activity. In *The Art of Consultation*, we told the story of a Labour government initiative in the field of housing that was given a high-profile announcement in the party conference. Many thought it was a forlorn piece of kite-flying, useful for a morning-after headline, but maybe less practical than it sounded. There followed a consultation to which about 400 local authorities responded, arguing more or less with unanimity that the proposals were unworkable or worse. When describing this case study, our complaint was the huge cost of exploring this idea. Some councils would merely have requested their officers to research the proposals and maybe write a response. Others would have sought to calculate the financial and operational implications for the council. Some would have called in their IT suppliers and investigated potential enhancements to their software programmes; yet others may have looked at the processes they might have been required to develop and new skills that might be needed for front-line staff. What might be the training costs? Should they sub-contract? And many, many councils of course would have convened meetings or set up sub-committees to form a view of the proposals and whether they should be supported. About £10 million probably just about covered it.

In the event, hostility to the idea led the minister to announce that the proposal had been dropped. Which is all well and good at one level, for it justifies the consultative exercise. Good idea consulted upon and found wanting; consultation does its job.

But the alternative interpretation is that this was always a non-starter and the intention was to give the appearance of activity without ever getting near to actually doing anything. The mantra that reorganisations often serve the purpose of giving the impression of activity whilst in fact achieving little maybe has a parallel in public consultations. Sometimes they are there to generate a lot of activity, but nothing more.

Thirdly, consultation can be used as a decision avoidance tactic. We mentioned *wicked issues* earlier, but there are some that are politically toxic. Governments, political parties and individual politicians try their best to avoid them. Some are capable of resolution but will result in a loss of political support for whoever makes the proposal. On other occasions, if a decision is inevitable, there is a search for someone, or anyone, to share the blame.

It can be an ideal form of procrastination, with the added benefit that it makes people think that those in authority are genuinely keen to hear alternative opinions before deciding what to do.

How else can we explain the long and seemingly never-ending saga of additional runway capacity in south-east England? The story is examined in detail elsewhere, but it is a splendid example of consultations over many years serving a purpose of spinning out the issue until a politically convenient moment where a decision might be taken with minimal electoral consequences. In 2010 the coalition government found itself deadlocked over the issue, or at least it did when it appointed Justine Greening as transport secretary, a minister totally committed to one side of the argument and opposed to further expansion of Heathrow. By then, however, the government had promised a consultation on future airports strategy and what was published after delay and equivocation was a document covering everything imaginable about future aviation policy... except of course where additional runway capacity might be.

It is admittedly a serious problem for parties when individual candidates adopt thoroughly inflexible positions on matters that clearly count for a lot in their constituency. Whether this should tie the hands of governments trying to take strategic decisions on national infrastructure projects is another matter. Successive administrations wrestled with that one, culminating in the 2008 Planning Act, where there was an attempt to reduce the political element in some of these decisions. It did not last and the policy was, in part, reversed in 2010, putting politicians firmly in charge once again. Except that, with choices as controversial as airports, they suddenly wished they weren't. The nation was subjected once again to a consultation, masking what maybe ought to have been the smack of firm leadership.

Professors King and Crewe, as noted earlier, argue that time is very often an important element in securing adequate deliberation, so there may be a fine line between rushing one's fences and taking too long. In the case of the south-east airports, almost everyone agrees that the take-off has been delayed too much already and we are still taxiing to a runway that may never be built.

Is this an isolated occurrence or are there other examples where politicians contrive to kick issues into the long consultative grass? The answer may depend upon your perspective. The fact is that many people suspect politicians of being more Machiavellian than perhaps they are. They look at the timing of some consultations and wonder whether they are dictated by the logic of the decision timescale or by political convenience and they marvel at the coincidence that consultations about unpopular measures seem to happen just after, rather than just before, elections!

Fourthly, politicians inherit a requirement to consult. Much of this is through legislation that commits them to consult. In contrast to the adage that Parliament cannot bind its successors, here is evidence that previous generations of MPs have regularly committed governments and public bodies of all kinds to consult before taking various decisions. It remains one of the biggest reasons why public consultations can become tokenistic, for parliamentarians have regularly made over-optimistic assumptions about the scope that might exist for the public or for stakeholders to influence decisions.

There are hundreds of statutory provisions that amount to a requirement on a minister or some public body to consult. We imagine that many owe their origin to a reluctance by Parliament to confer on them an unfettered discretion over something likely to prove quite contentions. The answer? *Make them consult.* It is a safe option for the parliamentary draughtsman for, in practical terms, the decision can be lawfully taken pretty well regardless of what happens in the consultation. And therein lies the problem. If politicians and civil servants feel that the consultation cannot oblige them to do anything different from what they had in mind all along, there is little incentive to do it properly.

Updating statutory instruments is a good example of where consultation can be written into the process. Just as some are subject to needing an *affirmative resolution* in one or both Houses of Parliament, others require there to have been a consultation. No less a body than the House of Lords Secondary Legislation Scrutiny Committee* has felt concerned by the cavalier way in which government departments have approached the task and cite a litany of abuses ranging from inadequate time through to a take-it-or-leave-it attitude. Sadly, there are too many cases like this.

Local government has often suffered from over-zealous exhortations to consult. The example of devolved council tax benefit schemes has already been given, but there are so many occasions when a power can be exercised only after a consultation has taken place. Included in the list would have to be the demanding rules that apply to licensing or town planning. What makes these difficult for local politicians is the in-built tendency for these processes to attract objectors rather than supporters. It is as if Parliament, when committing public bodies as well as government departments to these consultations, assumed that they would generate a balanced debate between supporters and opponents. Sometimes they do but often they don't and it can make politicians reluctant to engage wholeheartedly, for they fear creating an environment of opposition to cherished policies or projects.

---

* This committee examines the policy merits of regulations and other types of secondary legislation that are subject to parliamentary procedure.

As always, people doing something because they want to do it works better than doing something just because somebody else wants them to do it. Consulting stakeholders or the general public because the law says you have to is far less successful than when it is your own initiative and you are really keen to receive their advice.

So the overall picture is one where there are good compelling reasons why governments, their agencies, politicians and civil servants should all use public consultation constructively in policy-making. Frequently, however, they contrive to do so for rather different, less impressive reasons. Of course, there will be a mixture of motivations, but the danger is that a sceptical public is always ready to believe the worst rather than the best of those in authority.

Chapter 3
The legal framework

Statutory duties | equality law | legitimate expectations | judicial reviews: Building Schools for the Future, King Richard III, the rat run case, Greenpeace, Birmingham Council, library closures, Lewisham Hospital | Aarhus | Gunning Principles

Despite appearances to the contrary, politicians are not free to consult as and when they want, or in whatever way they please. They are, in reality, constrained by a fully formed legal framework that makes the law of consultation a considerable subject in its own right.

Parliament has, for years, imposed a range of consultation duties on ministers, civil servants and every imaginable form of public body it has created. Over time, the precise form of words may have changed, but often the requirement has been couched in vague terms that made it less likely that the courts would become involved. A favourite formula was to consult 'whoever appears to the minister to be appropriate', a loose piece of wording that seems almost deliberately designed to be incapable of enforcement.

Maybe politicians did this quite consciously. Maybe they appreciated the value of *normative legislation*, where Parliament is trying to influence behaviour by setting the standard through expectation: think wearing seat belts or smoking in public places. Alternatively, it might be that senior civil servants realised how easy it is to fall foul of anything too precise and wished to avoid exposing their departments to legal challenge.

Whatever the reason, they failed. There are regular attempts to show that consultations have been unlawful in one way or another. It is not a wholly welcome development, for many of these legal challenges are almost-covert ways of trying to undermine a public policy, opponents of which have decided that one of their best arguments is to question the propriety of the decision-making process.

The right to obtain legal redress is of course a fundamental part of the rule of law. If public bodies, or indeed any form of organisation, could with impunity disregard their obligations to consult, it would make a mockery of our democratic process and frequently frustrates governments through the unintended consequences of mistakes made as described by King and Crewe. Legal redress is considered so important in the context of major environmental developments that it forms part of the Aarhus Convention.* This treaty binds over forty countries to key principles of public engagement and consideration of likely impacts. Its three fundamental pillars are access to information, the *duty to consult* and, importantly, fair access to a legal system that will enforce the first two.

---

* The United Nations Economic Commission for Europe Convention on Access to Information, Public Participation in Decision-making and Access to Justice in Environmental Matters. Signed 25 June 1998 in the Danish city of Aarhus.

32

In the UK, judicial review is costly and attempts by the 2010–15 coalition government to discourage them will have done little to assuage the Aarhus Secretariat, which has ruled that the UK has been in breach of this third pillar since 2005. It is a moot point whether, in practice, this is a major barrier to justice. There are many instances where campaigners have successfully argued that consultation was either inadequate or improperly conducted.

For a time, there was a statutory *duty to involve*. It formed part of the 2009 Local Democracy Act* and followed years of cajoling local councils to take their consultation responsibilities seriously. It had three components – informing people, consulting people and involving them. In the following months many trees were felled to publish the welter of guidance that ensued. In Parliament, the Conservative opposition had argued against the measure on the grounds that good councils did all this anyway, and that those that did not consult could be rejected at the ballot box. This argument ultimately won, for the 2011 Localism Act repealed these provisions – and only dyed-in-the-wool enthusiasts even noticed, let alone mourned their passing.

In all probability, their demise made no difference, for such a 'catch-all' requirement was superfluous anyway. By now local authorities were governed by a Best Value regime, which stipulated that users of public services were entitled to be consulted, and the plethora of service-specific consultation requirements meant that few really important decisions could legally avoid an element of consultation. On top of this was the fusion of various anti-discrimination laws which became the 2010 Equality Act. It had a critical provision that became, almost on its

---

* Local Democracy, Economic Development and Construction Act 2009.

own, as effective a driver of public consultation as any number of other enactments.

Section 149 of the Act says that public bodies must give *due regard* to their obligations to achieve a range of socially desirable goals. This is known as the Public Sector Equality Duty (PSED) and includes eliminating discrimination, promoting equality of opportunity and fostering good community relations. The Act also identifies nine *protected characteristics*. Chances are that most readers of this book will be pleasantly surprised to realise that they are, in fact, protected. That is because your gender is there alongside your sexual orientation, religious belief, race, age or disability. The Act also protects those who happen to be pregnant and includes marital status and gender reassignment.

The way the Act works is to require that any public body taking a decision must be able to demonstrate that it has taken into account its responsibilities for those policy aims mentioned above. Initially, this was done by producing what was called an equality impact assessment (EIA) and became known as an equality analysis (EA). Its role was to try to anticipate how proposals would affect the interests of the *protected characteristics* and ensure that decision-makers acknowledged the implications of what they were about to do. Classic positive discrimination in the eyes of many! Rightly or wrongly, the courts have decreed that there is no necessity to prepare such a document – except in Wales where a statutory provision decrees otherwise. Total confusion! This is because it is also a fundamental premise of the law of consultation that organisations should have held a proper dialogue with those who will suffer adverse impacts from their proposals. If *due regard* is to be successfully evidenced, then such dialogues need to have been with representatives of the identified *protected characteristics*. How else can you be sure that your projected assessment of impacts carries conviction? That is the least they would expect.

That expectation has a significance that will surprise many. When judges are asked to rule upon whether a consultation meets the provisions written into an Act of Parliament, they are bound to rely on the normal rules of interpreting the words. This is called *statutory construction*. When, however, a legal challenge relies on common-law principles, the courts have more flexibility and instead pursue the goal of *fairness*. In this they are clearly guided by what is known as the *doctrine of legitimate expectation*. It has been around for many years, but seems to have enjoyed a recent upsurge in popularity as judicial reviews have tackled the legality of consultations in large numbers.

At its simplest, the idea is that citizens have a right to expect public bodies to act in accordance with the rules. If there is statutory guidance that tells a council, for example, how to interpret a piece of legislation, then unless there are good reasons to the contrary, the courts will assume that officials will act in accordance with that guidance. The same applies to policies adopted by a particular organisation. In essence, if you publish the way you are going to do business, then the public has every right to expect that this is how you will behave. A claimant lawyer we know enjoys telling public bodies that whenever she takes on a new case, her first act is to access the defendant's website to see what extravagant promises have been made, and whenever the reality departs from that expectation, her case is strengthened.

There is more. In the absence of a document, the *legitimate expectation* could be a promise made by a politician. In Chapter One, we illustrated this with a minister's commitment to consult on new nuclear build. But an expectation can arise just by examining how a particular relationship works.

Nothing demonstrates this better than the story of Michael Gove's cancellation of the Building Schools for the Future programme. This was a mega-investment kicked off in 2003, when times were good, and a flagship policy of New Labour. It was much disliked by the then Conservative opposition, which criticised it as being unnecessarily bureaucratic and wasteful. The numbers were mind-boggling. Almost every secondary school in the country was to be rebuilt or refurbished, so an average-sized education authority was expecting to spend tens of millions of pounds. Planning for this meant much research, examining all kinds of possibilities, sometimes identifying new sites, land purchase, lawyers and surveyors. Then we had the architects, the builders, the landscape designers and no doubt somewhere a candlestick-maker as well. At one point or another something called an *outline business case* (OBC) emerged, and it was upon the approval of this somewhat anonymous document that the Secretary of State alighted when trying to draw the line between what was to go ahead and what was to be cancelled. Those projects with an approved OBC survived, but those without were terminated, leaving councils with massive bills for wasted effort.

Six councils went to the High Court* to argue that they should have been consulted about the process of cancellation. The case was an extraordinary, somewhat unexpected victory for the claimants and a major endorsement of the *legitimate expectation* theory. Such was the complexity of the relationships between the army of civil servants working in the Department of Education

---

* R (*ex parte* Luton BC, Nottingham CC, Waltham Forest LB, Newham LB, Kent CC and Sandwell MBC) *v* Secretary of State for Education [2011] EWHC 217.

and the hordes of officials working in town halls that the judge felt it was inconceivable that a simplistic inflexible formula, so unsympathetic to local circumstances, could be fair. He then looked at the minister's responsibilities under the 2010 Equality Act. Had he had *due regard* to the interests of protected categories? Were there schools on the cancelled list that maybe should have gone ahead to avoid discriminating against those of a certain race? Were girls' schools more affected than boys' schools? And so forth.

The combination of the *doctrine of legitimate expectation* and the practical application of the Equality Act made the Secretary of State's defence untenable. And so it operates for most public consultations today. Fairness means taking steps to understand those affected and to analyse the forecast impacts, without which it is almost impossible to satisfy the *due regard* obligation. The reality, of course, was that no one in the Department had thought for one moment that consultation was a requirement. From its perspective, was it not crystal clear from the Conservative election manifesto and the coalition agreement that deficit reduction was to be the priority and was not Mr Gove merely implementing that policy?

Legitimate expectation is not something we can all claim just because we have expectations. We might just be optimistic. Such, we suspect, was the case of the Plantagenet Alliance of Great Britain – a group unknown to most of us until the excitement that surrounded the exhumation and reburial of King Richard III in Leicester. It led to a truly hilarious court case* during which the Alliance argued that it had a *legitimate expectation* that there should have been a consultation as to whether the royal remains be

---

* R (*ex parte* Plantagenet Alliance Ltd) *v* Secretary of State for Justice and University of Leicester [2014] EWCA 1662 (QB).

buried in York or in Leicester. Fans of *Blackadder** will be relieved to know that if they ever want for an additional script, they should look no further than the legal judgment handed down in this strange but sorry tale. It turns, in part, upon a discussion of what might have been the wishes of the deceased; there was also a separate argument as to whether the case was or was not out of time†. On our calculations, it was about 529 years too late.

High Court cases, however, are often important not for what they decide, but for what they say, and in rejecting the Plantagenet Alliance's claim, the judge gave us all a better insight into the precise role that the courts will play in ruling upon consultations. In simple terms, he said that there are four circumstances where, if a public body fails to consult satisfactorily, the courts will intervene. The first is where there is a statutory requirement to do so. The second is where there has been a promise to consult. The third scenario is where the nature of the relationship suggests a need to consult. The fourth – a masterful example of judicial invention, to be invoked only exceptionally – is where not to do so would *cause an unfairness.*

Now lawyers can have a field day exploring the boundaries of these circumstances and there are literally dozens of cases where campaigners who dislike a policy or a decision challenge on the grounds of inadequate consultation. As often as not, this is not a legal but a quasi-political step. The legal rules of consultation are

---

* A BBC TV sitcom starring Rowan Atkinson, known for hilarious depictions of historical characters and events. Its four series were originally broadcast between 1983 and 1989.

† A case for judicial review must be brought before the court quickly and in any event within three months of the decision or action being challenged. It is unusual for the court to accept late applications.

merely a pretext for the challenge. It is a proxy dispute – arguing about the process of decisions rather than the merits of the decision itself.

Unless human rights* have been infringed, the courts cannot and should not intervene in the substance of a decision if the process has been satisfactory. They have to be especially wary of controversial political decisions that go through a democratic forum. The trouble is that there are so many occasions when over-enthusiastic politicians or negligent officials have made mistakes that the list of successful judicial reviews has grown exponentially. Both the Greenpeace nuclear power and the Building Schools for the Future cases illustrated errors which were eminently avoidable, had the relevant government departments been better briefed.

There are few excuses, for the key principles of what is a lawful consultation have been established for years. For this we should thank Sir Stephen Sedley. In 1985, in the early stages of a distinguished legal career, Sedley was a barrister representing parents of a school in the London Borough of Brent who felt they had not been consulted properly about planned changes.† In this case he postulated a set of rules, which first became known as the Sedley Propositions. Gradually, as one case followed another, judges confirmed this set of rules and by now they are so well established that it is inconceivable that there should be any legal challenge to a consultation that does not, at its root, focus upon whether the rules – now known as the Gunning Principles after

---

* The Human Rights Act 1998 incorporates the rights set out in the European Convention of Human Rights, the enforcement of which can be through the British courts and, at the time of writing, the European Court of Human Rights.

† R (*ex parte* Gunning) *v* Brent LB [1985] 84 LGR 168.

the parents in the original case – apply and, if so, to what extent they have been followed.

It has often been observed that Sedley did no more than cobble together four statements of the blindingly obvious. First he said that proposals in a consultation should be still at their *formative stage*. This has been universally interpreted as meaning that decision-makers should not have made up their minds; another term much used is *pre-determination*. Secondly, he insisted that consultees must have been given sufficient information about the proposals being consulted upon as would enable them to give them *intelligent consideration*. Thirdly, there must be enough time for all those who have an interest to take part in the consultation. And finally, those who take the eventual decision must give the output from the consultation *conscientious consideration*.

Could anything be more straightforward? As always, the devil is in the detail. The requirement on timing, for example, resolves itself into a matter of evidence as claimants seek to demonstrate that the duration of a consultation exercise prevented or deterred people from having their say. Few cases have succeeded solely on the issue of timing. If public bodies find that their opponents have the better of this argument, they are normally wise enough to settle for a further period of dialogue rather than fight a losing battle in the courts. The odd intransigent council, poorly advised no doubt, tries to explain how Christmas or the summer holidays have little effect, but it ends up looking foolish.

Where the Gunning Principles prove troublesome for politicians and public bodies is over *pre-determination* and the tendency for both to use consultation as a rubber stamp on decisions they've already taken, rather than an aid to the decision-making in the first place. It is not always easy to regard a proposal upon which you may have been working for months or even years as being truly at a *formative* stage. Imagine a complex reconfiguration of hospital services, or plans to build a new high-speed train line. There is clearly an assumption that those involved in the project know what the answer should be. Under these circumstances, consultation is part of the checks and balances needed to ensure that nothing really unacceptable to the wider public proceeds without its voice being heard.

However, all this flies in the face of Sedley's common sense. If all is cut and dried and the decision is effectively a 'done deal', there is little or no purpose served by asking people's opinions. The law therefore confronts one of the biggest dilemmas for policy-makers and politicians alike: how do you consult honestly when you're pretty sure of the answer?

Elected politicians are caught between the conflicting desires to keep their pre-election promises and stay within the law of consultation. The leading case on this features Councillor Coleman who, as the environment portfolio holder for the London Borough of Barnet, sought to reopen a road called Partingdale Lane to through traffic.* To the satisfaction of local residents the previous administration had closed this well-known rat-run and added to the misery of motorists facing the inevitable delays of the morning rush hour. In the local election campaign in 2002, Councillor Coleman promised to reverse the policy and duly acted upon his manifesto commitment. Unfortunately the councillor overlooked the very clear legal requirement to consult the public before decisions like this could be implemented. Without taking himself out of the process completely -- which he

---

* R (*ex parte* The Partingdale Lane Residents Association) *v* Barnet LB [2003] EWHC 947 (Admin).

didn't-- it would be pretty difficult to meet the Gunning rule about *pre-determination*.

Those sympathetic to the councillor were firmly told by the judge* that 'public authorities, such as the defendant, are accountable to their electorates for the merits of their policies and their decisions; but they are accountable to the law for the legality of their actions.' In other words, no matter what mandate you have, if the law has assumed that no decision should be taken before relevant views have been heard, then this has to be observed. The councillor could have stayed within the law by doing one of two things: he could have removed himself completely from the decision-making process, or he could have couched his promises more carefully. Something like 'Subject, of course, to the required consultation, I will try to reopen Partingdale Lane...'

Another source of legal trouble for consultors is in providing enough information for people to respond in an intelligent way. We accept at once that there will be Cabinet-level politicians who genuinely wish to engage with the public and stakeholders, in order to share the main thrust of their proposals. They will take a broad-brush approach and fully expect officials to fill in the gaps and provide that level of administrative detail that should satisfy consultees. After all, is this not the value of a professional cadre of civil servants? In our mind's eye we conjure a vision of a nineteenth-century statesman-like leader – someone in the Gladstone mould, eager to prepare for the next piece of oratory and happy to leave to others the messy detail of legislation or bureaucracy. This is all terribly unfair to today's crop of earnest professional parliamentarians, but somewhere in the British system there still lurks the old idea that policy principles were

---

* Mr Rabinder Singh QC, sitting as deputy High Court judge.

something for the chiefs and the niceties of implementation for the Indians (language which today would not be tolerated).

The second Gunning rule (*intelligent consideration*) rarely causes difficulty over major policy principles; it is the detail that more frequently trips up the unwary. But there are exceptions. That seminal court case where Greenpeace challenged the government's energy consultation in 2007* partly turned on the consultor's inability to provide information that any outside observer might have considered essential. They were not trivial details. One was the commercial viability of new nuclear power stations. Another was the safe disposal of nuclear waste. This was hardly a new issue, and the experts had been trying to solve this problem for decades. It so happened that in parallel with the government consultation, the responsible department had set up a special enquiry to shed further light on the latest science. Sadly, its conclusions were not available to consultees, and in the event what did become available was only published after the end of the consultation. No wonder the government lost.

At this point, readers may like to speculate about the conversations that took place in the department when the High Court decision was announced. Did furious ministers lash out at hapless officials who had patently failed to secure the ship? Or had they been complicit in a conspiracy to try to push through a major change of policy by hoping that no one might notice massive gaps in the argument? In theory, neither scenario sounds credible. Neither can it have made sense for public money to be wasted defending such a weak case.

This, however, is with the benefit of hindsight. Back in 2007, before the rise in consultation-related judicial reviews, there was

---

* See Chapter 2.

a feeling that, provided the consultation paper was in the Queen's English and broadly made sense, no court would declare it unlawful. For certain, the Greenpeace decision was a shock to the civil service, and it is said it prompted an urgent rethink and the further rewrite of the Cabinet Code of Practice on Consultation in 2008. Seeing the decision make the main headline in the London *Evening Standard* also didn't help.

This was probably the first really high-profile consultation embarrassment for central government; it then found itself curiously wrong-footed by a succession of cases, which it was surprised to lose. Whitehall could understand the need to stick to the twelve-week rule set out in the Compact for most policy consultations; the mandarins could definitely grasp the *pre-determination* concept. But they were nonplussed at being criticised about the information they had published. They seemed fully accustomed to and comfortable with sharing that which they felt was enough to comment on – without recognising that what is enough depends upon where you are sitting. What you *need* to know if you sit behind a departmental desk is very different from what you *want* to know if you are a service-user and that service is going to change.

Cases about changes in public services came thick and fast, especially once the coalition government started a tough squeeze on public expenditure. It bore down heavily on local authorities and in the case of England's biggest council, Birmingham, led to a requirement to cut the social services budget by £57 million. It was decided that whereas services had previously been provided to people at the two top categories of need – *critical* and *substantial* – in future resources would be mostly directed only to those meeting the *critical* criteria. The budgetary arithmetic was complex and few understood it. The designation of those affected

44

appeared inconsistent; the alternatives on offer for those facing the withdrawal of services seemed uncertain and vague. Not unreasonably, the judge in this case* looked at whether the information provided was enough to allow those affected to make an intelligent response and struggled. He then had to consider whether the provisions of the Disability Discrimination Act, one of the forerunners of the 2010 Equality Act, had been followed. These included allowing decision-makers to see if the impacts of their decisions were likely to meet their obligation to have *due regard* to the need to promote equality of treatment and avoid discriminating against disabled people. What the judge found was a process where sufficient information had not been provided, so consultees could not reasonably have been able to comment intelligently.

It is at this point that we admit to a degree of sympathy for councillors and their officials. Faced with unprecedented budget cuts, little time to achieve them and a hostile client base who could scarcely have been expected to welcome reductions in their service, they tried hard to produce a storyline that made some sense whilst providing a practical way forward. Service change on such a scale was probably beyond anything attempted before; they were largely learning by doing. Of course one could pick holes in their case. Or so it might seem from the council chamber.

From the perspective of a disabled child and her carers, the process looked different. To them, a massive change in the child's lifestyle was being considered and when, as apparently happened, individuals likely to lose out attended meetings and asked 'What will happen to me?' they were asked to put that on one side and focus on the principle of the policy change instead. 'Sorry, we

---

* R (*ex parte* W and others) *v* Birmingham CC [2011] EWHC 1147 (Admin).

can't comment on individual circumstances. But tell us; do you think it is a good idea?'

In this and subsequent cases, the courts have regularly championed the underdog by insisting that public bodies and others tell the truth about their proposals and explain the likely impacts on those affected. There are times when this means cutting through jargon-infested PR spin of the kind that tells people how the loss of a cherished service is really good news. The second Gunning Principle has in this way become a beacon of brightness shining its light on the dark, murky and impenetrable obfuscation of a bureaucratic consultation. And the irony is that politicians are the first to find fault with such practices... unless they are done in their name.

Technical challenges to consultations provide opportunities for critics to demonstrate how people or interests have been unfairly affected, often more by accident than design. The classic argument is between campaigners unhappy that a consultation was not held for long enough and public bodies who feel certain that its duration was definitely sufficient to allow everyone who seriously wanted to participate to do so. Until 2012, there was widespread acceptance of the 'twelve-week' rule – an easy rule of thumb dating from the days of local government committee cycles. It was referenced in successive government codes of practice,* and became even more entrenched when the Blair administration committed to it in its Compact with the voluntary and community sector. It became a *de facto* standard and was simple enough to understand and monitor, something that cannot be said for the revised set of Consultation Principles introduced by the Rt Hon. Oliver Letwin (without consultation with anyone!)

---

* Published in 1999, 2004 and 2008.

in 2011.* These latter Principles advocated a flexibility for government departments to hold consultations for as long – or short – as they liked, and suggested a duration of somewhere between two and twelve weeks. Out went the relative certainty of the previous rule (though, curiously, the new Principles document went out of its way to reinforce the Compact). More confusion.

But although the third of the Gunning Principles is ostensibly about time, it is not quite what it seems. What the judges look for is whether people with an interest in the subject are given the right opportunity to participate, and that is far from being just a question of time. We have seen a great many exercises lasting three months, but for all the engagement they accomplished, it might as well have been three days. There are other short-lived consultations where a well-structured sequence of activities yields far more effective dialogues in a couple of weeks. It may all come down to the choice of dialogue methods.

Before everything speeded up, the leisurely timetable of a twelve-week consultation provided an opportunity to announce, publish and publicise a set of options or proposals before inviting consultees to attend meetings, complete questionnaires or maybe prepare a written submission. We could easily call these methods long-winded, but they have the advantage of giving people time to consider and to organise discussions with colleagues, members or other consultees. The thinking behind a faster process and a shorter period of consultation is no doubt influenced by the undoubted value of online methods, but to satisfy the courts, it is probably going to remain essential to demonstrate that everyone with a legitimate interest has a reasonable opportunity to

---

* The Principles were revised in 2016: see
http://www.civilservant.org.uk/library/2016_consultation_principles.pdf
(accessed 19 March 2018).

participate, offline as well as online. Indeed a 2015 case ruled against a council that placed too much reliance on its website for its local planning process.* It wasn't really a time duration case, but it came close.

One more Gunning Principle remains; one final hurdle for those who organise public consultations to overcome. Conversely, it is one more opportunity for those who wish to challenge such an exercise. If we suggested that the Principles are really about common sense, surely this is the most obvious of them all. Giving *conscientious consideration* to the output of a consultation is surely the most elementary requirement. Whyever would one not wish to do this? Indeed, why would anyone waste scarce public money and devote staff and time to run a consultation exercise without a genuine intention to be guided, at least to some degree, by what emerged?

Sadly, there have been hundreds of consultations where this is precisely what has happened. Interestingly, not many of them have been challenged in court, at least not on the grounds of the fourth Gunning Principle. This is because situations where there has been a demonstrative unwillingness to consider consultation findings are usually those where it is clear that the defendant body has already made up its mind. That being the case, it has normally been found easier to argue the case on the first Principle of *pre-determination.*

There is also the question of evidence. How does one prove that a committee or board of directors has truly weighed up the arguments in such a way as to convince a court that *conscientious consideration* has occurred? It is certainly possible. Revisions to an

---

* R (*ex parte* Kendall) *v* Rochford DC and Department for Communities and Local Government [2014] EWHC 3866 (Admin).

48

organisation's proposals suggest that a process of deliberation has taken place, though of course this does not necessarily demonstrate any causation between the changes and the preceding consultation.

We once watched live video-streaming of a council meeting from mid-Wales in which local councillors argued with each other – in public – over the fate of a proposed wind farm on an exposed hillside. Back and forth raged the debate. Supporters of renewable energy sources fought for the project; those wanting to preserve the existing landscape resisted and suggested alternative sites. Both sides of the argument drew on the data emerging from a recently held consultation. As is often the case, the views of the public as expressed in the consultation assisted both sides. This modern-day, broadcast democracy has much to be said for it.

Taken together, the Gunning Principles have given us a perfectly balanced set of standards against which public consultations should be judged. Why, therefore, are they not better known? It was a surprise when we discovered that most local government officers had never heard of them. We are pretty sure that Whitehall departments have, until recently, been similarly in the dark.

The reason is not hard to find. In the functionally formed structures of public bodies, this was a matter for the legal department, not for the departmental manager whose lot it was to consult on a particular policy change. Councillors or members of Parliament are regularly advised to be wary of making their minds up without taking proper legal advice, but very rarely have we seen or heard of such advice even mentioning the Gunning Principles. So disconcerted were we at the Consultation Institute to stumble upon such ignorance that we have sought at every opportunity to talk about them and to include them in our training courses.

It is said that lawyers hate it when their expertise is demystified and made more generally available. Our experience is that there are many in the profession who passionately care about the responsibility of public bodies to communicate better and consult honestly. Many of the High Court judgments we have read suggest that judges also – maybe to some people's surprise – take this view. In general they have vigorously promoted the concept of fairness and defended the citizen's right to be heard properly.

Politicians are ambivalent. If they disagree with a public body's actions, they are happy to champion the right to apply for a judicial review. If they support that body, and maybe if they are ministers of the Crown trying hard to make savings in our public services, they might well take a different view. The Rt Hon. Chris Grayling certainly did. When he was Secretary of State for Justice he tried hard to discourage such legal challenges. Apart from putting up the fees for various formalities, all kinds of other ideas were canvassed. One was to discourage applicants from pursuing claims supported by charities or other campaigning bodies. Another was to ban one public body from taking another to court. That was quietly dropped and although the government may have succeeded in minimising some judicial reviews, these changes are unlikely to make much of a difference.

The reason is many of the cases involving consultation are not really about the process anyway. As we mentioned earlier, what motivates many claimants is the loss of a popular service, or a disputed change of policy. Had they been able to go to court and argue about the merits of the case rather than the adequacies of the consultation, no doubt they would have done so. Sometimes they can. There may be statutory requirements such as exist for councils to provide a library service. If a council considers changing such a service, then the argument is about whether proposed changes actually breach a council's legal obligations. Once in a blue moon, lawyers try to use the *irrationality* argument, in essence seeking to show that a decision was so absurd or unjustified that no other public body or individual facing similar circumstances could have possibly come to that particular conclusion. It is called the Wednesbury rule after a 1948 case* and is trotted out every so often by barristers whose overall case looks a little weak. They could save their learned breaths, for the argument seldom succeeds and focus invariably moves onto the procedural side of things.

Claimants try hard to demolish the credibility of a consultation. They will point to all manner of technical failures: the questionnaire was biased, the website did not work properly, the advertised meeting never took place, some of the statistics were wrong et cetera. Consultation is not an exact science and it is always possible to find some flaw in what happened. But very few cases lose on such grounds. In the words of a wise judge in 2013, 'it is not the function of this court retrospectively to micromanage for perfection'.†

At the risk of repetition, we have concluded that most judicial reviews are not about the law at all. Not really. They are an attempt by critics of a public body's decision to overturn that decision. The critics choose to go to court because they sense that consultation is the weakest part of a decision-maker's case. If it was required to consult, did it do so properly and was it given a

---

* Associated Provincial Picture Houses Ltd *v* Wednesbury Corporation [1948] 1 KB 223.

† Turner J in R (*ex parte* Gate) *v* Lancashire CC [2013] EWCH 2937 (Admin).

complete picture of relevant views before taking its decision? Win or lose, campaigners gain a large amount of publicity. Plucky objectors have their day in court, literally. Like-minded people are attracted to the cause, and, if successful, they show the public body to be inefficient, untrustworthy, uncaring or worse. Successful legal challenges greatly enhance political opposition and can be a godsend to campaigners whose arguments on the substance of the case might be flagging somewhat.

So, many of these cases are really about politics. They are a rite of passage that can sometimes, though not always, be used to hammer home one side of an argument. We have dozens of examples where a judicial review formed part of a long-running dispute. One was the row about Lewisham Hospital,* with MPs and local doctors claiming that the Department of Health's Trust Special Administrator did not legally have the power to close significant services at Lewisham in order to save money elsewhere. To fight the case, NHS supporters nationwide contributed to a crowd-funded campaign, and built a war chest to pay for the best lawyers in the business. A petition acquired 51,854 signatures, and a parliamentary campaign secured debates and raised questions at every turn. The judicial review in this case played an important role in winning the argument, but it does not always work out in this way. Those who go to law take something of a risk and a significant financial liability. If the court thinks an important matter of principle is at stake, or if significant stakeholder rights are potentially jeopardised, they can offer a costs protection order. This can limit the fees that claimants have

---

* R (*ex parte* Lewisham LB and Save Lewisham Hospital Campaign Ltd) *v* Secretary of State for Health and Trust Special Administrator appointed to South London Hospitals NHS Trust [2013] EWHC 2381 (Admin).

to pay. Even then it can be costly, and prospective litigants would be foolhardy to rely upon a judge's sympathetic generosity.

By most standards, the courts have a good record of subjecting the executive to legal scrutiny. Judges have, on occasions, bent over backwards to ensure that claimants with an arguable case are able to challenge the decisions of public bodies if they seem high-handed or procedurally flawed. Those in the right-leaning media have often complained about this, arguing that the balance has swung too far and exposed public sector managers and civil servants to unrealistic criticisms. Some judges have been characterised as interfering busybodies duped by hard-luck stories and political rhetoric to find fault in what are in fact reasonable managerial decisions. Equality legislation is a frequent target for such sentiments.

It was Parliament itself that effectively gave the courts such a problematic weapon with which to monitor and adjudicate on the decisions of public bodies. The *due regard* principle is thought by many to be woolly and imprecise, and its interpretation unpredictable. For years, High Court decisions have gone in claimants' favour or been successfully defended on the most marginal aspects of evidence. A succession of six, twelve and eight principles in the cases of Judy Brown (2008), Sabrina Branwood (2013) and Bracking (2013) respectively, three seminal judgments on equality law, elaborated upon and sometimes contradicted each other. None have acquired the hallowed status of the Gunning Principles. The one consistent element has been a reluctance to insist upon an equality assessment, or equivalent, but in practice *due regard* can rarely be assured without such an analysis being to hand.

Even the terminology causes confusion. As we commented earlier, it was once called the equalities impact assessment or EIA, initials coincidentally also used for a parallel concept in the field of planning. There, the relevant document is the environmental impact assessment, a major constituent of any significant-sized development and a cornerstone of European planning law. Although they have very different histories, these two EIAs are tools to achieve a similar objective. In the one case, it is there to help us ensure that roads, railways, airports, power stations and the rest do not cause unacceptable damage to the physical environment. In the other, we try to minimise the risk of harm to the social fabric of our communities. Both rely on the principle that decision-makers have to appreciate the likely consequences of their actions, so everything depends upon these assessments being honest and accurate.

In defining the *protected characteristics,* the Equality Act 2010 required organisations proposing changes to try to anticipate what would happen when their plans were implemented. The law does not prevent them from taking steps that may disadvantage a particular group in some way, but is crystal clear in needing them to understand the consequences for these categories. This is the prompt for mitigation actions and evidence of such an approach will certainly help prove that there has indeed been *due regard.*

This is where consultation becomes relevant. It is one thing for a staff member to gather the relevant statistics, but another for the anticipated impact of various proposals to be openly discussed with these specific groups. There may be disagreement on a whole host of aspects. Figures may be disputed, existing practices may be poorly understood and future behaviour may be difficult to predict.

Any debate should ideally be within the context of any consultation that takes place. Equality, after all, is but one aspect of the entire case for change and although the regulations in Wales state that the equality assessment has to be published alongside or as part of the consultation, there is no such stipulation in England. All the same, Section 149 has to be satisfied and decision-makers have to have before them a convincing explanation of what will happen when they take their decision. In one High Court case,* a judge ruled that elected councillors need not necessarily have seen the actual assessment document, and that a generalised summary was sufficient. The Court of Appeal overruled him! In another case† when officers relied on a formula that obscured the likely impact of forty-seven separate budget cuts, claimants successfully challenged the consultation.

There are many who believe this all this sounds like bureaucracy gone mad. Others will think it bears little relation to the real world of tough decisions taken by hard-pressed public servants or elected politicians at a time of austerity. We think, however, that the judges have recognised this and seldom interfered where it can be shown that a genuine attempt has been made to follow the underlying principles of the Equality Act. With few exceptions, they have taken action only when governments or other agencies appear to be contemptuous of their responsibilities, or where the interests of certain citizens appear to have been overlooked or ignored.

Not for the first time, politicians have handed over to the courts a role in helping to bring about major social change. Ending

* R (*ex parte* Aaron Hunt) *v* North Somerset Council [2013] EWCA Civ 1320.

† R (*ex parte* DAT and BNM) *v* West Berkshire Council [2016] EWHC 1876 (Admin).

generations of discrimination against certain people is a noble cause and there is much support for a policy of ensuring that publicly accountable organisations play their part by taking important decisions in a particular way; hence the *due regard* rule. But someone has to police it and although there is a strong case for an administrative remedy, a mediation service or an ombudsman, without such mechanisms an aggrieved citizen has only the courts to access.

Between them, the *doctrine of legitimate expectation* and the willingness of the courts to insist on consultation when people's interests are at stake, the potency of the Gunning Principles once a consultation happens and the overlay of equality legislation make for a formidable set of rules for our bureaucracies to observe. As we will observe in the remaining parts of this book, they create a heavy backcloth of obligations that affect the entire landscape of our public affairs and have a profound effect on the politics of consultation.

Part Two

The Role of
Consultation in
Politics

Chapter 4 – Introduction

Beyond tokenism?

Tokenism according to Arnstein | power-sharing | right-wing and left-wing views | evaluating consultation | playing politics | the felling of a forestry minister

Few will argue that consultation has no role to play in the political drama. But there is plenty of disagreement as to what that role should be and what impact it might have.

Before we try to illustrate the realities as we see them, it may be as well to acknowledge that there is a vocal body of thought that believes the whole business is a charade. All the consultative mechanisms in the world are only a clever smokescreen to obscure the *realpolitik* that governs all decisions of importance. No one has articulated this scepticism better than the columnist, and ex-MP, Matthew Parris, who objected to pouring what he called 'bucket-loads of participation' over every group, every community and every question*.

---

* Matthew Parris, 'Don't ask my opinion; don't consult, engage or include; just lead', *The Times*, 26 February 2005.

Others point to an enduring analysis produced almost half a century ago, known to most as the *Arnstein Ladder*,* and, to our dismay, taught in colleges and universities to this day. Sherry Arnstein was a respected, left-leaning, American academic who, in retrospect, produced work that captured her distaste for corporate power and suspicions of municipal and federal governments. She dismissed consultation as 'tokenistic', a label that has stuck in the minds of many critics and which has regularly led to calls to abandon this clearly ineffective form of citizen participation in favour of something more concrete.

The trouble is, those alternatives are themselves hugely problematic. The Arnstein Ladder itself talks of *placation, partnership* and *delegated power* before ascending to the heights of *citizen control.* We have consistently preferred a more recent adaptation of Arnstein by David Wilcox in 1994, † which recognises that one can go beyond consultation by *deciding together, acting together* and ultimately *supporting* other organisations to which power has effectively been delegated.

All these models can, under certain circumstances, work effectively, so there is no objection in principle to any of them. So when politicians and academics sagely comment that, whilst consultation was once important but has really had its day because the world has moved on to a more participative culture, we smile sweetly and ask them to describe successful examples of these situations. They are not without merit, but do not always turn out to be what they seem.

---

* Sherry R. Arnstein, 'A Ladder of Citizen Participation', *Journal of the American Institute of Planners*, vol. 35, no. 4 (1969), pp. 216–24.

† David Wilcox, *The Guide to Effective Participation* (London: David Wilcox, 1994), available at http://partnerships.org.uk/guide/index.htm (accessed 19 March 2018).

The first time we heard the term 'neighbourhood planning'* it was after being harangued about the iniquities of the planning system and the inadequacies of the consultations inherent in it. Communities, we were told, were fed up with being asked their views and then ignored. No doubt that's true. But this unhappy state of affairs could be transformed at a stroke by allowing local people to decide for themselves and therefore never be overruled by busybody bureaucrats who, we were also told, needed to be abolished anyway – on principle. More later about planning and the arguments about neighbourhood planning – which, to its credit, has much going for it. But for now, it illustrates the hopes that many have expressed, that one could escape from the limitations of consultation and invent mechanisms that somehow allowed consultees something closer to real power.

The truth is that political power is precisely located and is difficult to spread around. Consultation survives as a concept because it is difficult to devise many formulae which enable your arguments to *determine*, rather than *influence*, a decision.

There have, of course, been attempts to force people to share power. The very concept of power-sharing is a fascinating experiment. It is probably seen by the public as an institutional form of knocking heads together and forcing friend and foe to sit alongside each other and secure consensus even when they profoundly disagree. In the UK and Ireland, we are most familiar with this scenario when studying the Northern Ireland power-sharing executive. It is an amazing tribute to the Northern Irish

---

* Neighbourhood planning is a right for communities introduced through the Localism Act 2011. Communities can shape development in their areas through the production of neighbourhood development plans, neighbourhood development orders and community right to build orders. See http://www.rtpi.org.uk/planning-aid/neighbourhood-planning (accessed 19 March 2018).

that thirty years of community conflict known as the Troubles, and the preceding centuries of mistrust, could culminate in the Good Friday Agreement,* which survives to this day – despite a rollercoaster ride towards more normal democracy.

Except that it is not normal at all. Obliging parties as opposed as the Democratic Unionists and Sinn Féin to work alongside each other required the fear of failure to overrule virtually every other consideration. By early 2018, there had been a year-long impasse and whether power-sharing could survive in the long term was a real question. The best view was that it would probably be sustainable only for as long as the preconditions that brought it into being persisted. So how did we get there? No amount of historic attempts to heed the arguments of a vocal but ultimately outvoted minority could appease Unionists. When their power was removed in favour of direct rule, a London government could consult as much as it liked but more was needed to secure the commitment of the Republican minority to being ruled within a Northern Ireland entity. In other words, there could clearly be situations when consultation, with its bias towards the existing power structure, cannot work and where different democratic constructs are needed.

Both political right and political left have found consultation an unconvincing option. From a right-wing, market-led perspective, the situational dynamic is sufficient to oblige producers and consumers to arrive at the optimum relationship. Top companies have survived by being better at addressing the needs of their customers than others. If this involves large expenditures in elaborate market research or even formal consultation with those

* Agreed on Good Friday, 10 April 1998, between the British government, the Irish government and the political parties of Northern Ireland, and implemented between April 1998 and December 1999.

customers, fair enough. No one here objects to consultation as an operational or managerial tool, but it is that and no more. It is up to each and every company to decide for itself whether or not this is the right way to proceed.

Apply this to political decision-making and the 'market' of the ballot box is invoked. If you have policies that people like and will support in elections, then that is all you need. It may be accepted that consultation has a role in helping to flush out the details of otherwise vague or still evolving policies. On the big questions, the right-wing view is that we identify and appoint those who know how to manage, vote for them if the opportunity arises, and make them accountable at the end of their terms for the wisdom they have or have not exercised. Those who dislike consultation often quote the defence analogy. We would never vote for our generals in the armed forces, we are told. And neither would we try to second-guess their major strategic decisions. If ever there was a cause big enough to warrant consultation, it should be by referendum. Was this maybe the thinking behind an in–out referendum on the EU?

From a left-wing perspective, the objections to consultation have been firmly based on opposition to the *status quo*. If your fundamental political belief is that existing power structures are wrong, then any process that accepts this and does nothing to disturb it cannot, by definition, add value. The objection goes deeper by suggesting that the very act of consultation can be a deceit, implying that those with power may claim to be willing to surrender some of it whilst in practice having no such intention. It is thus a confidence trick – a fraud on the genuine expectations of citizens.

The dislike of both political extremes has led to some unforeseen consequences. One is a relative dearth of good-quality academic research into public consultation. There are exceptions, of course, but research effort has concentrated on exploring and championing some of the more participative tools and techniques rather than understanding what happens in the traditional model of consultation. The key unanswered question is whether the millions of pounds spent on consultation yield a satisfactory return on investment.

It is not a simple question. How does one measure the impact of a typical consultation? Those who have tried to evaluate larger, more participative mechanisms have found it easier. In September 2005, the NHS launched a series of high-profile events under the brand name Your Health, Your Care, Your Say. It was designed to go beyond the normal boundaries of consultation, to engage with a wide range of stakeholders and give them a real feeling of involvement in big decisions that were, supposedly, imminent. An excellent evaluation of the entire exercise found that many of those 'soft' objectives were indeed met, but found it much more challenging to form a view on the 'hard' question. How much influence did these events and those who participated actually have? In this, and in many other comparable cases, those who have formed part of the process feel terribly optimistic that they have made a difference. Right-wing critics say they are deluded because their contribution would have added nothing to what was already largely well known; left-wing critics merely claim that whatever they said would have made little difference really – power was still concentrated in the Department of Health, which had commissioned the exercise in the first place.

The politics of consultation definitely complicates this question of measuring the effectiveness of a consultation. To take a simple but spectacular example, on the key question posed to the Scottish people in 2014's independence referendum, the Scottish Nationalist case was defeated. Politically, however, the referendum's achievement for the SNP was monumental, leading to its Scottish landslide victory in the following year's general election. Politicians of all hues will attest to the truth that fighting a losing battle often prepares one better for a more successful subsequent campaign. Maybe it is because so many of them cut their electoral teeth by standing in a hopeless seat with the aspiration of learning the ropes and being selected for a safer constituency years later. It means politicians learn to take the long view, in contrast to their being criticised so often for being short-termist.

Any analysis of modern consultations will find disputes and disagreements and ask about them the question 'Why did that become so controversial an issue?' The answer may often be that a particular politician, or a political party, or even a professional body found it in their interest to take a particular stance on this occasion. Consciously or unconsciously it would, at some time in the future, be seen to have helped their cause. It is at this point that conscientious civil servants and other public officials roll their eyes and reach for the whisky. Is this not exactly what justifies them in using the term 'playing politics'? They see politicians whipping up support for or against something and question whether the issue really warrants all the hoo-ha. Regrettably there are times when this kind of behaviour has some justification, but as we will observe in this part of the book, they are fewer than many would suppose. What actually happens is that a consultation offers the opportunity for something to be considered by a wider audience than the decision-makers themselves and the trend towards greater transparency is almost certainly unstoppable.

We therefore arrive at the conclusion that evaluating the impact of a consultation takes us beyond examining what happened to the issue itself. It looks at a wider political context and the role that a particular exercise might have played in the balance of that wider political argument. It might take years to know the answer!

Looking at the impact the process may have had on the issue itself is without doubt easier, but again is not wholly straightforward. Policies can undoubtedly be improved and plans can change – on occasions quite dramatically. The best-known example in recent years was in October 2010 when the Department of the Environment, Food and Rural Affairs outlined a series of proposals for changing the ownership of 258,000 hectares of state-owned woodland in England. The idea was to move towards a mixed economy of sorts, by transferring land from the Forestry Commission to a range of bodies, many of which would have been charities. When the consultation was launched, it unleashed an unholy row, with the twin forces of the National Trust and the *Daily Telegraph* prominent in a public campaign that included hundreds of local protests from the Forest of Dean to the Forest of Bowland. It was as if the government intended to steal the land from dozens of local communities, who until that moment had probably never realised how much they loved the Forestry Commission.

The story is used by the Consultation Institute to illustrate the pitfalls of neglecting to do the essential pre-consultation homework that is now the hallmark of well-designed consultation exercises. For now, we record that the result was an ignominious retreat by a government minister* and the firm intervention of a prime minister who was seriously embarrassed and who sacked the hapless Caroline Spelman when he conducted his first Cabinet reshuffle.

---

* In a statement on the Forestry Commission England website, Defra said: 'The consultation on the future of the Public Forest Estate in England was halted on 17 February 2011. It is clear that people cherish their forests and woodlands and the benefits they bring but are not happy with the proposals we set out. We want to thank those of you who have taken the time to contribute your thoughts and ideas.' See https://www.forestry.gov.uk/england-pfeconsultation (accessed 19 March 2018).

Chapter 5
Consultation and planning

Town planning | neighbourhood planning | developers |
housing | local plan-making | infrastructure planning |
nuclear power | energy-from-waste | HS2 | NIMBYism |
airports | fracking

Of all the subjects leading to formal public consultations, planning is close to the top of the list. Quantitatively, there are more consultations on this aspect of public affairs than are found in any other; qualitatively, they are often of the highest public profile and can arouse the most passionate debates.

Town planning is probably notable for having been the first public service to consult systematically. After the Second World War, the landmark Town and Country Planning Act 1947 and all that followed enshrined the statutory role of consultation as the UK sought to rebuild its cities, rehouse its people and re-engineer its infrastructure. * Its advocates saw it partly as a simple

---

* It is worth noting, however, that Penny Norton, author of the authoritative *Public Consultation and Community Involvement in Planning* (Abingdon: Routledge, 2017), believes that the real start of consultation in planning came in response

application of common sense. 'You would want everyone to help decide major planning issues, wouldn't you?' But among the enthusiasts were a large number of idealists, who saw their mission in life to use the planning system to achieve an economic redistribution of wealth; hence the enormous push for massive public housing and the popularity of top-down urban design and garden cities.

So spatial planning is inherently political, if not party political. Consider how nineteenth-century municipal leaders managed to build impressive buildings and infrastructures that enhanced their cities and the lives of their people. Some of the magnificent Victorian town halls we can visit today in Leeds, Manchester, Glasgow or Belfast were not the product of a public consultation. They were the response to political pressure and were frequently the grandiose expression of civic pride extolling the elected and the appointed. But we have to remember the social context: a very limited franchise, only rudimentary education and power structures that were simple but crude. Private buildings were usually commissioned by wealthy individuals, trade bodies or companies and designed to reflect the values and ideals their creators wished to convey to the world. The Victorians and their successors were far from naïve in their use of public relations!

We are not sure if the academic who suggested that urban planning only really became necessary with the invention of the lift was joking, but he had a point. Once it was possible to erect very high buildings, land values in the biggest cities rocketed so that a given piece of land was worth far more than the buildings that could traditionally be constructed on it. This made land a much more tradable commodity and one whose value depended,

---

to the 1969 Skeffington Report, which advocated the involvement of the public in planning.

to a great measure, on what you had permission to build. The rush to impose building controls in the late nineteenth and early twentieth centuries owed as much to the need to control untrammelled property speculation, as to citizens clamouring for some protection from the hideous and grotesque being built in the wrong place.

This diversion into social history, for it is a comparable story everywhere from Cincinnati to Sydney, is needed if we are to fully appreciate the unique relationship between spatial planning and the political process. Both are concerned with taking difficult decisions in an environment where there are few obvious answers and where the interests of conflicting stakeholders can be profoundly at variance. When Aneurin Bevan said that politics was about the language of priorities,* he could equally have claimed that the way your town or your county looks is the language of local preferences.

It is said that until 2013, when the BBC made and broadcast a series called *The Planners*, few people realised the extent to which our democratic processes engage with planning problems. In one episode, viewers were treated to the traumas of an elderly couple in Chester trying to secure planning permission for solar panels on a roof that was visible from the city's celebrated Roman walls. Then there was the village that deeply objected to a new housing development, and the lady who wanted to extend her house into her front garden...

Developers are increasingly required to consult local people even before they apply for planning permission. So-called pre-application consultations are meant to convince councils that the views of local residents have been taken into account by those

---

* At the 1956 Labour Party conference.

who prepare the proposals. They are something of a hit-or-miss affair. Councils have been reluctant to discourage developers whose suggestions they welcome, and the quality of these preliminary dialogues is seldom independently assessed or scrutinised by the planning committees that ask for them. At this level, what is going on is more public participation than public consultation. To the extent that local people are consulted, they are constrained by the overall plan which local planning authorities have agreed, and the principle that neighbours and others can raise objections if they find the specific proposals unacceptable.

This is bread-and-butter development control. The final decision is taken by councillors, thereby supplying the democratic element, who are bound by strict rules to ensure a minimum level of consistency and to discourage obvious forms of corruption. If Members of Parliament were to become regularly involved they would be swiftly shown the door by locally elected councillors, who would rightly resent their interference. Prudent parliamentarians try hard, therefore, to avoid becoming embroiled in disputes between neighbours – despite their surgeries being regularly used to voice the concern of one side or another.

On occasions, the issue is of principle. At other times it is its application to a particular piece of land. Nothing seems to excite local passions more than housing, and it is to this that we must turn if we want to assess the role of consultation in our decision-making.

It seems somewhat trite, writing in the early years of the twenty-first century, to say that everyone agrees that there is a shortage of housing. Speaking as authors with about fifty years of public awareness to recall, we cannot remember there ever *not* being a shortage of housing.

It is strange that housing disappeared from the top-line political agenda in the last quarter of a century. Being Minister of Housing was really important in the 1950s, and the Conservative Party is credited with general election victories due to the heroics of Harold Macmillan, when in that post, achieving the target of building 300,000 houses a year. But then the policy of council house-building became unpopular as poor design and even poorer planning led to enormous social problems, allowing the 'sink' estate syndrome to take root. Margaret Thatcher's response was to let enterprising tenants become homeowners with her policy of selling council houses at a discount, a policy so highly revered that thirty years later it is still felt to be a vote-winner.

This signalled a shift in responsibility for housing away from the government of the day and towards the free market. What it also meant was that planners would now have an even more important role. If the council won't build houses, someone else must, and all that society must do is to stipulate where, when and maybe what they might look like. For twenty years or more, house-building became the hidden issue and started to look like a regulatory matter rather than a political one.

All this time, there was a shortage and the Labour administrations of 1997 and 2001 basically addressed this in a typically regulatory way. Labour's idea was to strengthen regional development areas and give teeth to regional development plans. At one time its backers wanted to see a proper democratic legitimacy for such plans through regional assemblies. That went nowhere.

The regional bodies began to attract enemies. Some of these were house builders – especially those with local roots, or the bigger firms with the lobbying skills to deploy against local authorities that may have needed persuasion. On the other hand, developers were often thankful for a regional body able to take a wider view and maybe overrule a reluctant planning committee.

More significant, however, was the growing tide of resentment arising from communities themselves. This was particularly noticeable in the densely populated south of England, but was probably present throughout the country. People took the view that there was little point in voting for local councillors to decide on local planning matters only for them to be overruled by regional bodies a long way away. This was not a geographical sense of distance – but more a cultural sense of remoteness. When the Conservative Party published its analysis in the 2009 policy Green Paper *Open Source Planning*, a thousand villages would have rejoiced as they read it. The criticism that there had been a quiet, underhand power grab from local people on matters of intense local interest resonated far and wide and, try as they might, the planning profession could do little to stem the tide of censure.

It was, therefore, inevitable that one of Eric Pickles' first acts as the coalition government's man in charge of local government and planning was to publish a Localism Bill that removed the hated regional tier. Instead it encouraged planning authorities to push decision-making even further towards the grassroots by creating the idea of neighbourhood plans, * backed by referendums.

Remember, however, that we still had a housing shortage. Defenders of the regional development agencies (RDAs) just looked at the numbers. Their view was that, left to their own devices, very few local authorities would build enough houses to

---

* See Chapter 4.

meet their own requirements, let alone allo
growth. At least as long as RDAs existed, ther
say 'Yes', if too many councils were saying 'No'.

The coalition government begged to differ. Co
ministers may have been under pressure from leafy subu
traditional villages to say 'No', but their view was that some w
surely say 'Yes' if provided with the right incentives. The
introduced a new homes bonus – a modest bribe to encourage
reluctant authorities, but mostly they still said 'No'. When
neighbourhood plans were first mooted they were also seen as a
charter for the opponents of house-builders. Here was an
opportunity to spell out in comforting local detail where 'No'
would be the answer. Developers and old-school planners, still
chasing the numbers, were seriously concerned.

When, in October 2011, the government consulted about
neighbourhood planning, the experts all explained the chaos that
might ensue if neighbourhood plans were at odds with the
planning authorities' settled view of where they wanted to build.
As a result, neighbourhood plans were designed to be consistent
with the local plans already developed following long laborious
consultation and consideration. If a neighbourhood plan
attempted to contradict the council's existing plan, it would be
rejected and the public would not even have the opportunity of a
referendum, let alone vote for the new local alternative. This
popular vote was seen by many as the hallmark of the consultative
culture that Ministers were trying to graft onto the planning
system. And it was popular. Turnouts at these referendums far
outstripped those at council elections, and there remains a
powerful argument that a community that votes for its local
spatial plan is more likely to feel committed to its implementation.

ities of a community – a
ad rather a lot on the way you
question. Define an area in one
est a priority for business use
ther way and everything would
major housing development.

:d this problem. It obliged
on of an area and, frankly, we
v disputes. Maybe that is, in
part, explained by the fact that the majority of early
neighbourhood plans were generated in the south of England and
in rural areas. In one spectacular case, however, a dispute went all
the way to the High Court* and illustrated the politics of local
planning very well. It concerned a part of High Wycombe in
Buckinghamshire. The area had contained a Royal Air Force base
known as Daws Hill. Originally when the local community
seriously began preparing for a neighbourhood plan the site had
been released by the Ministry of Defence and outline planning
permission obtained for a development of hundreds of homes.
The Daws Hill community sought to draw the boundary of their
designated area to include this site and campaigned accordingly.
Consultation was perfunctory. Only fourteen stakeholders
participated and of these the principal developer, Taylor
Woodrow, was the most prominent. Intriguingly, however,
looking over the shoulder of the local district council was another
interested party – Buckinghamshire County Council. Its advice
was unequivocal. If the local people were able to include Daws
Hill in their designated area, it might not prevent, but could
entirely frustrate and delay, the construction of much-needed

---

* R (*ex parte* Daws Hill Neighbourhood Forum) *v* Wycombe DC [2013]
EWHC 513 (Admin).

housing in the area. After all, the county council knew we still had a housing shortage!

For reasons that faintly mystify us, the claimants chose not to fight their case on the inadequacy of the consultation, but tried to demonstrate how excluding the air force base was unfair to the local community. Their challenge duly failed, but not before exposing to all, the problems of defining an area in a way acceptable to its residents.

At the time of writing there were almost 2,000 neighbourhood plans at some stage of preparation. Countless referendums have been held and evidence is mounting of genuine engagement in communities all over England. The success of the policy has confounded many sceptics, but has also seriously disconcerted some in the planning profession. Once ministers decided to give primacy to the councils' adopted plans and reduce the potential conflict between them, all seemed straightforward – except that only half the councils had reached the stage when their plan could be adopted. It takes years. There was a mad scramble to accelerate those plans stuck in the mire of local disputes and indecision, with planners put under pressure, for otherwise the neighbourhood's own plan would hold sway.

In terms of increasing public participation and giving local people more say in shaping their immediate environment, this new innovation scores highly and seems here to stay. But the need for it largely arose from the interminable process of making plans the old-fashioned way.

In 2014 there was a test case that explored the delays and distractions along such a journey. A Mrs Kendall sought a judicial review against her local authority, Rochford District Council.* She alleged that a crucial consultation before the examination stage of the local plan had been invisible to her and her fellow residents. It had also been largely inaccessible as it was entirely conducted through an online questionnaire. For years we had been waiting for the courts to pronounce on the growing practice of relying solely on internet-based consultations. When it came the decision was clear cut. The courts found that the council had acted unlawfully, because the consultation was inadequate. It is worth quoting from the judgment, paragraph 82, explaining what is alleged to have happened:

> The council never directly notified any individual members of the public – not even those on its planning policy mailing list – of its consultation on the draft plan together with the sustainability appraisal. It never published any details of those consultations in *Rochford District Matters* or in any other local newspaper. When it did consult the general public it relied solely on its website. This was contrary to the council's promise in the Statement of Community Involvement that it would use 'electronic media' in consultation 'only in conjunction with other forms of participation'.

> Even for those who did have access to the internet, navigating the website to find the page … was far from straightforward … The inhabitants of Rayleigh – would not have been aware that consultation under the SEA [Strategic Environmental Assessment] regulations was taking place unless they happened to have heard about it by chance.

* R (*ex parte* Kendall) *v* Rochford DC & Department for Communities and Local Government [2014] EWHC 3866 (Admin).

Here we have a process deliberately designed to settle differences between competing local interests, but it is made so bureaucratic and inaccessible that even the most active community campaigners can scarcely mount an objection. As an aside, we need to note that although Mrs Kendall won her argument on the specifics of relying on the online survey, she failed to stop the plan or indeed quash the decision. The judge felt that the inadequacies of the consultation did not, on the evidence of this particular case, suggest that the outcome would have been any different had it been better conducted.

But there in a nutshell is the problem. Successive bouts of consultation embedded in an overall plan-making process of mind-numbing and arcane complexity destroy the all-important causal connection between effort and reward. Without this, most people cannot justify spending their time and taking the trouble to respond.

Few consultations have the magic formula of, say, the Scottish independence referendum of 2014, where a clear decision followed immediately after participation. Such instant gratification is clearly missing from local authority-based plan-making, with dire consequences for the reputation of planners. We feel sorry for them. Despite the coalition's much-trumpeted bonfire of planning regulations, including a reduction of approximately 1,000 pages of guidance to about 50 pages, planners are still bound by a statutory system that proceeds at a snail's pace.

No wonder the housing shortage got worse. Not even Labour's top-down regional target-setting foresaw the combined effects of shrinking average household size alongside unplanned immigration. The established model of spatial planning takes too

adly, there is something of a conflict between being
ative and being quick. The reason the process takes a long
time is because it requires councils to listen at several different
points. All totally logical, but maybe lacking the urgency that the
housing shortage demands. Ministers clearly understand this and
regularly bring forward ideas for tinkering with the system, but to
limited effect.

A few years ago, we were invited to facilitate a large-scale public
meeting in a village called Bodelwyddan in Denbighshire. The
system in Wales differs in detail, but is fundamentally similar. The
county council sought to satisfy a Planning Inspectorate desire to
see 800 units a year of new housing and the residents had been
worried by a suggestion that 1,500 of them would be built in their
village. Anyone familiar with this glorious part of north Wales
knows that suitable building land is not easy to find, especially in
the mountainous majority of the county. Equally, anyone who has
visited Bodelwyddan, nestled between the smallish coastal plain
from Abergele to Rhyl and the hills that rise up to the south,
knows that it was once a truly delightful village, with a white
marble wedding-cake church. Admittedly the presence of a major
hospital and the A55 trunk road spoilt things a bit, but not to the
point that the local community lost the wish to protect themselves
from further development.

The evening saw over 200 people packed into the village hall.
BBC Cymru Wales and the local constabulary stood outside and
residents sat from 18.30 to 22.00 without a break to express their
displeasure. In a memorable intervention, the campaigning
committee asked to see the facilitators before proceedings began,
to protest that the agenda contained a mid-point 'comfort break'.
'Not needed,' they said. 'We don't want to waste a single second
and lose the opportunity to tell the county council how absurd

this proposal is.' So, they sat there, cross-legged, and vocal as only the Welsh can be. It was a bilingual event and we heard all manner of objections. To this day we recall the local vicar, with all the gravitas of his calling, in a deep baritone reminding his parishioners that whenever it rained (it usually does in this part of the world) burials in the local cemetery meant pumping water out of newly dug graves. Clearly the land was flood-prone and unsuitable for housing development. Everyone agreed.

It is easy to parody this Dibley-esque* scenario, but it is no comedy. Residents were in deadly earnest and at the end of their tether. The meeting in question had been requested three times and the county council was technically right to point out that the formal procedure only required residents to state their objections and submit them for councillors to consider. They had, of course, done all this and more – but knew that most of the councillors came from the mountains and with their friends could outvote Bodelwyddan's supporters. And they grasped the housing development truth that a councillor voting against a distant proposal could end up having the same unwelcome proposal in his or her own backyard.

This dilemma can be replicated all over the country and has added venom when the proposals involve the once-untouchable Green Belt. Social media has greatly enhanced the ability of community groups to campaign. It is nicely ironic that many of those who object to councils over-relying on new technology are among the best at exploiting it themselves. Public bodies are often ill equipped to respond rapidly to the speed with which modern grassroots mobilisation can take place. At one level this is a magnificently liberating development, opening up the corridors

* *The Vicar of Dibley* is a BBC TV sitcom that originally ran between 1994 and 1998, starring Dawn French in the title role.

81

of power to unprecedented influence. At the same time, it places a real premium on the organising skills of various groups, rather than the quality of the argument. One thing, however, is certain. New tricks of the social media trade ensure a steady stream of innovation, giving competitive advantage to those who learn them quickest.

It can set council against council. The most spectacular example is the long-running saga of an incinerator in Norfolk. It is a perfect illustration of local politics at work and has lessons for planners and politicians alike. It began with the county council being required, in common with other top-tier authorities, to produce a waste management plan. It consulted. So did others. Unfortunately, not many people noticed. Norfolk is England's fifth largest county by area and it is a long way from Great Yarmouth in the east to King's Lynn in the west. Suffice to say that when, following the aforesaid consultation, the plan was adopted and required the council to build an energy-from-waste plant, nobody in North-West Norfolk District Council paid much attention.

Suddenly, however, the original assumption that the facility would be based close to the county's largest centre of population, Norwich, was changed. Instead the county council proposed to build it in King's Lynn and the chosen contractor, Cory Wheelabrator, duly went about its business and sought planning permission. At once the community's alarm bells sounded. Now that waste management had become what planners call site-specific, all hell broke loose. The Conservative-led district council called a referendum on the issue, using little-known powers given to councils some years earlier and largely unused since. The question it asked was whether local people were in favour of the proposed facility. So intense was the public interest that an impressive 61 per cent of the population cast their vote and of those, 92 per cent were against the proposal.

We asked the district council chairman at the time to explain his thinking. He was, to say the least, sending more than a shot across the bows of the county council, also Conservative-led; in fact, he was sending a whole battleship. The propaganda war had its effect. Soon the Department of Communities and Local Government demurred in grant-aiding the project. Then there was an unsuccessful High Court case and, in due course, the county council found itself faced with enormous costs. If it pulled out of the deal with Cory Wheelabrator there would be millions to pay in commercial costs and compensation. If it ploughed on with an increasingly unviable project, it faced further financial issues and political unpopularity to boot.

That political unpopularity cost it dearly. In the 2013 local elections the Conservative Party lost a total of twenty seats on the county council, ending its twelve years of majority rule. UKIP took fourteen seats. The defeated Conservative leader, Bill Borrett, ruefully said, 'We need a consensual approach going forward ... So I hope my consensual and collegiate approach is something that fits with what people perceive is required.' A failure to consult better on the original waste plan and an inability to build a wider consensus were the root cause of his problems.

In their different ways both Bodelwyddan and King's Lynn illustrate how communities can fight against proposals that affect their areas. The rights and wrongs of the argument play a relatively small part in the dynamic. Of course there was a case for housing on the coastal plain of Denbighshire – and we understand that houses have been built. And similarly, a waste facility of the kind proposed for King's Lynn will probably be built, in spite of the arguments advanced by those who believe the technology to be both unviable and a health risk.

What we are witnessing is a retreat from pure planning into politics. Of course it was never that pure, and in 1995 the Committee for Standards in Public Life introduced the Seven Principles of Public Life,* known as the Nolan Principles after the committee's first chairman, Lord Nolan. They operate as an anti-corruption measure and oblige decision-makers to behave appropriately without taking sides. Everyone joining a planning committee is solemnly advised that it is a 'quasi-judicial' process and that their decisions must conform to strict planning laws which might result in legal challenges. That is asking a great deal from elected members whose constituents expect them to take a particular stance on matters of local controversy. It takes personal courage and a commitment to a fair hearing for all shades of opinion, and is possibly threatened by the current vogue for pinning all politicians down to definitive answers. It is becoming increasingly difficult to say 'I don't yet know'.

It is very problematic to find anyone to take responsibility for those most unpopular decisions. So challenging in fact, that the Blair administration finally accepted expert advice. They tried to take out of politics the most awkward infrastructure planning projects. The 2008 Planning Act put this into effect and provided for a set of national plans for various aspects of infrastructure. One would be for roads, another for rail, yet another for docks or water. They were all meant to settle upon an overall strategy, subject to consultation and a full nationwide debate. Apart from suppliers and specialised stakeholders, no one noticed. Far more interesting for everyone was the creation of the Infrastructure

* See Learn to Be a Leader website, http://www.learn-to-be-a-leader.com/nolan-principles.html (accessed 20 March 2018).

84

Planning Commission (IPC) with elaborate processes for handling the biggest, most important strategic projects. It is these that grab the headlines and often occasion the greatest amount of opposition – as in the cases of HS2* and Heathrow airport. Prominent in both of these cases are strong objections from councils representing several million people. However, they are fighting a government anxious to build a major prestige project, and with probable parliamentary backing for its plans. Within government, however, there are often tensions and arguments and this results in hesitation or postponed decisions. It all feeds into the popular notion that the UK is hopeless at building or replacing its infrastructure.

Professional planners and the construction industry welcomed the 2008 Planning Act. There was a genuine belief that we might overcome this malaise and that insulating the IPC from high-level politics was the answer. Taking the decisions out of the hands of politicians was seldom mentioned; instead the argument focused almost entirely on the need to overcome the UK's traditional tardiness in these matters.

Had it continued it would have been an extraordinarily interesting experiment. The *quid pro quo* was always that, in return for surrendering the decision-making power, the IPC was obliged to operate within a rigid process framework that required a very substantial element of public and stakeholder consultation. Quite right too. It is a measure of the planning profession's understanding of the balancing judgements required for these tough decisions that there were relatively few objections to the long and convoluted timetable of dialogues. Replacing the

---

* HS2 (High Speed 2) is a planned high-speed railway linking London and Birmingham, with further extensions to the East Midlands, Leeds and Manchester.

previous pattern of multiple applications for a range of permissions with a single development consent order was a major prize – and planners were happy to consult *ad nauseam* to reach it.

The IPC introduced a welcome revolution in transparency. Its website published details of every major infrastructure project once it had been received into the process. It provided links to the hundreds of relevant documents and to this day shows precisely where each one lies in the process at a particular time. In addition it published in some detail the questions, the answers and discussions taking place with a scheme's promoter as well as a welter of general advice as to how to navigate the complex process set up by the 2008 Planning Act.

All this was, of course, part of a search for planning objectivity – a vast experiment in evidence-based policy-making. In practice it ensured that the public have enjoyed unprecedented access to information and process insights that greatly enhances their ability to participate. At a stroke, an immense amount of information has been handed over to campaigners and objectors so that they can examine in fine detail the proposals of project-promoters and the way in which they are being presented to stakeholders and the public alike. Without doubt this is a tremendous advance – even if it makes life more difficult for infrastructure-suppliers and planners.

But to improve access to all this information, whilst at the same time trying to remove the political dimension from the equation, might well in retrospect appear a little optimistic – some might say naïve. In its 2010 general election manifesto, well before the IPC had got close to taking a single decision, the Conservative Party pledged to reverse the policy and abandon its independent status. Subsequently Eric Pickles' Localism Act amended the

2008 Planning Act and restored the traditional role of government ministers as the final arbiters on major projects.

Seasoned infrastructure-builders groaned. Would this mark a return to political fudge, interminable delays and inconsistency? To its credit the coalition government did rather well. Possibly, it was assisted by the austerity climate of its first years in government, and also the length of time everyone seemed to take to comply with the process. Although this probably discouraged a number of project-promoters, the first development consent was granted in 2011, but because the IPC's role by then was being transferred to the Planning Inspectorate (itself part of the Department of Communities and Local Government), it necessitated a special parliamentary process to try to prevent the independent IPC's decision being challenged. It did not stop a series of High Court cases that only concluded early in 2015.

This case itself illustrates perfectly the politics that can affect any of the 100-plus projects that have at various times pursued the process for major infrastructure. It concerned another energy-from-waste proposal, this time for Stewartby, in Bedfordshire. It emerged at a time when expert opinion was already moving away from this technology as the solution of choice, which provided a cue for the mayor of nearby Bedford, Liberal Democrat Dave Hodgson, to mount a vigorous campaign to oppose the plans. With the demise of Bedfordshire County Council in 2009, the selected site was within the area of the new Central Bedfordshire unitary authority. The nearest centre of population is Bedford, but its council was now a separate unitary authority, under different political control.

Hodgson had unsuccessfully used the consultative process to try and dissuade the IPC from approving the application, but continued to campaign. Declaring that none of Bedford's own waste would find its way to the new facility, he sought to undermine the economics of the project. We are not sure how important a factor this might have been but in 2013, the project promoter – an established and experienced American Company called Covanta – announced its withdrawal from the UK market. Its record in obtaining planning permissions for the technology was probably no better and no worse than those of its competitors, but its departure was an important signal that even if we might have cracked the problem of taking decisions to build, such decisions are a long way from being a guarantee that the facilities being sought are in fact built. It took some years before Covanta re-entered the fray and only in 2018 did it start construction on the site. The Environment Agency raised a permit for the waste incineration plant, despite vociferous local opposition from residents. Bedford Borough and Central Bedfordshire Councils jointly objected, claiming in a letter dated November 2017, 'This has made it difficult for both consultees and the public to engage with the process and as such we would consider the process flawed and very misleading'.'

Thus there can be many a slip between the consultation and digging the first trench. Nuclear power is another case in point. In 2012 the IPC approved a new nuclear power station at Hinkley Point in Somerset, long after the government had successfully overcome a Greenpeace legal challenge to its public consultation. Short of ploughing through hundreds of pages of analyses and recommendations, it is almost impossible to visualise the extent and complexity of the documentation. Reading the 324-page tome that is the report of the planning inspector's examination team, one can only be impressed by the consideration patently given to the wide variety of claims and assertions made by consultees in the various stages of consultation undertaken as the proposal matured.

But still the project was not home and dry. Hinkley Point is expected to cost £37 billion, and once-canvassed ideas that the private sector could build the next generation of nuclear plants without public subsidy disappeared a long time ago. The government had to conclude a 35-year deal with a guaranteed 'strike price' that many people regarded as totally unwarranted. Without such a deal, however, the plants would simply not be built!

Then there was a further legal challenge – this time from Ireland.* The judicial review challenged the UK government's decision by claiming that under international treaty obligations, it should have consulted a neighbouring country that might conceivably be impacted in the event of a nuclear accident. Whilst the case finally turned on the political interpretation of the word 'likely' (when the eventuality being guarded against was rated by experts to be less risky than that of a devastating meteor strike on planet Earth) it raised the awkward question of who precisely needed to be consulted.

As technologies like nuclear have demonstrated, the consequences of disaster are no respecters of state boundaries. Think Chernobyl. The claimant in the Hinkley Point Case was An Taisce, the National Trust equivalent in Ireland, and it lost its case in the British High Court. Nonetheless, this further delayed matters and demonstrated again that streamlining the planning

---

* R (*ex parte* An Taisce – the National Trust for Ireland) *v* Secretary of State for Energy & Climate Change and NNB Generation Company Limited [2014] EWCA Civ 1111.

process does not of itself solve the problem of maintaining and replacing infrastructure.

Whilst writing this book we looked at the list of proposed major projects shown on the National Infrastructure Planning website; it changes day by day. Of the 147* detailed on the website at the time of our visit, 69 of them had received a permission to proceed from the Secretary of State. Once responsibility for the IPC moved to the Planning Inspectorate, decisions were taken at a significant rate. This confounds the pessimists who argued that giving back power to the politicians would slow down the approval rate. But ministers realised full well that, as in the cases of Stewartby and Hinkley Point, taking the planning decisions is only part of the process.

Politicians have come to understand this very well. Skilled campaigners see opportunities to argue their case at several points. Those who object to nuclear power stations can present their arguments as part of the national debate on energy needs and how to satisfy them. But they have another bite at the cherry when proposals become site-specific. It was exactly the same with the King's Lynn waste facility. What makes Britain's infrastructure planning so challenging is the separation of national policy consultations from the approval mechanism for a single facility.

The great majority of projects initiated to date involved energy or transport. Although there are similarities, these market segments can behave rather differently. Road and rail schemes have been magnets for controversies for generations and there is scarcely a bypass around a single British town that did not attract at least

---

* National Infrastructure Planning, 20 March 2018,
https://infrastructure.planninginspectorate.gov.uk/

some degree of local debate. For years, the railway enthusiasts complained that the so-called roads lobby had the ear of Whitehall and that the business case for motorways took no account of environmental and other non-economic costs. Years later, we heard a similar tale, but with the roles reversed as plans for high-speed trains were questioned on similar grounds.

Note that HS2 did not meander through the infrastructure planning process; it had the benefit of a private Act of Parliament. The 2008 Planning Act covered infrastructure projects across a wide spectrum but was primarily designed for site-specific installations where a community of stakeholders could be reasonably identified. The process is far more difficult when a greater good is sought by inflicting environmental and/or social disruption on a long list of communities. HS2 affects a large number of towns and villages along its route. As an analogy, consider the challenges faced by those who build our electricity transmission systems. Pylons are never popular and we are told that the public preference for underground distribution is not as yet, at any rate, viable. In 2013 the Irish equivalent of the UK's National Grid, EirGrid, consulted large parts of the Republic of Ireland as part of its plan to build its second North–South Interconnector. It sailed into a fierce political storm, which culminated in a parliamentary inquiry as to how such an important consultation was so badly mishandled. We have no doubt that mistakes were made and that process improvements were there to be identified and implemented. But the fundamental issue remains: everyone wanted to see the Interconnector built, 'but please can you locate your pylons in the neighbouring parish, not ours'.

For projects of this kind, the NIMBY phenomenon is clearly alive and well. But it is often misunderstood. The term 'not in my

91

backyard' appeared in the *Christian Science Monitor* in the 1980s although there are claims for its use since the 1950s, but it is generally applied rather loosely and with an implied criticism that those who object to something are, in some way, selfish and denying the rest of society some useful investments that we all, collectively, want. However, excellent academic research has helped us understand NIMBYism rather better.* Apart from confirming that labelling objectors in this way almost certainly adds to the problem, it shows that public attitudes are fashioned by more than straightforward perceived self-interest.

It emerged that we are all affected by our views on three direct aspects of a proposal. First is the technology underpinning the project. If it is something which we inherently approve of and applaud, we are more likely to support it, but, as in the case of nuclear power, for example, where there are deep-rooted fears and anxieties, we are less pre-disposed to favour its development. Many renewable energy projects start with a favourable public image. In principle, we all seem happy to support the sun, the wind and the tides as means to generate our electricity. Maybe this is why the first tidal lagoon project in Swansea sailed through its initial public consultation phases, with scarcely anyone noticing.

So why have onshore wind farms proven to be so unpopular? The academic research pinpointed a second factor which influences

---

* Professor Patrick Devine-Wright is an environmental social scientist who draws from disciplines such as human geography and environmental psychology. He acted as principal investigator for the 'Beyond Nimbyism' interdisciplinary project, researching public engagement with renewable energy technologies. The project was evaluated as 'outstanding' in the end-of-grant peer review by the Economic and Social Research Council. Its report was published in 2009 and is available on the ESRC website at http://www.researchcatalogue.esrc.ac.uk/grants/RES-152-25-1008-A/read (accessed 20 March 2018).

our attitudes: it seems we care about the image of the project promoter. In the case of wind power, rightly or wrongly, the public perception has become distorted by a vision of large-scale, multi-million-pound conglomerates seeking to make money by ruining our landscape and making us all see and hear skyscraper-sized turbines towering above our green and pleasant land. We can contrast this caricature with the resounding public endorsement of wind in other parts of Europe. But we understand this was, in part, because local communities were themselves the initiators of those wind farms and were, therefore, committed from day one to a venture without an evil commercial enterprise to attract criticism.

Finally, we are apparently much influenced by our perception of the planning process. Confidence that decisions will ultimately be taken in a way of which we approve and by persons we believe to be appropriate can make us more forgiving of some of the disadvantages of a planning proposal. Consider HS2. The scheme's supporters had looked enviously at comparable projects in France, Spain or Italy and admired how relatively trouble-free their planning had been. Opponents also looked at these countries and disputed the benefits said to accrue from the shorter journey times enjoyed by high-speed passengers. A faster train from London to Birmingham, they said, afforded a busy businessman between twelve and twenty minutes of time saved. They then argued that much of the government's business case had ignored the reality that the time saved was probably not worth the alleged cost saving, for since the original calculations were made, the widespread availability of onboard WiFi has meant that such travellers can work on the train and will suffer less of a penalty if it goes slower.

This is the typical stuff of consultation. Its virtue is providing time and space for competing claims and counter-claims to be argued out transparently. So why did the consultation process for HS2 attract such vehement opposition? In all we counted sixty-two separate campaigning bodies, sprung up along every section of the proposed route. Almost without exception, they felt the process was unfair and eventually they supported a gigantic legal challenge that sought to prove that environmental as well as consultative standards had been breached. Not all these were community organisations inspired by the literal threat to their backyards! They included major local authorities, such as Warwickshire County Council, not otherwise known for disputing policies of a government coalition led by the same Conservative Party that ran the council.

The reason, of course, is that among citizens and councillors the argument had not been won. Parliament was a different matter. Apart from select committee quibbles about the business case and a general concern about the environment, High Speed Two enjoyed majority support from the big political parties. When, instead of taking the project through the 2008 Act process, a special parliamentary bill was sought, the measure went through both Commons and Lords with little difficulty.

Even so, the politics can be difficult. With a route that traversed marginal constituencies, parliamentary arithmetic could yet have blown the project off course. Local Members of Parliament struggled to make the case for the greater good of nationally efficient railways when their constituents would experience grief and disruption but little or no direct benefit. No gain; just pain.

In the case of HS2, the government showed political resolve, but the same cannot be said of its approach to airports in the south-east of England. Here the political calculation was different and a history of vacillation and procrastination has ensured that no full-sized runway has been built within campaigning distance of London for sixty years. Here there is nothing to mirror a line of disaffected communities along the blighted corridor of a proposed rail route. Instead there is merely the problem of a major hub airport that is deeply unpopular with large sections of the West London population, whose politicians have individually and collectively tried to torpedo any suggestion of its expansion.

A third runway at Heathrow was proposed around the turn of the twenty-first century. This led to a ferocious battle with residents of the immediate area, who succeeded in a court case* that ruled, among other things, that the government consultation should not have excluded the expansion of Gatwick: a scenario ruled out by a previous administration, which had promised the residents of nearby Crawley that no second runway would be built there for fifty years.

For much of the Labour government's thirteen years in office, the case for more runway capacity in the south-east became stronger. However, by the time it had its infrastructure ideas developed and the 2008 Planning Act was on the statute book, the world's financial system was in meltdown and demand for airline travel had shrunk, along with much else. After the coalition government came to power in 2010, it recognised, to its credit, that this was not an issue that could be avoided forever and promised to consult the public on their preferences. This was not the first such exercise. Back in 2003, there had been an attempt to gather views on capacity issues nationwide. In the earliest days of the

---

* R (*ex parte* Wandsworth and Hillingdon LBs and others) *v* Secretary of State for Transport, Luton, Stansted and Heathrow airports, BAA and others [2005] EWHC 20 (Admin).

Consultation Institute we waded through eight volumes of maps, diagrams and forecasts examining the future demand for airspace and airports. In the event, the economic recession from 2008 undermined every one of the consultation's conclusions.

By the time the coalition government felt able to publish a new consultation on the intractable south-east problem, it found itself hobbled by a Liberal Democrat commitment not to expand Heathrow and a noisy clutch of Conservative MPs totally opposed to the idea. A not very elegant solution was found by consulting the Great British Public, not on their preferred site for the elusive new runway, but on the criteria they thought relevant to the decision. Enter Boris Johnson. By now the Mayor of London, he was using his wit and charisma to advocate an alternative designed to appeal to residents of every one of the protagonist sites. His concept of an estuary airport, of inconvenience only to migratory birds, was, of course, not a wholly novel proposal. A previous suggestion for an airport at Cliffe, near Rochester in Kent, had been mooted and dropped in 2003. But, whatever your politics, you cannot deny Johnson's sheer chutzpah; his intervention threw enough fog into the channel of communications and there seemed an inevitability that the government would kick the issue firmly into the long grass of yet another independent inquiry. Howard Davies's Airports Commission took relatively little time to dismiss 'Boris Island' as a realistic option and no doubt to the Treasury's delight, it soon started to assemble an impressive amount of evidence in favour of one particular solution.

Even this commission, however, felt obliged to hedge its bets. Recommending Heathrow became impossible without a string of caveats related to air quality and the environment, enough to make the airline industry choke at the prospect. As ever, the argument became one between environmental and economic realities and between vested interests on both sides. As we write, Heathrow has launched a glossy consultation of its own, seeking views on its plans for a possible additional runway and admitting that it might entail consequential investments such as rebuilding a substantial part of the M25 London Orbital motorway.[*]

There must be at least some question marks over the use of public consultation as a major determinant of public policy here. Unlike, say, high-speed rail, the case for greater airport capacity carries more popular support. We nearly all fly; we will not all go from London to Birmingham. What the formalities of a consultation do is to provide a platform for various arguments to be made and debated. In the case of airports, however, it becomes a somewhat lopsided discussion. Many people want the solution, but it is the local residents who suffer the noise, the air pollution, the traffic and other inconveniences. When one side becomes associated mostly with one political party, there is a tendency for those who might ordinarily be happy to engage in the process to conclude that their time could be wasted. The decision would in due course be taken on old-fashioned party political grounds anyway. Is there a case for saying, therefore, that the public consultation is irrelevant and better to accept a purely parliamentary process?

We think not. Local popular and political opinion must be heard – even if Whitehall mandarins or think tank policy-advisers believe that other considerations carry more weight. Either to forgo a consultation or to hold a transparently ineffective one

---

[*] On 5th June 2018, the UK Cabinet finally decided to approve the Heathrow options. Readers are invited to speculate as to whether this finally ends the story of delay and procrastination.

would merely stoke up immense community resentment and probably diminish such support as there might have been for expansion in that area.

Airports policy demonstrates the pitfalls of building expectations that might not be capable of being fulfilled. By the time decisions are made, there will be few among local protagonists who think they were given a fair shout.

Such arguments probably lie ahead with the contentious matter of shale gas extraction, or fracking. Once again, the debate is between environmental campaigners and policy-makers, with the latter now largely convinced that fracking is an essential ingredient in the future mix of energy sources. What is interesting about fracking is that it presents itself in the public mind as a brand new issue, without the decades of history that contaminates the debate on airports – and even a new language. Ten years ago, who had heard of fracking? Even among those who use the word freely today, who understands exactly what it means?*

Note, however, how the government was very quick to perceive its potential value – but also its potential for political trouble. With what some saw as undue haste, the coalition government bowed to pressure and agreed an opposition shopping list of safeguards and conditions with which planning permission for both exploration and extraction facilities would be encumbered. The big parties wanted to avoid saying 'No' to a potential energy bonanza. But they were equally keen to avoid being seen as too eager. The problem, they knew, is site-specific, but those campaigning against fracking attract sympathy from a much wider body of community-level opinion than, say, those along the route

* The process of injecting liquid at high pressure into subterranean rocks, boreholes etc. so as to force open existing fissures and extract oil or gas.

of HS2. Much of this is because of *new technology anxiety syndrome*. People watch a television programme or find an internet site that tells them how disastrous fracking has been in parts of the USA and some are unprepared to accept reassurances from the Environment Agency, scientific or academic circles.

Despite opposition, the English Department of Communities and Local Government has given an amber, if not shading to green, light to fracking. Contrast this with the situation in Scotland, where its government was far more hostile to fracking and organised a consultation to test public opinion on the subject. In what the industry regarded as a manipulated narrative the consultation paper stated that health experts could not guarantee the safety of the process. Inevitably the public response, in 2017, overwhelmingly rejected the technology.*

It reminds us of the sentiment surrounding genetically modified foods ten or fifteen years ago. No longer is it necessary for opponents or sceptics to demonstrate that something is dangerous: the burden of proof has been placed firmly on the advocates of new technology to show that their plans are totally safe. That can be difficult; one is sometimes trying to prove a negative – that water aquifers cannot be contaminated – or, as in the case of allegations of autism near power lines years ago, that health issues do not arise.

All these cases point us in one direction. The public will become sceptical whatever planning laws and practices may say. In engagement and consultation, those who want to build will also have to persuade. On site-specific questions, local people will often win the argument, but overall, if society decides it needs

---

* *Talking 'Fracking': A Consultation on Unconventional Oil and Gas*, Scottish Government, January 2017.

something for the good of the country as a whole, it will have to convince enough people to carry out locally unpopular decisions from time to time.

Spatial planning remains one of the most fiercely contentious issues, bound to provoke demands for full and fair public consultation. Politicians have learnt to tread very carefully in this area. And that caution has itself led to unforeseen consequences. One of these is a reluctance to decide. Another is the slow pace of infrastructure build. It remains to be seen if the nation at large is content with such an outcome.

Chapter 6

Consultation and health

Loving the NHS | engagement mechanisms | a surfeit of
abbreviations | organisational complexity | Mid-Staffordshire
| local engagement | patient pathways | Foundation Trusts |
children's cardiac surgery (Royal Brompton Hospital judicial
review) | hospital reconfigurations

Please ensure you have a recent *Abbreviation Vaccination Certificate*
(AVC) in order to make sense of this chapter.

In any event, this should be a much wider discussion than just the
services currently delivered by the National Health Service
(NHS). The issue is dominated by the UK public's attitude to this
so-called national treasure. It almost means that rational analysis
is impossible. Such is the evident impact upon public perception
that no one can start to understand public consultation on health
without first grasping the nation's relationship with the NHS.

No other public service evokes a sense of community ownership
like the NHS. In parts of south Wales and the north of England,
one can still point to buildings erected with miners' or other
workers' subscriptions and left well beyond their usable date, as a
token of how difficult it can be to tamper with the public's hard-

won investment. We do not have to dwell upon Aneurin Bevan's* legacy or travel to his political homeland to discover the same kind of generation-by-generation allegiance to the idea of the NHS. Politicians who have genuinely seen this as doing more harm than good have been repulsed in the last thirty years; so the orthodoxy has developed that no one is elected in the UK without demonstrating that they love the NHS. The analogy with the role of religion in the USA is very tempting. No wonder, therefore, that the NHS has frequently been described as the religion of British politics.

What follows from this analysis is the public's innate belief that they should have a say in what happens to this cherished service. This is something that has grown up over time and was far from being a cardinal principle at its inception. Indeed, health is one of those services where the *culture of the expert* has always been alive and well and where the public has traditionally shown due deference even when it is far from deserved.

This distinction between a service planned and run by clinicians and an oversight role for the representatives of the community lies at the heart of the NHS relationship. There has always been a tension between the two dimensions but for as long as the community had confidence in the clinicians and they in turn were given sufficient money and resources, it was a manageable equation. What has happened in recent years is that both these long-standing working assumptions have been challenged.

Long before this, however, there were attempts to tinker with the practicalities of public engagement and accountability. The

---

* After the landslide Labour victory in the 1945 general election, Bevan was appointed Minister for Health, responsible for establishing the NHS. On 5 July 1948, the government took over responsibility for all medical services and there was free diagnosis and treatment for all. *Per* BBC History.

Conservative administrations of Margaret Thatcher and John Major had encouraged what they regarded as innovation, through such concepts as fund-holding general practitioners.* In part, this was seen as an attempt to limit the power of managers and bureaucrats, who were held to be too susceptible to influence from local community activists and politicians. Twenty years later, Andrew Lansley, the then Secretary of State for Health, repeated the call for the service to be run by doctors and created clinical commissioning groups on a similar platform in England and with much the same intention. In both cases, the practical issues of running the ultra-complex NHS made this particular policy difficult to work and even the most passionate advocates of handing power to clinicians have stopped short of telling the public to keep away and leave it to the professionals.

For twenty-nine years England and Wales had community health councils (CHCs), a safeguarding mechanism with the power to enter and inspect NHS premises. We have no doubt that this irritated managers, who saw it as unnecessary interference by well-intentioned but often clueless busybodies. Managers' continuous lobbying for the abolition of CHCs finally found, in England at least, willing ears in a Blair government that was keen to modernise the NHS by removing unreasonable burdens from the shoulders of modern managers. In their place, a new quango was proposed. It would recruit individuals to take part in what were called public and patient involvement forums (PPIFs), with a remit much like CHCs but lacking some of those powers that had upset many of the managers. Members of the CHCs were furious – especially those who saw themselves as the people's

---

* GP Fundholding was created in 1991 as part of the 'quasi-market' created in the NHS by the National Health Service and Community Care Act 1990. *Per* Wikipedia.

champions. They were not much impressed either by the creation of special-purpose health *overview and scrutiny* committees (HOSCs) in the 1999 Local Government Act.

Maybe they should have been. In the years that have followed this initiative, it seems to us that they have had a much bigger and generally more beneficial effect on the conduct of public engagement than the CHCs ever had. *Overview and scrutiny*, though, was a brand new concept. Nobody understood it, least of all those who belonged to its committees! In any case, it was seen as part of the changes being made in the governance of local authorities. The move to cabinet government was already unpopular with backbench councillors. Now stripped of status and the power they once wielded in the committee system, very few saw the HOSCs as the potent accountability mechanism that they eventually became. Even fewer predicted that chairing a high-profile HOSC would command a great deal of political kudos and that NHS managers would fear its interventions more than most other mechanisms of public engagement.

Back in 2003, there were high hopes that the PPIFs would attract fresh blood. New national machinery, the Commission for Patient and Public Involvement in Health (CPPIH),* would create a better-quality dialogue about forward directions, priorities and overall resources rather than an attempt to micromanage by local committees. That was the theory. Despite being called forums, the PPIFs were actually committees and found it a real challenge to recruit enough people to make the new system work. We remember meeting key people and heard them

---

* The CPPIH was set up in January 2003. It was an independent, non-departmental public body, sponsored by the Department of Health. The Commission's role was to make sure the public was involved in decision-making about health and health services in England.

describe the efforts they were making to attract the right ethnic or socio-economic balance. It cost a small fortune and before long there were dark mutterings about differences between the minister and those running the PPIFs.

It was not the politicians' finest hour. Having removed the well-established, if not much cherished, CHCs, they then proceeded to undermine their own replacement mechanism and destroy its credibility with both local authorities and NHS managers.

What happened next was a classic piece of reflex policy-making. A committee of engagement experts was convened and given the brief to find something better than the ill-fated forums. Somehow they managed to recommend something even more unwieldy – local involvement networks, which soon became known as LINks.* In one sense they were brilliant and possibly ahead of their time. In a practical sense, they were little better than hopeless.

This model recognised the well-founded reality that the number of organisations and individuals keenly interested in the NHS runs into tens of thousands and that local committees will face a challenge to represent their varied viewpoints. Committees were in any case becoming unpopular, even when called forums. Those who invented the LINks model were much impressed with the explosive growth of social media and its ability to create *communities of interest* on the web, hence their use of 'networks'.

So far, so good. Trying to build local coalitions of health-related voluntary and community groups would surely be easier than going onto the streets, clipboard in hand, trying to persuade local

---

* LINks were to work with existing voluntary and community sector groups, as well as interested individuals to promote public and community influence in health and social care.

people to sign up for a patient voice role. Some local groups actually welcomed the initiative, but the truth is that there is less of a tradition of successful co-operation between these kinds of bodies than one might suppose. Abandoning or diluting your own channels of communication and persuasion in favour of a wider body is not necessarily an attractive option, unless, of course, you feel you are not currently being heard. In short, if you already had influence in your own right, the appeal of participating in LINks was rather marginal.

Despite this, the willing members of the 574 PPIFs were politely thanked for their efforts and local LINks were established on a model that, from day one, prevented them from being effective. The Labour administration was, by now, in full retreat from its initial Blairite command-and-control philosophy, with hundreds of targets to drive up standards in local authorities and other services. By 2006, the new mantra was to devolve decision-making and encourage a commissioning approach. For that reason, councils were told that they could not run LINks themselves, but instead had to find and pay for a host organisation to do the job for them. Apparently the thinking was to eliminate the overtly political element in some NHS-related issues at local level. There seems to have been a concerted attempt to remove elected members from the new arrangements – no doubt a continuing legacy from the antagonism that had led to the demise of the CHCs in the first place.

It would be nice to recall that most councils found satisfactory hosts. The truth is that far too many of them failed. Some took an inordinate time to find anyone willing to shoulder the responsibility, for there were so many uncertainties and unclear funding guarantees. One of the experts' criticisms of the local forums had been that they had an over-prescriptive, centralised model which had nevertheless been inconsistently applied. LINks compounded the problem. To avoid telling local networks exactly how to run their affairs, the Department of Health just told them to get on with it. Guidance was sparse and most hosts floundered on their inexperience and the inherent vagueness of the networking concept.

The results were predictable. The voice of patients and local public involvement, terminated abruptly by the abolition of the PPIFs, degenerated into a year or two of impasse as host organisations strove to agree suitable governance arrangements and tried to develop an effective *modus operandi* for their networks. Some never made it!

All this occurred as the economy passed from times of plenty to financial free-fall and as the pace of change in the NHS accelerated. Patient and public voices were, let us be frank, muted, and nowhere is this better illustrated than in the sad tale of the hospital in Mid-Staffordshire and the campaign so impressively, if controversially, run by Julie Bailey* to uncover the most shocking case of mismanagement ever seen in the NHS. So much has been written about this scandal and the culture change recommended in the subsequent Francis Report† that it is easy to overlook some of the mistakes in listening to public and patient voices. The sad truth is that between 2005 and 2008, when much of the worst happened, the machinery in place was faulty and this was the direct result of ministerial decisions to tinker with the system.

---

* Founder of a pressure group, Cure the NHS, after experiencing unsafe care for her mother, Bella Bailey, who died in Stafford Hospital in 2007. She was awarded a CBE for her contribution to uncovering the scandal.

† Robert Francis QC's damning 2013 report into a catalogue of failures, which ensured that no one emerged with credit.

The tinkering continued. The coalition government had its own reasons for disliking LINks and proposed yet another new incarnation – this time called Healthwatch. This was intended to remedy the problem of the arm's-length host organisations and promised better use of public money to secure a representative view of public and patient opinions. More chaos and confusion occurred as one more CHC replacement was abolished and a transition programme took place.

It says much for thousands of volunteers and local pressure groups that they have maintained a degree of willingness to participate despite this lamentable tale of blunders, and worse, in England. Contrast this to the relative stability of the situation in Wales and Scotland. The Welsh retained their CHCs and the Scots built a single, impressive body called the Scottish Health Council to oversee a system that has enjoyed broad political and public support for a decade or more.

England's experience is, however, a real shocker and tells us much about the ambivalence of the political class towards public and patient involvement in the NHS. Every document bearing a ministerial signature speaks eloquently about the commitment to hear public views, but actions have rarely supported the fine words. It is not easy to discern particular acts of sabotage – except maybe the petulant abolition of the CPPIH, when Sharon Grant, its chairwoman, upset Labour ministers. What we see instead is a total inability of politicians to leave well enough alone and allow new structures to develop properly over time. No matter how ill suited have been the successive models imposed by government on increasingly demoralised volunteers, most of them could have become effective if allowed to mature.

Eventually, the Welsh Government succumbed to similar pressures from civil servants and centralisation-minded ministers and it proposed abolishing its CHCs in 2017, after what some members allege to have been several years of systematic undermining and destabilising. Insofar as its aim was to seek machinery for public and patient involvement to cover both health and social care, it had a point. Its problem was the same as that which faced the English. Could it find an acceptable alternative that would speak on behalf of local people without causing government ministers even more embarrassment?

Political rhetoric on public and patient involvement has become a real problem. In 2006, when it announced the abolition of the CPPIH, the Department of Health, ironically in a publication called *A Stronger Local Voice*,* declared that it wanted to strengthen the legal *duty to consult*. Section 11 of the 2001 Health and Social Care Act had laid out a very clear *duty to consult*, but what the government did was to water down this requirement with a new form of words deliberately drafted to weaken the commitment. That new wording became enacted as Section 242 of the 2006 NHS Act, and survived to become part of the 2012 Health and Social Care Act, which implemented Andrew Lansley's contentious reorganisation. It replaced the *duty to consult* with a 'duty to involve (whether by being consulted or provided with information or in other ways)'. Lawyers have speculated that if legally challenged, a judge would rule that any response to information provided by the NHS would lead to a legal *duty to*

---

* *A Stronger Local Voice* set out the government's plans for the future of patient and public involvement in health and social care, including the establishment of LINks. The package of plans was designed to promote the importance of user and public involvement at all levels of the health and social care system, and to create a system which enabled more people to become involved and have their voices heard.

consult. The fact is that politicians have so committed themselves to consultation that regardless of what the legislation actually says, it would be a brave part of the NHS that sought to interpret the Section 242 provisions too narrowly.

We have no doubt that officials have repeatedly advised ministers that it may be better to use the terms 'involve' or 'engage' rather than 'consult'. Involvement and engagement are looser, more elastic concepts and do not carry with them the rigorous requirements of the Gunning Principles.* The political reality, however, is that when a Member of Parliament gets up in the House of Commons to express concern about local NHS services, he or she never complains, 'My constituents have not been *involved*.' The language used on the green benches is always the same – 'My constituents have not been *consulted*.' In response, minister after minister, whatever party they represent, calmly offer the reassurance that, of course, consultation is what is intended.

In the meantime, politicians created yet another parallel form of public and patient involvement, this time in and around Foundation Trust hospitals. These new creations were to have members so that a substantial body of users and indeed the wider community could influence them. As usual, extravagant claims were made for this innovation and again, in theory, there was real potential for harnessing some of the practical experience undoubtedly found among the thousands of people who registered for membership. The numbers were quite impressive. We once visited the Royal Devon and Exeter Foundation Trust – one of the first to build a large membership – and heard how effective it had been by inviting in-patients to become a member

---

* See Chapter 3.

110

as part of the discharge procedure. 'Sign here, please – and you can go home!' However, once they had accumulated 16,000 or so members, half of them NHS staff apparently, there arose the question of what exactly to do with them.

As an audience to receive the positive messages of the communications team and as a pool of knowledge from which to recruit volunteers for various projects, the Foundation Trust membership format should have worked well. But no one could claim that this was in any way a representative body and were it to act as such, it might quickly appear, wrongly, to be usurping the role of the admittedly troubled CHC replacements. Having thousands of people identifying with a Foundation Trust was clearly a positive asset, but very few of the trusts put in place the staffing and processes necessary to leverage real involvement from these structures.

We believe that this is where successive governments, and their advisers, have got it wrong. Creating and modifying various structures carries an administrative overhead; when times are tough it is not surprising that there is a reluctance to incur what many managers believe is an avoidable cost. It also takes time and requires patience, which ministers have rarely shown. In fairness, the Foundation Trust structure has survived longer than most others, but still shows little sign of fulfilling its potential to sustain a long-term dialogue with local communities.

The term that best captures the aspiration of ministers and officials in this space is *continuous engagement*, and although absent from the legislation it has featured in one way or another in guidance documents for years. The NHS in Wales is particularly fortunate to have developed a very comprehensive set of guidelines* which rightly place this notion at the centre of its thinking. Even this did not prevent successive ministers from complaining that there were too many legal challenges to their plans to change the NHS, and that this must have been due to failures in that *continuous engagement*. We were far from convinced about this. We suspected that Secretaries of State for Health and their counterparts in Wales, Scotland and Northern Ireland had been caught out by the confusion between *engagement* and *consultation*. Consultation, they feared, led to conflict, whereas engagement, they hoped, produced the balm of consensus.

A remarkable number of parliamentarians and ministers cling to this naïve belief. It has led several to wonder why they can't jettison the idea of consultation in favour of a more permanent dialogue that may save them from the unpopularity of taking tough decisions. We have seen several civil service papers speculating as to whether *continuous engagement* can reduce the extent of community opposition. In every case, it is the triumph of hope over experience. The problem is not just that the politicians' penchant for tinkering with public and patient involvement structures have denied us the stability that might have made them work, but that the accelerating agenda of change creates a complexity that inhibits the growth of any kind of consensus. Not even the clinical professions are of a single mind about many issues.

That complexity manifests itself in the creation, proliferation and amalgamation of bodies and agencies that form part of the fluid management jigsaw that completely baffles the general public. It has the same effect on employees – and even the politicians that created it.

---

* 'Guidance for Engagement and Consultation on Changes to Health Services'

In addition to the Foundation Trusts that increasingly manage our bigger hospitals, those same politicians created a regulator, Monitor, whose job it was to regulate them and other health providers. To do this it was given a wide range of powers particularly in setting tariffs or other commercial frameworks for service delivery. This was real power, and although Monitor's literature talked fondly of exercising it to protect consumers and patients, NHS managers were sceptical. Instead they viewed Monitor as an arm's-length tool of ministers, shaping and influencing the development of the NHS away from the glare of publicity. It eventually merged in 2016 with yet another agency and is now, optimistically, called NHS Improvement.

Monitor is only one of several bodies that have come and gone in recent years. Hands up if you can explain the distinction between Monitor's role and that of NHS England in respect of clinical commission groups. And where, before it disappeared, did the Trust Development Authority come in?* Then there is also the Care Quality Commission (CQC) with its higher profile since the disaster that was Mid-Staffordshire.

All these bodies, excellent in their own ways no doubt, had placed upon them statutory requirements to consult. Quite rightly so, for their functions called out for a degree of public involvement. Take NHS Improvement, just for one example. Part of its remit is to assess the impact of any of the NHS's actions if they are likely to significantly affect health providers. And users of the service. Finally it goes the whole hog and adds the general public. On our interpretation, that means everyone. However, no one has

---

* For the record, it was not a financial services regulator to improve fiduciary relationships! Instead it was meant to lubricate the journeys of NHS providers into becoming trusts, and will mostly be remembered for its role in the ill-fated plan to rationalise Lewisham Hospital – stopped by a judicial review.

yet satisfactorily defined what 'significant' really means, so in theory this regulator should be assessing changes to virtually everything. Such impact assessments cannot, of course, be undertaken without consulting those deemed to be affected, so, again in theory, NHS Improvement should be continuously consulting on virtually every change in the Health Service.

Now let's look at the CQC. Again, few people disagree with its principal objective and it has done much to ensure a better-informed debate by publishing more and enhanced data on its inspections and its regulations. Look closely at its goals, however, and you will notice that it not only has to listen to patient experiences but also must be seen to be 'involving the public and people who receive care in our work'. No one disputes that this is a perfectly sensible management aspiration, and consultation will certainly be one method of fulfilling this goal.

Next let us consider NHS England, which initially supervised the Clinical Commissioning Groups (CCGs) created in 2013 that were meant to cover similar areas to the old Primary Care Trusts. NHS England also acts as a kind of catch-all body to run, or more accurately, *commission* those services that cover the whole country and lie beyond the jurisdiction of individual CCGs. We hope you are following this, and if you aren't, you are in honourable company. But the point of this sightseeing tour around the NHS is not to admire the geometry of the organisation but to note that every one of these bodies needs to consult and indeed does so. It is a classic example of several initiatives, which of themselves are perfectly logical, combining to produce a nonsense.

In practice, co-operation between these overlapping structures means that common sense prevails. The fact remains, however, that in principle the public could be asked its views about the same issue – but by at least five or six different bodies. Consultation fatigue is the least of the perils!

Many of these organisations have a nationwide role. Much of their engagement is with key stakeholders, such as the Royal Colleges. In one fell swoop in 2015, NHS England sought the views of clinicians and patients on changes to clinical and service pathways for more than thirty specialist medical conditions. Other actions by these bodies have a more local impact and it is at this time we must mention the remaining piece of this intricate jigsaw.

Health and Wellbeing Boards (HWBs) are run by top-tier local authorities. In England this means there are about 150 of them. Looking back over the evolution of the NHS and the arguments about accountability, we feel sure that the intention was to make each HWB the architect of and final arbiter on the health service within its locality. They are usually chaired by local councillors, but essentially they are committees of chief officers alongside CCGs and other interest groups, and all in the presence of Healthwatch. The process of establishing precisely what each area needs is, of course, well established and long pre-dates the HWBs. It is called the Joint Strategic Needs Assessment (JSNA) and the idea must have been to force the local managers to pursue an agreed strategy and do so transparently.

We have seen many worthy attempts to deliver on this process. JSNAs tend to be 100-plus-page documents full of facts and figures, graphs and histograms analysing health needs. They are not user-friendly, but of course they are not intended for an audience of the general public. Their job is to inform a local plan, which is owned by, and in theory the responsibility of, the HWB. The weakness is that these attempts to localise the operation of the NHS lie within a very tightly managed nationwide system with such intricate inter-dependencies that the discretion available to HWB members is very limited. Trying to do something new or different cannot be easy, given that the other institutions, including NHS Improvement, NHS England and the CQC, all have power and financial control over what actually happens.

Arguably, the Lansley reorganisation added to the difficulty, by fragmenting the service and ostensibly giving CCGs control over the money spent in their areas. Sums are allocated to the CCGs, which then commission the services they require from a range of providers, often dominated by the local hospital. They are accountable to the public for this expenditure but their available resources are determined by an obscure formula created by NHS England. They have seats on the HWB and report their progress to it. But in no practical sense are these CCGs beholden to the more representative HWBs, which sadly have become limited to receiving strategy documents, talking about them and proposing limited initiatives. They are not quite impotent, but they have clearly not established themselves as perhaps their original advocates wished.

This is not to say that determined local politicians cannot have an impact. A local authority near us has an elected mayor, who has placed himself as chairman of the HWB and does so almost certainly to secure maximum influence on local health issues. Other councillors have, however, found the *overview and scrutiny* committees a more effective forum for such influence, for unlike the HWBs with their membership and focus on the local management of the system, these committees have the right to refer matters to the Secretary of State. In truth, however, local authority members have had minimal influence on local NHS management. No wonder that progress towards integrating health and social care in England has been slow.

In any event, CCGs are a problem. The idea of discarding thousands of apparent NHS pen-pushers must have sounded attractive to the coalition government when it came to office in 2010. Although the Conservative Party had said it would not force through another top-down reorganisation of the service, it did inherit something of a time bomb. This was a House of Commons Health Select Committee report * into health commissioning that was published in 2010 – after the parties had written their election manifestos. The committee had heard evidence that made it doubt whether the existing primary care trusts (PCTs) could deliver the commissioning model that everyone, including Labour ministers, by then thought was a good idea. It went further. It made the fateful recommendation that this popular way of developing the purchaser–provider relationship could not possibly succeed whilst the PCTs remained as they were.

The report was an open invitation to abolish PCTs and, looking back, it is easy to see that many had failed to perform adequately. But they had strengths, which maybe had not been sufficiently noticed. One of them was an identity with local communities, developed over many years and supported by small groups of staff that looked after patient and public involvement. Their job was to help fulfil the legal requirements for consultation and engagement we mentioned earlier. Compared with its counterparts in the local council office down the road, the PCT effort was rather puny. Whereas a local authority might employ dozens of staff in a large number of departments, all with experience of local engagement and public consultation, the

---

* House of Commons Health Committee, *Commissioning*, Fourth Report of Session 2009–10, HC 268, 30 March 2010.

average PCT had two or three people at most. But they knew the local patch.

Just a few had made a strategic investment in community relations. We once worked with the PCT that served the centre of Birmingham, covering almost 300,000 people in one of the UK's most diverse areas in terms of ethnicity, religion and culture. Its primary care was delivered, in part, by a bewildering network of single-doctor practices, many of whom catered for the particular needs and preferences of various groups. Managing such an offering, alongside a more conventional service, required intense community liaison and the PCT, recognising this, invested appropriately. When we met the team, their local knowledge was impressive – as was their ability to work with other agencies and across organisational boundaries.

In Birmingham and elsewhere, much of this know-how was swept away in the convulsions that overtook the PCTs as they were disbanded to make way for the slimline CCGs. Those who were worried about the loss of expertise and the consequences for local community involvement were, of course, brushed aside, but in the light of the legal requirements to involve and consult, could not be ignored altogether. The answer was the creation of commissioning support units (CSUs) – much needed anyway to undertake critical business support services like IT which were not realistically manageable at the level of the CCGs and many of which had been run on a regional basis for years already. The CSUs were asked to provide a communications and engagement service for the CCGs, and to do so on a commercial basis, the theory being that the CCGs would not waste money buying anything they did not need. Almost twenty CSUs were created at the beginning, but they faced problems from the start.

118

Removing a task that has traditionally been done on a very local basis and operating it from further afield always causes problems. Almost any private business that regionalises faces the same opposition from staff and customers and only in the best-managed situations are the outcomes really successful. In the NHS, it must be said, there is a similar lack of appetite for such changes, and in the case of public engagement, there is good reason to be sceptical. Core competence in this specialised field means knowing the local area really well. Descending upon a CCG from miles away was never going to be satisfactory.

Wise CCG leaders recognised the need for active local dialogue, as part of determining the services that should be provided. We might, therefore, have anticipated the emergence of the most consultative organisations ever devised in the NHS. Instead, they were given mostly inadequate resources and funding. To obtain the specialist skills, they needed to rely upon the CSUs, quite often many miles away.

In defence of the CSUs, we accept that it is possible to regionalise aspects of communications in the Health Service. Much of what needs to be communicated, from public health campaigns through to signposting patients to services, can be done by professionals who are able to address these issues regardless of where they are based. The same is not true of *community engagement*, where the essential know-how is a deep understanding of the intricate dynamics of the local area. These people are the ground troops of public engagement and they are needed in order to lubricate the wheels of consultation on matters large and small.

It was not long before some CCGs realised the need to retain these people; but too late, and there was something of a scramble to sign up some of the better engagement specialists who had gone to the CSUs and offer them jobs in house, providing the same advice as they may have previously done. In this, as in other respects, the Lansley aspiration to remove bureaucracy failed because it had not sufficiently worked out what to do with essential functions when the PCTs were disbanded.

Regardless of who helped them, the public engagement buck stopped with the CCG board. Putting clinicians in charge meant that originally enthusiastic GPs who agreed to become CCG chairs were overwhelmed by the demands made by the management tasks they absorbed. The average budget of CCGs in 2015 was £304 million and few of the key people had the slightest experience of managing on such a scale. The problem was compounded when government policy deliberately made massive, international-scale hospitals dependent for their funding on CCGs, made up of GPs whose previous experience had been to run their practices as small businesses with turnovers of around £1 million–£2 million.

No wonder that successful CCGs recognised that their life became easier if they could obtain and keep a degree of confidence and support from their local communities. One way is through the force of personal leadership. For all its faults the reorganisation did, after all, give some GPs a remarkable opportunity to lead the change towards better services in their areas. Clinicians we have met rank high among the most impressive public servants around – able to provide a vision of how the NHS can become better, and some have the ability to articulate it. Faced with a possible withdrawal of some hospital services in his area, a CCG chairman we know asserted that he would 'die in the ditch' rather than let those changes take place without his local community being consulted.

The most visible element of primary care providers listening to patient voices in England ought to be the patient participation groups (PPGs) run from most general practices. As a focus for local brickbats and bouquets, these PPGs can be useful, but it would be a mistake to over-emphasise their impact. Generations of local GPs had little, if any, experience of meeting patients other than on a one-to-one basis. Consultation, for them, meant the ten minutes allocated when we visit the surgery. Over-worked GPs saw the PPGs as another bureaucratic imposition, but the Department of Health offered them money and they started to be organised! Many PPGs were poor; others took time to learn how to be effective. What should trouble us is that it took until the second decade of the twenty-first century for the notion of a user committee of some kind to take root in primary care. There are still PPGs where the doctors send their staff to attend or run meetings, assuming that there may only be a succession of complaints about appointments, opening hours or the condition of the waiting room.

Any specialist in customer satisfaction will confirm that what are called *hygiene factors** are immensely important to people, but will know that the real value lies in creating a safe space for views and ideas on a much broader range of issues to be aired. Provided no one interferes and they are given time to develop, PPGs can be useful channels of dialogue in the NHS. In London and other large cities, they have joined forces to form an umbrella body capable of talking to several CCGs at once about the GP service. And well they might, for there is now little doubt that so many of the challenges faced by the health economy as a whole stem from failures or problems affecting those front-line services. Maybe

---

* *Hygiene factors* are the aspects of work (enough pay, job security, reasonable work–life balance etc.) which make for greater contentment.

PPGs are one way to alert managers that action is needed in this area.

Our experience is that changes and improvements in GP surgeries go reasonably well if there is a good attempt to involve local people and elected representatives. A frequent topic is the amalgamation or relocation of surgeries to accommodate the increasing range of services demanded of them. In rural areas this is an especially thorny problem; if those who need the service most are faced with journeys of five miles or more with little or no public transport, they might be unable to use it. Early dialogue by CCGs or their equivalents in Scotland, Wales and Northern Ireland can usually identify 'least worst' solutions, but the track record of ameliorating such inconveniences is not wonderful. England has the added disadvantage that the actual GP service is still mostly run by doctors as independent contractors, even though the CCGs' commissioning activities influence virtually everything it offers. Conflicts of interest initially led NHS England to assume responsibility for managing the individual practices, but it was not long before this had to be delegated.

This over-complex, fragmented organisation simply could not drive the changes needed. So Simon Stevens, chief executive of NHS England since 2014, rightly concluded that he needed a solution of some kind. Parliament was of no help. The very thought of a further statute-based NHS reorganisation made everyone feel queasy. He therefore divided England into forty-four areas and in a burst of misplaced label creation made them responsible for Sustainability and Transformation Plans (STPs). The label aside, this was a sensible approach. Size-wise CCGs may be appropriate for delivering primary care, but many of the required service improvements and cost savings needed to be implemented across a wider area than a single CCG. The average size of an STP area was over a million people – probably about right for this. Stevens's other objective was to speed up the integration of health and social care by ensuring that each STP was agreed between local authorities, NHS providers and the local CCGs.

Sadly, he then made a series of mistakes. Firstly, his officials drew lines on a map, and would have been much wiser to have engaged with local councils and local NHS bodies before presenting them with a *fait accompli*. Some areas had always worked together as a unit. But others, including our own local area, found their NHS and social care plans drawn up for a non-statutory geography dreamt up by NHS England alone. Stevens then sought to steamroller the whole strategy too quickly and faced howls of protest from local councillors who felt they had had little or no say in the plans. These plans were, apparently, crafted by part-time secondees selected by NHS England or, in some cases, sub-contracted to external consultants who produced a mixture of unintelligible or self-serving models of care supported by no one and drafted with little or no consultation. By autumn 2016, NHS England realised that few of the initial plans were satisfactory, so it published guidance exhorting all the STP areas to engage with their constituent organisations and produce better plans. Faced with outrage from Members of Parliament of all parties, harassed ministers gave a promise that local people would be consulted on the STPs. In reality, only a handful of areas consulted. All the others admitted that they did not yet possess proposals which were in any position to withstand public scrutiny.

Despite this, STPs provided the shock to the system that Stevens probably intended. They became 'Sustainability and Transformation Partnerships'. Some of them consisted of twenty-plus organisations and reaching any consensus must have been a daunting challenge. Without such a mechanism, however, it would have been virtually impossible to produce any proposals for change that would not immediately have faced outright opposition from other partners. The STPs recognised that Parliament had bequeathed managers an over-complex, fragmented structure, and one can only applaud sensible attempts to create something more manageable.

But there is clearly a missing ingredient, and that is public and patient involvement. As we have outlined in this chapter, the separate component structures still retain the obligations to engage and consult. The new partnerships have neither a legal basis nor the concomitant requirements to consult. Therefore, the moment they embark seriously on significant changes to the service, one of the existing organisations has to organise a proper consultation. Those at the top see salvation in a new mystical creation called accountable care organisations (ACOs). This has muddied the waters even further, and eventually the robust intervention of Dr Sarah Wollaston MP as chair of the parliamentary Health Select Committee persuaded the government to offer this latest big idea for public consultation. The ACOs may well prove a reasonable way forward but they offer yet another illustration of self-build structures emanating from Whitehall. We think there is somewhere an IKEA-style warehouse of words where new organisations can be assembled from a flat pack of standard components; they sometimes last, but not always.

Irrespective of structures, there is the knotty problem of deciding who exactly becomes involved in examining alternative options and developing the proposals – much more difficult in the larger areas covered by STPs. Many people believe that it is at this point that public engagement and patient dialogue matter most. This is because making collective provision for something as personal as healthcare requires insight into the compromises people make. One of the best developments in pursuit of this understanding is the advent of 'expert patients', recognising that no one knows better what is involved in medical procedures and the way the system handles individual cases than those with first-hand experience.

There are thousands of condition-specific groups who usually campaign for more or better resources for their particular concerns. They have spawned immeasurable clusters of patients, able and willing to give their views. Moreover, there is a well-funded pharmaceutical industry with a commercial incentive to create similar machinery – all around consulting patients about their illness and their experience.

We hear much about 'patient pathways'. This is a rather good phrase, we think, for many people see their experience with the NHS as some kind of journey. Truly excellent work has been done to modernise these pathways, for it is really amazing how some have not changed for years. Laypeople like us scarcely comprehend the traditional sequence of visits, referrals and other interventions involved in a serious illness. A renewed emphasis on improving this sequence saves money, improves outcomes and delivers better satisfaction all in one. Our politicians should be rejoicing. It is everything they wanted. Unfortunately, few of them have delved sufficiently into the detail to see how much of an impact these improvements make.

In contrast, politicians certainly know of a variation on this theme that is called *co-production*. The label is used rather loosely but refers to those occasions where change emerges from the involvement of patients, or other stakeholders. It finds its way into ministerial speeches and has been particularly promoted in Scotland and Wales, where doing something different from the London-based NHS is always popular.

It is not a surprise that politicians like the sound of the term '*co-production*'. It resonates alongside co-operation or collaboration, as a universally approved value with which they wish to be associated. We also like the principle of *co-production*, but need to point out some important weaknesses. One is concerned with the legitimacy of the group that assembles for this purpose. It is not unknown for single-minded clinicians or managers to gather around them a group of people who agree with them. Secondly, there is the danger of having a wholly unrepresentative group of stakeholders – there, maybe, because of experiences which do not mirror those of the majority of service users. Finally, *co-production* blurs the accountability for a service. That is because the term covers a multitude of variations from *co-specification* to *co-design* and sometimes as far as *co-delivery*. Everyone wants to take the credit for changes and improvements that prove effective and popular. But if they are not so regarded, who is responsible? *Co-production* can lead to an element of passing the buck, hence the need to have a group that is perceived to be legitimate and representative.

'*Co-production*' may be an inelegant term, but it raises one of the most serious issues affecting public consultations in the NHS. Failure to tackle this issue well enough was spectacularly illustrated in a saga that rumbled on for years, and it is worth detailed treatment as a case study in how to antagonise elected members, the medical profession and highly visible members of the general public all at once.

The story is the attempt by successive governments to rationalise the number of hospitals undertaking cardiac surgery for children.

Admittedly this was a *wicked issue* that had been postponed too often, and a difficult, emotive one at that. Operations on little babies command enormous public interest and cardiac transplants themselves made celebrities of internationally renowned surgeons such as Christiaan Barnard or Magdi Yacoub.* The UK has excelled at such innovations and over the years acquired formidable expertise, though distributed throughout the country. By the turn of this century, there were eleven paediatric cardiac centres in England, from Newcastle upon Tyne to Southampton. Distressed parents of children needing extensive and often successive procedures naturally sought their nearest centre for ease of visiting and support. Outside the south-east there was a natural reluctance to travel continually to London, despite the capital having three such centres in Great Ormond Street, the Evelina Children's and the Royal Brompton hospitals, and notwithstanding all three having enviable international reputations. Conventional wisdom held that such complicated surgery should be concentrated in fewer centres and following a report into failures at the Bristol facility in 2001, the Department of Health began work on a rationalisation programme.

But how does one address such an issue, when, politically, it is clear that local communities – in this case regions of five million people and more – will fight hard to retain what they regard as an important NHS service? It was not an enviable task, and when the Department of Health convened a group with the title of the Joint Committee of Primary Care Trusts, one could immediately

---

* Dr Christiaan Barnard performed the world's first human-to-human heart transplant in South Africa in 1967. Sir Magdi Yacoub is a professor of cardiothoracic surgery and pioneered heart and lung transplants. He worked at the Royal Brompton Hospital from 1986 until 2001.

detect the tensions that were bound to arise as each fought for the retention of their own. As is often the case, the solution was to appoint a panel of experts who would then work with a respected consultancy to gather data and to develop options for a future configuration of hospitals to undertake this work.

At this point, we think, things started to go wrong, though few people knew it. Only upon publication of a damning report by the Independent Reconfiguration Panel (IRP) in 2013 did they come to light – even though there were two high-profile judicial reviews on the ensuing consultation in the meantime.*

When discussing *co-production* earlier, we noted the importance of legitimacy. This matters especially in the eyes of other key stakeholders. At once, the Royal Brompton Hospital became alarmed with the composition of the panel of experts. It appeared to them to be biased, as the panel contained people associated with the other two London hospitals, but no-one familiar with their own. Although in the judicial reviews the judges refused to regard this as bias in the legal sense of the word, it raised eyebrows. Two years and millions of pounds of legal fees later, the IRP found that

> membership of the Steering Group, although ostensibly based on representatives from professional associations, included people with a connection to all of the surgical centres included in the review with the exception of the three that were subsequently selected for de-designation at the end of the process.†

---

* R (*ex parte* Royal Brompton Hospital) *v* Joint Committee of PCTs [2011] EWHC 2986 (Admin) & [2012] EWCA Civ 472.

† 'Advice on Safe and Sustainable Proposals for Children's Congenital Heart Conditions', Independent Reconfiguration Panel, 30 April 2013, paragraph 4.16.7

The IRP uncovered a sequence of other errors ranging from inaccurate or at least disputed facts and figures to misunderstandings that almost certainly mis-stated the Royal Brompton's research endeavours. When anxious parents from West Yorkshire sought clarification as to how the published 'scores' that portrayed their local Leeds Infirmary as being significantly worse than Newcastle, they were rebuffed. Well after the Royal Brompton had legally challenged the findings and tried to resist being de-designated, the Leeds parents formed themselves into a campaigning organisation called Save Our Surgery Ltd and challenged the department once again. Whereas the Royal Brompton lost, the Leeds parents won. They secured a landmark judgment with the judge, Nicola Davies, literally laying down the law on the need for transparency in such matters.* From now on, experts cannot hide behind their expertise and refuse to share with others the rationale for their judgements.

The Royal Brompton fought its case by arguing that the decision-making committee had clearly made up its mind and was therefore in breach of the first Gunning Principle. † The consultation paper postulated four alternative configurations, but in all four of them, the two selected London survivors were the Evelina and Great Ormond Street. The judge at first instance found in its favour, though based upon such convoluted logic that the Court of Appeal had little trouble in setting it aside. The Royal Brompton, Their Lordships claimed, should have fought its corner in the cut-and-thrust of the consultation rather than rush to its lawyers and mount a legal challenge. When discussing the disagreements about the facts, and the underlying research that

---

* R (*ex parte* Save Our Surgery Ltd) *v* Joint Committee of Primary Care Trusts [2013] EWHC 439 (Admin).

† See Chapter 3.

had informed the decision to reduce the number of hospitals to six or seven, Lord Justice Richards said that a consultation should be 'self-correcting', a phrase that has intrigued us ever since. But in the context of this particular story, it made sense. That is because clinicians will regularly disagree from the best of motives. So do other professionals; think of civil engineers, IT specialists or even tax consultants. The role of a consultation is to expose these disagreements to open and transparent debate rather than keep them hidden behind closed doors. What concerns us in this story is that when the truth finally emerged, the Secretary of State for Health was obliged to come to the House of Commons and withdraw the entire package because of fundamental flaws in the approach taken by the decision-makers. The tax-payer had paid £6 million for the exercise, and it had to start all over again.

Not all reconfigurations pose anything like the same problems as those faced in this case. It was a nationwide exercise; it unleashed professional and regional rivalries. It also provoked serious disputes about the underlying evidence and turned the courts, albeit tentatively, towards a growing role in ruling upon whether options offered to the public have been fairly developed and presented.

Local issues actually are not dissimilar. When there are two or more hospitals in a city, it is not unusual for the supporters of one to campaign furiously at the expense of a neighbour. If there is also an overlay of sectarian allegiances, as was the case in Belfast in 2000,* the problem is even harder. The scenario there, as in many subsequent cases, involves the need to focus hospitals more

---

* In the High Court of Justice in Northern Ireland, Queen's Bench Division (Crown Side), in the matter of an application by Kathy Hindes for judicial review [2000] 2153 Ref COGE3292.

precisely on a given number of roles and to stop being all things to all patients.

In fact, the model of the district general hospital (DGH) is rapidly becoming obsolete. Politicians and local communities obviously prefer a single point-of-contact, do-everything hospital and for half a century, building a DGH to serve 200,000 people or more worked well. But as the incidence rates of various illnesses and conditions have changed over time and the skills and technology required have made different demands on hospital facilities, a degree of specialisation is inevitable. Actually, a surprising amount has been accomplished without the hue and cry that typically attends proposals affecting emergency services or maternity.

One of the unheralded success stories of recent years has been to centralise stroke and cancer services in London and other areas. Most of the proposals were, as is traditional, worked out by clinicians based on good, well-researched evidence and supported by ministers anxious about the UK's deteriorating position in the world rankings for effective treatments. Of course, there were local controversies, but faced with a persuasive case and strong clinical leadership, many of the relevant charities and other influential stakeholders backed the principles.

Adult cardiac surgery was more contentious. The 'golden hour' rule for strokes applies in much the same way to heart attacks, making communities very aware of travel time as an issue. We remember taking part in a particularly difficult radio debate on the proposals to downgrade cardiac treatment at Kendal Hospital in the Lake District. An NHS manager had done his best to explain why this was a necessary move, but we then heard an Oscar-worthy bravura performance from a local campaigner. Her

131

message was that 'patients would die in the ambulance' whilst being transferred to Lancaster or Barrow-in-Furness, taking twice as long in the traffic-clogged summer holiday months.

It is difficult to exaggerate the importance in local people's minds that travel times play in forming their views about hospital reconfigurations. They are rightly suspicious of quoted 'average travel time' figures and it has taken a long time for consultation specialists to recognise that they have to provide better information. It is not just travel time. The rationale for change has frequently been badly expressed. Maternity services are a good case in point. Mothers-to-be do not understand why long-standing arrangements at reasonably accessible hospitals should change. They cannot accept that there is a shortage of relevant consultants; if there is, they deem it to be the fault of managers or politicians. Either will do. They just know intuitively that it is not a situation where the mothers-to-be should be penalised.

We once saw this argument played out in Scotland, where a mishandled consultation in the Vale of Leven Maternity Service led, in part, to a reference to an independent body. In Wales, the downgrading of the maternity services at the Withybush Hospital, Haverfordwest, obliged pregnant women to travel to Carmarthen, 40 miles away, except in extremely straightforward cases. Wherever staff shortages are cited as a reason for centralisation, the public believe they are witnessing real mismanagement. They then see hospitals mounting international recruitment expeditions to the Middle East or beyond and complain about the waste of money caused by inadequate manpower planning at home.

The NHS has been forced to rely expensively on temporary staff, and high-profile media coverage of the issue has angered campaigners trying to retain threatened services. It erodes any confidence that managers are competent and casts doubt on other assertions they make. Staffing levels are particularly contentious. Following the Mid-Staffordshire scandal, it became evident that many parts of the NHS did not employ the necessary numbers and profile of staff to ensure a safe and clinically satisfactory service. The Department of Health initially fought against the imposition of minimum staffing quotas for nursing, but in the end had to agree to guideline numbers. But all this made the public and backbench MPs extremely wary of promises that new arrangements would work well. When the Welsh Government revised its guidance on public consultations in the NHS in 2011, it is said that the then minister added one extra item to the list of mandatory information regarded as necessary in a consultation paper. The item in question required managers to 'set out how sustainable staffing levels are to be achieved'. Shrewd.

Had this requirement been demanded of English reconfigurations, we suspect it might have led to even more controversy. The plain fact is that forecasting revenues and consequently staffing levels in the NHS has been an inexact science for years. Much of this is because staffing tends to be driven by the available finance rather than the other way around. The planning question appears to be 'How many people can we afford to employ?' rather than 'How many people do we need to deliver a safe and effective service?' As a result, the least reliable parts of the case being taken to the public are the numbers – and campaigners know this.

We have sympathy for the planners, though there are now fewer of them and many of the business cases for change are nowadays prepared by expensive consultancies. This fuels the concerns of die-hard NHS staff who fear a covert plot to privatise whenever these firms become involved. Whoever they are, those designing a new configuration of hospital and allied services face a daunting task – seeking to guess or, more technically, model a range of variables years ahead. To compound this problem is the uncertainty over many partner organisations. Withdrawal of funding to much of the voluntary and community sector also makes it hard to be sure about their future roles, but the biggest problem is local government.

Just before Sustainability and Transformation Plans were invented, a large northern city proposed extensive changes to the historic role of some of its hospitals. These entailed bed closures. It therefore needed to show how domiciliary community services would be provided to meet the needs of those who might otherwise have been treated in hospital. In this case, there were several councils involved and they mostly proved unable to explain the replacement services. The most they could commit to was to consult the public when their proposals were ready; each council would be different. Inevitably the hospital reconfiguration was controversial and political opposition flared up from place to place. The NHS could not wait, but the local councils were not ready. No wonder Simon Stevens had to create the STPs.

If it is difficult for managers, it is equally difficult for politicians. No Secretary of State wants to close hospitals – not even at a time of austerity. So there is a natural desire to delegate the blame – or at least find somebody to share it. In England, the Department of Health has been fortunate to hit upon an effective mechanism in the IRP. As the children's cardiac case study shows, its unwillingness to become a rubber stamp for departmental decisions has undoubtedly contributed to a deserved reputation. Over the years we have examined most of its referrals and find difficulty disagreeing with its findings. Obviously technical judgements are best made by clinical specialists on the panel, but we find that the IRP has been consistently right about many of the process failures that affect many plans to change the NHS.

The 1999 Local Government Act gave health *overview and scrutiny* committees (HOSCs) the power to refer proposals involving substantial change to the Secretary of State on three grounds. One is a failure to consult, the second is 'inadequate' consultation and the third is the catch-all claim that the proposals are not in the best interests of the health and wellbeing of the local community.

This third option seems to be most popular, as it enables communities some latitude in how they interpret their own best interests. It is also, however, most difficult to prove as it pits laypeople's gut instincts against the views of professional clinicians. Inevitably, it revolves around clinical outcomes more than access to services.

In any such debate, much depends upon the credibility of those who argue for change. When respected doctors take time to outline the case for change, they are very likely to win the argument. When they shy away or leave the explanations to others, they run risks. Most experienced politicians taking a populist 'hands off our NHS' stance will win such arguments with managers, accountants or bureaucrats. But, all else being equal, in a straight fight between clinician and politician, it is the medic who wins. In spite of everything, they have retained a degree of public confidence, whereas politicians, with honourable exceptions, are generally less respected.

For a HOSC to refer its grievance on the other, specific consultation-related, grounds should be more straightforward. A failure to consult, after all, is a factual situation, capable of being proven one way or another. More problematic is the idea of consultation having been inadequate, for it opens to argument the standard of public dialogue that one could reasonably expect. In practice, HOSCs have acquired what is tantamount to the power of veto over CCGs that want to make service changes. No one calls it a veto but its effect is similar. The relevant regulations require a CCG to notify the HOSC of the changes it wishes to make and it must then seek agreement with local councillors as to the nature and extent of consultation that is appropriate. If they agree, then a sound working relationship should ensure that the NHS delivers what was expected.

Supposing, though, that there is no meeting of minds. It occurs quite often. A case we considered concerned closing a small unit offering very specialised services that could clearly be offered to a higher standard in a neighbouring clinic. Everyone on the HOSC appeared relaxed about the proposal, except for one councillor, who represented the single incumbent patient who was unhappy. She fought her corner for this constituent and effectively prevented the committee, which preferred to work by consensus rather than by majority, from approving the change. She demanded a full-scale community consultation, almost certainly inappropriate for the precise circumstances of this case. NHS managers wondered what to do. They were under no obligation to conduct a high-wide-and-handsome exercise for a service change agreed by everyone except one patient. Yet they feared that the HOSC could refer the problem to the Secretary of State on the grounds that they had failed to consult, or had consulted inadequately.

So what exactly is *adequate consultation*? Answering that question may not be quite as difficult as defining a *significant* change, but it is clear that there will be different views as to what each set of circumstances warrants. We remember once appearing in front of a HOSC in the north of England. The chairwoman was as formidable a local councillor as we could recall meeting in many years. She had the bit between her teeth. NHS managers had promised to carry out a thorough exercise seeking the involvement of as many residents as possible. Yet the numbers were far too low for the chairwoman's liking. Based on comparable data, we thought the CCGs had actually done rather well, but as the meeting progressed one elected member after another rose to complain that the exercise had not been adequate. Our abiding recollection is of the impassioned speech made by another councillor who explained that her experience of selling poppies for the British Legion over many years had taught her that engaging busy shoppers was twice as successful as they entered or left the supermarket if she stood on the right side of the entrance rather than the left! She had, apparently, passed on this intelligence to the NHS consultation team, but the advice had been ignored. No wonder, she concluded, that the consultation was inadequate.

It is easy to be amused by such tales, but in many ways they capture, in microcosm, the dynamic at work when local people are given influence over the way they are consulted. Far better this than the antagonism created when the conduct of the debate seems dictated from high up, or from far away.

No better example exists than in the sorry tale of Lewisham Hospital.* The politics of the situation was considered earlier but, in this context, what matters is the extent of opposition to the way in which the consultation was conducted. No matter how

* R (*ex parte* Lewisham LB and Save Lewisham Hospital Campaign Ltd) *v* Secretary of State for Health and Trust Special Administrator appointed to South London Hospitals NHS Trust [2013] EWHC 2381 (Admin).

contentious the Trust Special Administrator's proposals were, what caused offence to local doctors and to the clinicians working in this hospital was the way in which the consultation treated them as second-class citizens – even on their own patch. Now there were reasons for this. The NHS was, after all, seeking to address a large financial deficit over a wide area and saw a change in the role of the hospital at Lewisham as a way to solve the problem. Such a situation had been anticipated by Whitehall bureaucrats and the appointment of the Special Administrator was made under legislation brought in by the previous Labour government. Critically, it included provisions to reduce the duration and the extent of consultation, thus creating a position where, at a time of greatest potential change, the process of dialogue was curtailed. No wonder local people were incensed. For them, their hospital was being downgraded in order to solve someone else's problem, and they saw the fast-track process as a means of railroading local clinicians to support an unwelcome scheme.

There was a similar scenario developing less than a hundred miles away. Two large towns, 15 miles apart, had rising populations and each had a hospital that was struggling both financially and clinically. Neither wanted to lose facilities to the other and each had been in on–off talks with its rival for years. Suddenly, the financial picture worsened and the CCG was told to call in one of the top private-sector consultancy firms to work out a future plan. Clever people can always produce a plan, but their presence casts a shadow over local relationships. The HOSCs started getting twitchy. Ditto the Health and Wellbeing Boards. Healthwatch became anxious. Such destabilisation came about not because communities were unrealistic or did not acknowledge that there were problems to be solved. It did so because the timetable, the

138

methods and the messages of the dialogue appeared to be dictated from above.

As the Sustainability and Transformation Partnerships acknowledged, the integration of health and social care involved inherent conflict between a top-down management ethos in the NHS and the more locally based, democratically accountable services run by local authorities. Budget cuts, high-profile failures and the media vilification of social workers had in any case weakened councils' capabilities and their discretion. Governments of all recent hues have had to step in when dramatic failures have occurred and some councils have had their care departments taken over by Whitehall-appointed managers. Weak councils made uncomfortable partners for the NHS, so public legitimacy was increasingly reliant upon sound consultation with everyone, rather than the words of elected members.

After all, it was politicians that decreed local people should have a say. Until STPs provided a single, multi-local focus, the complex set of more immediately local bodies caused continuous confusion. Communities had to scratch their heads to figure out who was really behind the proposed changes. It boiled down to trust, and a suspicion of consultations written by one or more of the NHS organisations but with another three whispering off-stage. Somehow, the people suspected they were not being told the whole truth.

In 2012 one of the health boards in Wales consulted its public on a wide range of changes and presented a paper that covered almost every aspect of the NHS and social care service-mix. It ended up in court * when campaigners fought one of the

---

* R (*ex parte* Flatley) *v* Hywel Dda Health Board [2014] EWHA 2258 (Admin).

proposals – to reduce the opening hours of an accident and emergency department in Llanelli Hospital. One of the arguments was that protestors had uncovered a secret plan. This was a paper written some years earlier and ostensibly recommending precisely the change that the board had made. Local people cried foul, claiming that the discovery proved that managers had misled them. They argued that this was a breach of the first Gunning Principle, suggesting that the decision had already been taken and that the board had capriciously omitted to reveal its plans when it conducted its consultation.

In court, the protestors failed, for there was no evidence that the planning paper had been seen by key decision-makers, let alone been endorsed by the board as a whole. But this was a salutary experience for everyone and sent shock waves through the community of highly challenged planners whose task it is to forecast future demand for NHS services. It highlighted the need for almost all their papers and reports to be written *subject to consultation.* Loose drafting and some doubt as to the status of the document cost this particular health board hundreds of thousands of pounds in legal fees. More significantly, it typified the climate of mistrust that exists in some communities when changes in health and social care are contemplated.

Fortunately this does not apply everywhere and there are areas where relationships are excellent and levels of mutual trust are high. The aim of STPs surely is to build, over time, viable inter-agency bodies with strong public engagement obligations. If they are to last, they will need to be placed on a statutory footing.

By the end of 2017, and in spite of austerity and political arguments, the government could claim reasonable satisfaction levels with the NHS, which was still held in high esteem by the public. However, their love affair with NHS services did not extend to its management. There is little doubt that organisational complexity has always been one of the main reasons for this, and STPs cannot solve it.

There may also be an argument that whatever structures are created, an environment where indispensable services are perceived as being under threat will always arouse deep passions and the public's concerns are understandable. Public engagement on health and wellbeing in Britain is therefore likely to remain, alongside spatial planning, one of the most visible instances of UK community involvement and consultation in the foreseeable future.

Chapter 7

Consultation and governments

Schools and education | Sunningdale Institute | government
blunders | council structures | double devolution |
community websites | participatory budgeting | council
budgets | symbolic consultations

The reason why health and planning feature so prominently in the
landscape of public consultation is that we are all, in a sense,
stakeholders; as such, we feel entitled to a say in decisions. Other
services also have this characteristic – changes to schools, libraries
and fire and rescue services can all become controversial. But a
further range of services, including the more obscure welfare
entitlements, somehow lack the capacity to excite communities in
the same way. For the more contentious issues, there are well-
established processes of consultation – many of them specified
by statute. The politics is not necessarily at the point of service
delivery. As in the NHS, there are a host of public services where
politicians argue out the policy choices, but other agencies,
notably local government, have the operational role. No wonder
people are confused!

Schools policy is an excellent example of seismic changes having taken place. Yet most people would be hard pressed to remember whether they were consulted on their local comprehensive becoming an academy. This is because, in our system, changes of this magnitude are seen, rightly, as the domain of the national political discourse. Its forum is Parliament. Only when the policy is rolled out, sometimes years later, does the reality become visible to most people. Politicians understand this well and have been adept at lighting the blue touch paper and retreating from view, leaving the operational agencies to consult as part of the implementation process.

When asked if you think the local school should become an academy, it seems clear that in reality, there is not much in the way of a choice. It is a yes-or-no, take-it-or-leave-it proposition, which one day we may see challenged in court under the first Gunning Principle. In comparison with other services, education has been quite transparent, with many recent initiatives designed, in part, to take account of stakeholder views. Traditionally, this would have focused on parents and pupils, but suddenly in the late twentieth century the debate widened. Part of the critique of our schools at that time was that they were failing to deliver to the business community the profile of skills it deemed desirable. Businesses therefore demanded a degree of involvement, and having schools converted into academies seemed one way to reach out and secure their participation.

Ironically, the system that directly-funded academies were intended to replace was one where consultation was supposedly built in at the point of design. The idea of local education authorities was that the influence of elected members would ensure a responsive, locally accountable system, one that was also able to spread the risk by providing common services or specialist

144

facilities where the need was greatest. Was there perhaps too much consultation? Were critics of this long-standing formula right when they complained that innovation was stultified and political in-fighting hampered schools' attempts to raise standards? Regardless of who was right, the emerging model has seen academies and free schools largely able to determine their own strategies, but also required to consult the local community and the parents. Have we now built a local politicians' bypass?

One matter upon which Parliament has been quite specific is school admissions. Long seen as a pivotal policy and with a history dating back to the divisive 11+ exam and councils' attempts at social engineering, this has been specifically legislated upon. It has even been judicially reviewed, when the London Oratory School defended a somewhat inadequate consultation.* The judge looked at the statutory provisions which, being recent, required only that the school publish its draft admissions policy on its website. The schools adjudicator argued that the logic of Parliament's intention was that the whole community should have the opportunity for a dialogue about this subject. He was, therefore, promoting a view that this policy was one that mattered to a wider audience – not just obvious stakeholders such as existing and prospective parents. The court shared this view and ruled in the claimant's favour. Not for the first time, there was tension between targeting specific stakeholders and promoting a dialogue with the wider public.

There is no denying that there was a public dialogue over university tuition fees. Issues as prominent and divisive as this do not need a public consultation, though the existence of clearly enforceable rules might have helped ministers manage the

* R (*ex parte* Governing Body of the London Oratory School) v The Schools Adjudicator [2015] EWHC 1012 (Admin).

process rather better. When, in 2011, the government instigated a substantial increase in tuition fees for students at English universities, opponents alleged a breach of human rights legislation. The High Court rejected the claim.* Claimants did better by proving that the minister had not given *due regard* to the foreseeable impact of the policy on poorer students and those from certain disadvantaged groups. Officials had under-estimated the need to dot the i's and cross the t's of the 2010 Equality Act, then only recently enacted.

The politically explosive issue of student tuition fees obscured other important changes to the tertiary sector. Note how consultations on these matters rarely hit the headlines. Unlike health, the fate of academics and their interests excites the media rather less than what happens to clinicians and their patients. Nonetheless, these issues were very visible in the academic community itself. Comparable claims can be made for the arts community. Or the scientific community. Or the defence community. Or any other defined group of stakeholder interests insofar as public policy directly affect them.

Government agencies have become adept at building consultative relationships with specific client groups. This is a double-edged sword. On the one hand, these groups help policy-making ministers and civil servants understand the issues better and see the impact of their decisions at ground level. On the other hand, departments have often been accused of being too close to particular interest groups and we remember how the farming lobby lost some of its influence with government when the Ministry of Agriculture, Fisheries and Food disappeared into the

---

* R (*ex parte* Hurley and Moore) *v* Secretary of State for Business, Innovation & Skills [2012] EWHC 201 (Admin).

Department for Environment, Food and Rural Affairs after the 2001 foot and mouth epidemic.

In 2009, the once-influential Sunningdale Institute published a paper called *Engagement and Aspiration: Reconnecting Policy Making with Front Line Professionals.** The authors – Sir David Omand, a former Cabinet Office permanent secretary; Professor Ken Starkey of Nottingham University Business School; and Lord Adebowale, with a host of experience in the charity sector – had impeccable credentials, and their analysis was well expressed by the paper's subtitle. The paper tackled the perception that civil servants and ministers lived on another planet and rarely empathised with people and organisations affected by their proposals. A case was made for a new generation of staff they called *networked public officials*. They would spend substantial periods on secondment working with stakeholder organisations, changing places with others travelling in the opposite direction. All this would require a new approach to training civil servants.

Their analysis might have been reasonably accurate but their timing could not have been worse! Written, no doubt, before the full extent of the economic meltdown and its impact on public services were appreciated, it sank without trace. The National School of Government, of which the Sunningdale Institute formed part, failed to survive the purge of inessential bureaucracies swept away by the incoming coalition. Far from embracing a Whitehall makeover, most policy-making civil servants hunkered down and prayed for survival. Such luxuries as a closer relationship with stakeholders became synonymous with the profligate Noughties. Even the term 'stakeholder' was

---

* Available at
http://webarchive.nationalarchives.gov.uk/20100505174116/http://www.ca binetoffice.gov.uk/media/182021/sunningdale.pdf (accessed 22 March 2018).

banned, in an attempt to rid government announcements of impenetrable jargon. Sir Humphrey Appleby*might not have approved!

We looked closely at the Sunningdale proposal and concluded that a complete revamp of officials' training was well over the top. What was needed was for civil servants to stick to the consultation guidance that the Cabinet Office had already published. At that time, it called for extensive pre-consultation with affected stakeholders. What was all the fuss about? The answer lay, and still lies, in the distinction between technical and political issues. Most weeks of the year, Whitehall publishes six to ten consultations, rather more when senior officials clear their desks to go on summer or Christmas holidays. About half will be technical in the sense that they raise few if any matters of contention or policy choices. They are often amendments or updates to secondary legislation; many have been implementations of European directives. Almost all of these will have been the product of discussions with specialists and are unlikely to be of interest to the general public.

The challenge is to ensure that the levels of skills and knowledge possessed by public officials are roughly equivalent to those of the lifelong specialists in particular industries that they are dealing with. In *The Blunders of Our Governments*,† Anthony King and Ivor Crewe identified the root cause of so many public project failures as being an asymmetry of knowledge between purchasers and providers. They drew upon an avalanche of evidence, including a

---

* A senior civil servant in the satirical BBC sitcoms *Yes Minister* (1980—84) and *Yes Prime Minister* (1986—8), characterised by a reliance on bureaucratic terminology.

† Anthony King and Ivor Crewe, *The Blunders of Our Governments* (London: Oneworld, 2013).

148

2011 National Audit Office review of 184 of its investigations,* finding that an alarming proportion of the problems were caused by skills shortages in the ranks of the civil service. If anything, the situation has become worse. Opinion surveys of senior officials have confirmed that there is deep concern that they do not have the expertise required to work with their commercial counterparts. In the fields of defence and IT, it has almost become a cliché; in high-profile embarrassments like the massive Connecting for Health† project for the NHS the litany of mistakes is literally mind-boggling.

All this means that although government departments with a knowledge deficit face risks on small-scale technical issues, their problems are compounded when they embark upon the bigger, more politically sensitive projects. Here a lack of specialist know-how is usually tackled by increased reliance on outsourcing to major consultancies, with sensitive commercial issues and negotiations undertaken by external lawyers – often from the same range of companies. This creates conflicts of interest, but has also diluted the civil service's traditional caution. King and Crewe suggested that IT companies have sometimes displayed a degree of hubris. But it is worse than that. They quoted a witness giving evidence on the NHS IT system to the Public Accounts Committee – someone who had tried to warn his superiors in the Health Department about the failure at the outset to consult clinicians! We often consult excessively on small, relatively inconsequential issues and sometimes neglect to consult at all when there are massive changes afoot. Whoever claimed it was

---

* National Audit Office, *Annual Report 2011*

† Connecting for Health was part of the Department of Health Informatics Directorate. Its role was to maintain and develop the NHS national IT infrastructure. It ceased to exist on 31 March 2013.

like consulting about the disposition of deckchairs on the *Titanic* whilst the liner was starting to sink had a point.

Government consultations, as a result, can be extremely variable and it is not immediately obvious whether they are the product of long-term, high-quality informed dialogue with representative and authoritative stakeholders, or a back-of-an-envelope quickie done as a box-ticking exercise. There are clues, of course. Those that have had the benefit of substantial discussions will no doubt cross-refer extensively and usually provide details of who has been involved. They may even append a list of stakeholders – though we are often surprised and disappointed by who's missing! Those offering only one option or whose questions start 'Do you agree with us that...' rightly arouse more suspicion and merit closer scrutiny.

Just because a public body's consultation is on proposals that seem complex and highly engineered does not necessarily indicate that there has been dialogue. Technical issues frequently box officials into a corner where the range of options is constrained. We remember once coming across a consultation which basically amounted to a choice between implementing a EU rule of some sort, and not implementing it. 'By the way,' the consultation paper mentioned, albeit in dense bureaucratic gobbledegook, 'one of the options would be breaking EU law.' One wonders what the point might be, save that, if in doubt, Parliament these days veers towards the failsafe of giving the public the chance to comment. Presumably in this particular case, the exercise – if it managed to engage the right people – would probably have uncovered any fears or anxieties about the proposed implementation. In which case, it might have been more honest to consult on the impact of the regulations – not whether to make them in the first place.

150

If we look at subjects that obviously excite the public, we see a clear pattern. Large, life-defining mega-propositions such as Scottish independence, whether to remain in the European Union or even the future of the BBC understandably command their attention. At the other extreme, local issues similarly stimulate a degree of involvement. It is the ones in between that cause difficulty. For example, politicians have long discovered that general public care very little about the structures of public administration. Successive waves of local government reorganisations only capture the imagination when proposals start interfering with people's sense of identity or their traditional tribal allegiances. When these are combined with perceived changes to services, it makes for a heady cocktail. Some years ago, an ambulance call centre for north-east England was going to be moved from Hebden, just south of the Tyne. One imagines there may have been disquiet anyway, but once it was revealed that the new centre was destined for Middlesbrough, the balloon went up! It is as if fans of Newcastle United or Sunderland were asked to abandon their clubs and support the rival on Teesside.

In English local government, the move away from the traditional two-tier model has now been in progress for over twenty years and has been accepted with reluctant nostalgia in many areas. Who now mourns Bedfordshire County Council, Cornwall County Council or Shropshire County Council? When, however, it was proposed to convert Norfolk and Devon to single-tier unitaries, unhappy district councils took the matter to the High Court* and managed to demonstrate that their residents had not been properly consulted. The case turned on the poor quality of information provided by the Boundary Committee, but no one

---

* R (*ex parte* Breckland DC) *v* Boundary Committee for England [2009] EWHC Civ 239.

except the district councillors and a few activists seem to have found this a priority issue.

The same apathy was seen when the idea of local authority mergers first appeared. Impressed with the galvanising impact of high-profile American city mayors in New York, Washington, and Boston, ministers suggested we adopt a similar model. It seemed to work in London, so why not elsewhere? The answer is that in large conurbations like the capital, power has to be distributed so there remains a role for the ordinary councillor. In smaller places, the arrival of a dominant figure with a popular mandate was a threat to many careers. Until 2000, local government was run on committee principles, conveniently spreading the accountability around and making it difficult for council taxpayers to pin the blame for unpopular decisions. Councillors with reservations about mayors are not unlike MPs who dislike the idea of an elected second chamber. What they both oppose is the prospect of rival mandates.

Not that any mandate in local government amounts to much. Turnouts at municipal elections have hovered between 20 and 30 per cent and when people in ten English cities were asked in a referendum in 2012 whether they would like a mayor, few turned up to vote. Only Bristol voted for a mayoral system as councillors elsewhere campaigned to keep their hands on the levers of decision-making.

When cabinet government was introduced in the 1999 Local Government Act, it seemed to many that the average backbencher was reduced to lobby fodder for votes in full council. Power was with leaders and portfolio-holders who effectively determined all key policies and ran the council alongside the chief executive and the paid staff. Some council leaders, who quite fancied being bosses, decided in one of the more bizarre episodes in local government to fire these chief executives or maybe ask them to manage the staff of one or two adjoining councils as well. In part, this was a reaction to some foolish excessive pay packages rightly condemned by Eric Pickles in his hair-shirt phase. Management suddenly became a dirty word and power was concentrated increasingly in cabinets, which could be very partisan where local politics were finely balanced and councils could change control.

Austerity politics is so difficult for local authorities. Voters don't easily rally around the slogan '*Vote for me and I'll close your library*'. Instead they prefer to imagine that there are thousands of non-jobs cluttering up the town hall, which can disappear without anyone noticing. Maybe there were, for over the course of five years, councils obediently cut their expenditure drastically. The cash settlements of the coalition government were harsh but the irony was that satisfaction levels with councils remained high. Still everyone craved for something more positive and it was at that point that George Osborne had his big idea and floated the concept of local government devolution. Actually the thought had occurred to the previous Labour administration, who labelled it 'double devolution' but never managed to make it happen. Never mind, it was now Osborne's.

First he went to Manchester and proposed a fully integrated health and social care organisation based on a single mayoral super-council. It was what many people had called for, but it is full of operational problems, as the NHS dislikes working under the direction of elected members. The £3 billion budget would not be the only carrot. Osborne had championed the idea of the Northern Powerhouse and, with a constituency in Cheshire, knew the need for renewal of its infrastructure and the deep mistrust of

153

London-based decision-making. He offered to devolve a raft of economic development, housing and transport powers and make available large-sounding sums to foster enterprise and economic growth. The money was, in fact, relatively small as it was to be spread over thirty years but it made for good headlines and the plan received a good press just in time for the 2015 general election.

Emboldened by having the first Conservative majority since 1992, Osborne cranked up the engine and offered everyone else the chance to engage in devolution. Having an elected mayor was a pre-condition, but most councils, especially the old metropolitan councils, found that bearable if they were to acquire new powers and, of course, the money.

Almost every council found it could bid for devolution. Some had historic or cultural claims to stand alone. Therefore, Cornwall had a 'deal' in the bag and even escaped the mayoral requirement. 'Devo deals', as they became known, sprang up all over the place and it seems council leaders were most enthusiastic. But the public were not. Some voices were heard saying that there was a democratic deficit. Did the various councils in the Greater Manchester area want to subsume their roles to a massive new authority under a new mayor, without knowing more about the compromises that would have to be made? In any redesign of public administration there are perceived winners and losers, but, according to those outside council leaders' offices, no one seemed to have a clue as to who won and who lost. The Communities and Local Government Select Committee decided to take an evidence session in Manchester and found that encouraging reactions to the advent of new powers and money were almost totally wiped out by criticism about the lack of transparency. Where, people demanded, had there been 'consultation'? Where indeed? Councils appear to consult about almost everything from the location of a park bench to the routine patching of potholes. Yet, come the biggest shake-up in local government for decades, no one asked the people.

The select committee duly reported how delighted everyone was with the powers, and the money, but pointedly condemned councils' failure to consult. A few of the others that were in the devo-queue made half-hearted attempts to elicit electors' views, but in the main negotiations proceeded between council leaders and the Treasury, and mostly behind closed doors.

What transpired was a patchwork quilt of merged or semi-merged (sub-merged?) councils, mostly with mayoral leadership but with differing powers. It made the previous untidy two-tier system a model of consistency and clarity. What also emerged was that council leaders were at a loss to know how to consult their populations. What could they ask them? Almost all the 'deals' were take-it-or-leave-it agreements. They could hardly go to the public and offer them a choice of this or that option. To make matters worse, the public would ask questions to which council leaders realised that they did not know the answers. Who would have final say on infrastructure investment decisions? Could a mayor overrule planning decisions by district councils or other planning authorities? And how would all these decisions be scrutinised? How would accountability work? These and other questions had not been considered in the 'devo deals' and astute councillors realised that any consultation would struggle to meet the Gunning Principles. Just consider: the deals had effectively been done. Gunning One requires consultations to be at a 'formative stage'; Gunning Two requires all the relevant information to be available. As we have noted, it was not! We can satisfy Gunning Three by making the consultations last as long as they like but, frankly, there was little councils could do to engineer a lawful consultation.

In time, no doubt, there will be a reasonable level of engagement with community interests but the whole devolution saga illustrates the lopsided nature of consultation at local level. In contrast, planning and health, as we have shown, command public attention and consultations are taken seriously – after a fashion. Council structures just make the public yawn.

Elsewhere in Local Authority Land, things are a little hit-or-miss. Middle-class articulate citizens will inevitably engage to oppose closures to library services and the 'culture' lobby will always appear to defend entertainment facilities against cuts. But, beyond this, we struggle to find consistent dialogues. This is a worry, for there are many causes and concerns affecting disadvantaged or under-privileged groups for whom there are fewer advocates. To cope with this imbalance, many councils rely upon a framework of *continuous engagement* machinery, designed to ensure that elected members and officers hear different perspectives as they discharge their duties. One of our future challenges is to find ways to measure the effectiveness of such machinery.

In the meantime, vigorous debate on services can be found in our local newspapers and their associated websites. Scarcely any town these days goes without a citizen-run site that seeks to stimulate discussions about local matters. The power of these to form instant bandwagons is immense. Just before Christmas, some years ago, a well-meaning participant of our home town's local affairs and gossip page on Facebook started posting fascinating old photographs attracting many comments and several active discussions about the town's past. Then, on New Year's Eve, some killjoy posted unpleasantly that some of these 'might be subject to copyright' and in any case, the policy of the local history society was not to publish them on free access social media. How dare this individual, who apparently belonged to the society, violate its policy? Our embarrassed enthusiast apologised, thanked everybody and announced he would leave the forum. We then witnessed a collective outburst of online anger. Before we had rung in the New Year, more than 300 local people had vented their anger at the killjoy, who retreated into sullen inactivity before finally being persuaded by other history society members to withdraw the accusation of malpractice. It was all over within hours. Obviously this is a trivial example of small-town community dynamics, but tiny dramas of this kind are an everyday occurrence in virtually (that's the correct word!) any town or village across the UK. In them, petty jealousies, historic injustices and implacable enmities compete for mindspace with pleas to help find a lost dog, recommendations for a suitable pub, appeals to support charitable events and the latest marathon run.

It has not been lost on the police, the emergency services, the NHS or progressive councils that these social media sites offer superb insights into the attitudes and concerns of residents. Rightly, it is called community intelligence in some quarters. Equally the sites offer unprecedented possibilities for two-way dialogues on matters of local controversy and are, therefore, becoming the methodology of choice when seeking to understand the views of local people.

It is a problematic direction for us to travel. Those who use Twitter, Facebook and all the others to give opinions on current affairs are still a minority. It is one thing to share those views with 'friends' or 'followers', but another to express them to a public body, especially if the rules state that anonymity cannot be guaranteed. Experience is showing that the scale and nature of participation suffer if consultors try to be too clever. The KISS principle (Keep It Simple, Stupid) appears to be the best advice. Some years ago, Bristol City Council, one of the pioneers in online consultation, experimented with something called deliberative polling. It is based on encouraging respondents to consider various aspects of a problem as they refine or maybe change their opinions. In this case, it posed the question: 'Should we encourage the erection of tall buildings in Bristol?' Depending upon the answer, the respondent would then be given information from the other side of the argument. For example, if the respondent said 'No', the website would display the argument that major employers in the area might have to reconsider expanding their operations in the city if restrictions of this kind were imposed. Conversely, for those who answered 'Yes', information was provided on the potential threat to the town's existing skyline. And so forth. Supporters of this technique join those who are keen on deliberative events as a methodology that produces more nuanced outputs that are of much greater value to policy-makers and politicians than a straight yes or no. One might add that there are those who reflect upon the EU referendum of June 2016 and wonder if a similar approach should not have been attempted.

Bristol's experiment showed that although such techniques have their uses, they are not yet workable on a day-to-day basis. There are several reasons for this. It seems that many people heartily dislike being challenged and seriously resent being questioned about their views. They think it is an impertinence and an attempt to suggest they do not know what they are talking about. Instead they prefer a simple question because that relieves them of the responsibility of thinking through the implications of their decisions. That task, as they see it, is one for the elected politicians and their officials. It makes routine local consultations subject to the old truism that it is easier to find out what people oppose than to discover what they might want instead. It is yet another compelling reason why the best local consultations offer a range of options from which the public can choose.

One of the purest examples of this is the rise and fall and rise again of *participatory budgeting* (PB).* In principle it consists of involving the general public – defined as anyone who *wants* to get involved – in allocating public money. Somewhere in our archives there is a great video of the people of Keighley† back in 2008 when some money was set aside to experiment with these participation-based methods of consultation. Alan Budge, a great innovator and facilitator of these initiatives, introduced the video. He explained that some weeks earlier, voluntary and community bodies in the town had been invited to submit bids for community projects – much the same as was done in hundreds of other towns. What happened under normal circumstances is that councillors met to decide how to allocate the council's money. They based their judgements, no doubt, on their views of local needs and the contribution the projects might make. If there was a concept of a return on investment, it was likely to have included political investment as well as the benefit to the community. It is this element of politics that PB seeks to bypass. Instead of politicians making financial decisions, the theory is that the community itself makes the choices. PB has its origin in the city of Porto Alegre in Brazil, where, after decades of corruption

---

* PB is about local people making decisions directly over how local public budgets are spent: see pbnetwork.org.uk

† The Keighley PB pilot in Bradford ran from 2006 to 2008 with £130,000 of neighbourhood renewal funding. 250 people attended a 'Decision Day' event to vote on how money was spent.

and mismanagement, local people took charge of the situation and met in large groups to decide their own priorities. The story went worldwide and there have been countless attempts to build on the original experiment.

In the United Kingdom, the focus has been very much on the small-grants model, such as in the Keighley experiment. The video showed the big public event held one Saturday to choose between competing projects. Keighley has a highly diverse population and bids were received from dozens of ethnic and religious groups, from Muslim, Hindu and Sikh groups right through to the Church of England. There were lots of sporting projects from women's football to taekwondo, arts and crafts proposals and activities for older people. Up they came in turn to make their case, each one vying with others to entertain as well as to argue the benefits of receiving the money. It must have taken hours. Everyone who attended – about 250 in this case – had a vote and experienced users of PB will claim that one of the magical things that happens is that people genuinely base their votes on what they believe to be the merits of the case rather than just supporting their own bids. In the end money was distributed among eight to ten winners but even the unsuccessful seemed happy that they had seen their bids considered by the community as a whole rather than discussed behind closed doors by local councillors.

Logically this should not work. Bidders could pack out the meeting with their own supporters. How representative of the community are the ones who turn up? How do they know whether the organisation seeking funding has the management capability to run their project successfully? Who is accountable for their performance? What happens if things go wrong? These and a hundred other questions steer the traditional local bureaucrat away from PB. Yet the bidders accepted the result. No one complained and the community integration benefits seemed immense. On film, one of the bidders explained how she had never realised the good work being done with young Muslim boys in parts of Keighley, or the efforts being made by voluntary youth workers trying to devise activities for bored young people from deprived backgrounds. Maybe the principal contribution of PB is to enhance community cohesion. It is not the decision that matters, but the educational and consensus-building process that leads up to it.

So if PB can work on this scale and if those that become involved enjoy this feeling of shared ownership, why can't it work with the larger decisions on public expenditure? One can quickly move beyond 'we haven't got a room big enough' to attempts to apply the underlying principle – which is that anyone who wants to participate can do so. Back in 2000 the English Department of Communities and Local Government decided to back PB and agreed to set up a small unit in Manchester to promote it. When the recession arrived, funding quickly disappeared and despite a resurgence of interest in the north-east, most of the action moved to Scotland. The SNP government in Edinburgh identified *community empowerment* as being strategically important and found techniques like PB a useful alternative to the more traditional ways of consulting people as to what should happen in their local areas. It is absolutely right of course and maybe the experience of the independence referendum has added to people's confidence that their involvement truly makes a difference. Time will tell if the equally divisive EU referendum brings about similar changes in the mood music south of the border. In both cases, though, we wonder whether PB will ever become truly mainstream unless it shows its usefulness on a wider basis – particularly local government finance.

Consultation on council budgets is a particularly thorny matter. In theory, as an issue, it should be top of the list for local people. Money spent on local schools and colleges, roads, children's services, libraries, day centres and the other 300-odd services provided by the bigger council clearly matter. An opportunity to influence the allocation of money should surely be an attractive option for the civic-minded citizen. Well, it seems not. With a few exceptions, as with municipal structures, the public take little notice.

We cannot blame them. Local government finance in England must be one of the most abstruse, obscure, incomprehensible constructs ever devised. Looked at from the perspective of needing to explain it to laypeople, in order to consult them, one flounders under its contradictions. Local councillors are, for example, accountable to their local electorate for what they do, yet the bulk of council money comes in the form of the support grant from central government, whose intricate formulae mean that no-one understands how or why the grant goes up one year and down the next. Then the discretion councillors have is highly circumscribed by laws and duties imposed on them by a Parliament that has for decades willed the ends without willing the means. The problem of budget literacy has been highlighted for years, not just for the general public but also for councillors themselves.

There is no statutory *duty to consult* council taxpayers in general about a local authority's budget. All we find on the statute book is a provision dating back to John Major's government that requires councils to consult small businesses. When this provision was introduced, most authorities could not see the logic of talking to one stakeholder group but not others and soon found themselves following Audit Commission guidelines and consulting everyone.

There is good reason to do so. Unlike central government, which has a whole nation of consultees in theory, local authorities have a defined area and a greater sense of who's who. Most councils have lists of organisations and businesses that make up the economic and social fabric of the local community. They are the ones that normally matter when local politics throws up a knotty problem or a conflict of priorities. They are the local movers and shakers and no doubt they come closer than anyone to understanding what local government finance is all about. Or they would, if they had the chance. The trouble with the Audit Commission's advice is that it took insufficient account of the budgetary calendar. What happens is that the sums given to each council are announced in November for effect the following April. By the time the arithmetic is done, councils are in danger of consulting the public over the Christmas period, so they invariably do it in the spring with inadequate time available to make much use of people's input.

Councils are often quite good at telling local people about specific service change options. Over the years they have learnt how to ask which libraries to close or which street lights to switch off to save money. One authority presents the public each year with a list of forty services and for each one there are choices varying from minimal change to drastic reductions in service. The problem with this approach is that those who object to serious change feel cheated that no one asked them about the principle of reductions to that particular service in the first place.

Libraries are a case in point. Once a council starts reducing the number of libraries, their supporters' first line of argument is 'Why has the libraries budget been cut by so much?' The answer, of course, is that the council cabinet has already made its decision, faced, as they all were, with finding unprecedented savings. There usually will have been tough negotiations between different portfolio-holders as to where the axe might fall. They are two distinctly different processes. One is about the *shape* of a budget, or what is spent on what. The other we can describe as the *substance* of the budget, meaning the services to be delivered, which may need to be changed. A failure to consult on the shape usually means problems with the substance. The budgetary calendar, however, allows councils little scope to consult on the various departmental allocations and many will just argue that this is the task for elected members and that the public has no part to play in the process.

Best practice has now evolved to a position whereby wise councils consult on their budgets all the year around. No sooner do they start the new financial year in April than they kick off discussions about the following year. The advent of a three-year financial settlement has helped in terms of knowing the general direction of financial travel, but too much else, especially in the way of new statutory duties or changing operational assumptions, limits the value of this overdue reform.

Two examples show the difficulties councils face and the need for almost continuous dialogue on these matters. One was the introduction of the Care Act in 2014. It sought to update the framework for social care, but councils argued that the government short-changed them on the money needed to implement it properly. Ministers refuted this, but their case depended upon assumptions that councils would have addressed long-standing issues relating to staffing or facilities. Frankly, some had and some had not. By far the best solution for council leaders trying to introduce radical new policies and services whilst balancing the books, was to gather all the local stakeholders together and try to use the latest *co-production* or *co-design* techniques to find the optimum way to spend the money that would actually be forthcoming.

The same approach served well with our second example, which is the transfer of the public health function from the NHS to local authorities in England. This was a straightforward moving of £3 billion of public expenditure from the management autocracy that is the NHS to a democratically accountable council and it was clear that over time priorities might change. The pressure point came when the Treasury demanded a significant reduction in funding. In percentage terms, it was not huge by the standards of contemporary austerity, but it was enough to jeopardise existing programmes and warranted a rethink by many councils. Doing this in a hurry antagonises stakeholders and produces idiosyncratic results. So a reasonably permanent dialogue has much to commend it and this seems to be the best-practice standard that has evolved for budget consultations in general.

Some councils widened the dialogue to help everyone participate, so instead of asking for people's comments on published service change options, they asked them to outline their priorities for local public expenditure as a whole and to explain their choices and maybe propose novel solutions. Questionnaires are of limited value, though they reveal interesting patterns of preferences. Rarely do they reflect the more compassionate side of society. Few people place caring for disturbed youngsters or helping gypsies and travellers high on their list of priorities. It is not always easy to detect whether this is a function of the respondent profile for such broad-brush consultations, or whether there is a deep-seated truth to Ben Page of Ipsos MORI's* frequently quoted finding that people are in favour of austerity, provided it means cutting *someone else's* services. Slightly different results emerge from focus groups or deliberative events where people have time to consider the value and the outcomes of different services. Whatever method is used, councils can then enter the budget-making process not so much with a list of priority services, but with far more insight into who values what – and why.

All this works well enough for routine budgeting, but recent years have seen far more radical changes. The nearest that budget consultations came to an authoritative judicial ruling was in the strange case of Mrs Nash in 2013. This doughty campaigner took the London Borough of Barnet to the High Court† to try to set aside the council's decision to outsource £350 million of its services, in the then biggest deal whereby councils became commissioning bodies rather than service-deliverers. She faced a daunting task for there was something of a supertanker to stop. Her difficulty was that the original decision to pursue this strategy was taken several years earlier. Consultants had been briefed; committees had examined their reports. Proposals had meandered to and from directorates, procurement had been undertaken and by waiting until the point at which Barnet was about to sign a contract with Capita, Mrs Nash risked being well beyond the timescale when one can mount a legal challenge. So,

---

* Ipsos MORI is the second largest market research organisation in the United Kingdom, formed by a merger of Ipsos UK and MORI, two of Britain's leading survey companies, in October 2005.

† R (*ex parte* Nash) *v* Barnet LB [2013] EWHC 1067 and [2013] EWCA 1004.

she lost, not once but twice, the second time in the Court of Appeal.

However, at the first time around, Lord Justice Underhill took the unusual course of dealing with the merits of the case, even though he refused her application for being out of time.* In effect he was saying 'Just in case I am wrong', a sentiment not too frequently heard in the High Court. And he had another reason for doing so. Lurking on the statute book since 1999 had been provisions about Best Value, long observed by local government officials but never effectively tested in court.

The whole Best Value concept is rather interesting from the perspective of public consultation. The idea was Labour's reaction to the much-hated Lowest Competitive Tender regime that had led so many councils to sub-contract their services to low-cost, poor-performance companies. Best Value was intended to focus minds on a greater range of variables – including consultation with the users of the service. That is what the guidance required, but the actual statute was somewhat more obscure and provided little by means of redress. What Mrs Nash's case did was base the claim upon the requirement that councils had to satisfy the tests of Best Value in the way that they organised themselves. She argued in court that none of the council's budget consultations had even raised the possibility that it would outsource such a massive part of its budget. The council tried to say that these consultations would have allowed anyone with strong feelings about its policy to express their views. But its arguments were weak. The budget consultation in 2012 really amounted to an internet-based money allocation 'game' that only

---

* A case for judicial review must be brought before the court quickly and in any event within three months of the decision or action being challenged. It is unusual for the court to accept late applications.

about fifty people had used, with little insight into who they were! The council's other consultation method had been public meetings, many of which were cancelled due, according to the council, to a lack of interest.

Full marks to the judge for stating that such consultations simply do not stack up. Had she not been out of time, Mrs Nash would have won. The Court of Appeal let Lord Justice Underhill's judgment stand and it is now good authority for the proposition that, in respect of the rather vague Best Value legislation, the public now has a legitimate expectation that councils will consult properly on their budgets.

We have often wondered what might happen if the Chancellor of the Exchequer was under a similar obligation. Most Budget statements actually announce consultations on technical matters, usually so that the financial services industry can probe plans for new taxation or other initiatives; up to twenty such exercises can emerge from the Chancellor's speech. But as for financial or fiscal policy, these are rightly the province of elected ministers and parliamentarians and we see no case to extend the principle of consultation in this direction. The Chancellor's Autumn Statement (since 2018, a Spring Statement) on public expenditure is rather different, as spending programmes impinge much more directly on citizens' services. Here there is already a tradition of subjecting radical changes to public consultation.

Another trend has been for governments to seize upon the news agenda and demonstrate their concern by instigating a consultation. What causes certain issues to leap up the public's agenda is a mystery best considered by PR professionals and lobbyists. It is well illustrated by the country's profound interest in the spring of 2018 in pollution caused by plastics. Some attribute this to the popular BBC television programme *Blue Planet II** and its highly respected presenter, Sir David Attenborough. Without the growing media profile for this issue we question whether the Chancellor of the Exchequer's Spring Statement would have included the announcement of a consultation on 'tackling the plastic problem',† curiously called a 'call for evidence' on 'using the tax system or charges to address single use plastic waste'. HM Treasury wanted to consider a variety of probably unpopular or unworkable options, but hoped to ride the wave of public support and demonstrate its willingness to listen. In a different example, only a week earlier was the symbolic launch of a consultation on strengthening the law of domestic abuse. Timed to coincide with International Women's Day, it was assured of better coverage in the broadcast news. It was a great example of consultation being used not just as a tool of policy-making, but also as a not-too-subtle signal of governmental values and direction of travel.

To summarise, government in all its forms and at whatever level is deeply imbued with the culture of consultation. It may not always do it very well, but we can probably vie with any advanced democracy in our willingness to subject our plans and proposals to the scrutiny of an effective consultation process. The next part of the book explores the way in which politics can influence the effectiveness of what is otherwise an impressive feature of our democracy.

---

* Originally aired between 29 October and 10 December 2017.

† 'Tackling the Plastic Problem', gov.uk, 13 March 2018, https://www.gov.uk/government/consultations/tackling-the-plastic-problem (accessed 22 March 2018).

Part Three

The Influence of
Politics on
Consultation

Chapter 8 - Introduction
Is anyone in charge?

Silo mentality and the drive for centralisation | politicians *v* technocrats | who's in charge? | select committees | reluctant stakeholders | stakeholder mapping | a brief history of consultation guidance | parliamentary ping-pong | the Whitston case | BBC consultation | Whitehall gets it right?

If we take politics to mean the exercise of power, then there are interesting questions over the way it influences the processes of consultation.

In principle, consultation is intended to inform those who are in power, in the sense that they make the ultimate decisions. The difficulty is that it is far from being an exact science and the way that politics intervenes and political manipulation occurs makes their effect complex and unpredictable.

This part of the book looks at the impact this has on public consultations. It is certainly not intended as an attack on politicians or their causes, but an attempt to understand the forces at work.

We need to focus on public affairs to appreciate this impact. Office politics occurs in all organisations and territorial battles happen as frequently as disputes about policies. If consultations are planned or executed deep within departments where there is a culture of autonomy, we hear the phrase 'silo mentality'. It has connotations of officials pursuing their own agendas without taking account of others. The criticism may well be unfair but has led many public bodies to establish the central co-ordination of public engagement, much to the fury of strong departmental heads, who brook little interference of this nature. As often as not, they claim that it is needless bureaucracy and a classic example of head office micromanaging and trying to retain as much power as possible in the centre. Power struggles of this kind have taken place for years. The advantages of pulling together the silos of public engagement are obvious and a centralised unit can ensure consistency and the observance of standards.

The same debate goes on in Whitehall. The 2008 Cabinet Code of Practice on Consultation envisaged Departmental Consultation Co-ordinators able to supervise and ensure compliance with the Code. They did not all last. Parts of the government machine found they were useful in controlling further-flung parts of their empires. At one time, the Department of Education had a specialist Communications and Consultation Unit in Runcorn, Cheshire, which brought together and co-ordinated a wide variety of public engagement. Like others it fell victim to the headcount reduction of the coalition government as posts were gradually eliminated.

Wherever the centralisation debate occurs, two things stand out. One is the fear factor that makes council leaders or senior civil servants wary of accidents happening further down or sideways across a large department. Another is the belief that if you centralise communications you may also need to centralise public engagement and consultation. Both have a grain of truth if consultation is badly done. If it is done well, it matters not where organisationally the function is situated.

But there is another more 'political' reason for centralisation and it can be a worthy one. True leaders, whether national or local, know how important it is to stamp their vision upon their administrations. That means influencing even if not controlling the public engagement agenda. These are the people who can talk convincingly of 'making the weather' or setting public sentiment pointing in the direction they prefer. In his book *The Myth of the Strong Leader,*[*] Archie Brown points out that many of the most successful have eschewed overt tub-thumping and concentrated instead on creating conditions sympathetic to their policies.

For such leaders, it matters that stakeholders and the public see the difference between those things that the leader has already decided and those matters upon which he or she is open to persuasion. Of course, in a totalitarian context, there is no consultation. But in a mature democracy, it is built into the system and true leaders know instinctively that they can use it to shape the agenda.

Without this form of strong political leadership, consultation can easily fall into the hands of the technocrats. Our civil service and local government officers would not welcome this description. What we mean is that the public engagement and consultation becomes part of the bureaucratic toolkit and less of a political act by decision-makers who genuinely want the views of consultees. Some years ago we studied the way in which consultation operated in local government and found that only in a minority of councils did elected members take the lead. Consultation for

---

* Archie Brown, *The Myth of the Strong Leader: Political Leadership in the Modern Age* (London: Bodley Head, 2014).

175

most of them was something officers advised the members that they ought to do '…and please can we get on with it?' We think this is unsatisfactory. Consultation is far more likely to be taken seriously by those who commissioned it in the first place. If politicians feel it is an unnecessary embellishment, foisted on them by an uncomprehending Parliament or obfuscating officials, it is not surprising that they are half-hearted about listening to its output. A few local authorities have considered making all public consultations report to their overview and scrutiny committees. The thinking is that a consultation commissioned by a council cabinet may well be structured so as to support its desired outcome, but it is questionable whether it is realistic to attempt to do this. The argument is also, however, that the voice of the people, as expressed in the consultation, is not the sole property of the leadership but is a knowledge/insight resource available to the community as a whole. And, of course, to the council as a whole too.

If we apply similar thinking to the national picture, there is a case that Parliament should consult – rather than the government. That is possibly going too far, but for some consultations it may be appropriate. A disadvantage is that the public perceives MPs as being the worst possible choice if we want a respected, relatively neutral consultor. It is quite ludicrous that Parliament lacks a budget to undertake its own consultations. In 2014, Graham Allen MP, then chairman of the Constitutional Affairs Select Committee, had the inspired thought to consult his fellow citizens on their aspirations for a written constitution. This was to coincide with the 800th anniversary celebration of Magna Carta. Allen's committee managed to find a researcher and produced a gargantuan consultation paper reminiscent of public consultations twenty years ago. It had the benefit of little or no professional advice, save what was donated *pro bono*, and predictably the entire exercise failed to gather any meaningful traction. Admittedly, this was before the constitutional traumas of the Brexit referendum but it could and should have commanded far more public attention than it did. For Parliament to be unable to support initiatives like this says much about the way MPs see their roles. Managing public consultations is clearly not one of them.

And this is probably right. The nearest Parliament comes to eliciting the views of consultees is the well-established practice for select committees to invite 'calls for evidence'. These are mini-consultations, except that it is not for committees to ask for views on a set of options. More typically, they will list a series of questions and ask for submissions. Committee clerks then trawl through them and select suitable organisations to appear in public. Naturally there is criticism that the process of selecting witnesses is itself a highly political act and reveals much about the committees' thinking. A consultation, it is argued, would avoid such blatant bias in the way that output is handled. But we are not so sure. There is a strong case for decision-makers at all levels to hear at first hand what stakeholders think. At least MPs are prepared, through the select committee process, to meet the witnesses in person and to hear their views. Too many in power tend to hide behind the consultation and some, especially where no politicians are involved, never meet a consultee from one year to another.

The influence of politicians on a consultation is, therefore, an aspect of governance. Who is in charge of the exercise? Until recently consultations were seen as a project to be organised by paid officials and answerable through the chain of command. Much of this is clouded in secrecy and a legitimate grievance of stakeholders is often that there is a manifest lack of transparency in the way that a consultation is designed and its output considered. The malign aspect of politicians is when their choice of whether or not to participate in consultation governance is a deliberate act of distancing themselves.

We have a classic example of the obscurity that confuses and irritates stakeholders. Health and Wellbeing Boards* were set up through Andrew Lansley's 2012 Health and Social Care Act and were intended to be responsible for what the NHS was called upon to deliver in their areas. The key point about these boards is that, although they give seats to the various professionals delivering the services, the chair is usually a local politician. A plausible theory is that this lies at the heart of the disappointment with these boards. Many of them have so far failed to grasp the nettle of the changes needed in the Health Service. As a result, in 2016, the NHS had to institute its own planning process to accelerate progress.

We have already chronicled the saga of the Sustainability and Transformation Plans/Partnerships, and their failure to consult local people. Whilst this occurred, however, clusters of clinical commissioning groups, NHS providers, the odd council and such miscellaneous regulators as happened to be passing, produced one plan after another and intermittently launched public consultations.

Politicians deliberately stay away from such planning exercises. Close involvement with tough choices is a challenge and few Members of Parliament are happy to take the risk of being seen to be too close to bureaucrats who may be blamed for bad news. We constantly hear from officials in town halls, the NHS or other

---

* See Chapter 6.

public services how much they would like to be able to involve their local members in addressing the dilemmas of fitting quarts into pint pots. If professionally trained, they would have undertaken an exercise called *stakeholder mapping*, figuring out who is likely to be affected by or have an interest in the subject matter.

The intention is to 'map' these organisations or individuals so that the best way to engage with them can be devised and implemented. Inevitably local politicians feature in these analyses. Rightly they are categorised as having a high degree of interest, meaning they have a considerable stake in what happens. They are also usually earmarked as possessing a high degree of influence. Who can disagree with that?

The technique itself was originally developed and used by the World Bank and has been applied, with variations, ever since. By taking the two dimensions of interest and influence, it enables one to show in a Boston Square chart* those who are almost certain to wish to become involved in a consultation – as well as those whose profile looks somewhat different.

In the Consultation Institute, we particularly use *stakeholder mapping* to identify people or groups with a high stake in proceedings, but whose influence is low; these are often hard-to-reach or, more appropriately termed, seldom-heard bodies who are passionately concerned about the subject (high interest) but who need quite a lot of help if their voices are ever to be heard (low influence). The model also shows those stakeholders who are largely indifferent or who are little affected by the proposals (low interest). But even here, one has to be careful for they might,

---

* A Boston Square chart, as used by the Consultation Institute, is a rectangle divided into four quarters with axes for Interest and Influence, on which you 'map' key stakeholders accordingly. The original presentation method was used by the Boston Consulting Group in 1970s for marketing purposes.

despite this, carry a lot of clout (high influence). Traditional media, such as newspapers, are frequently found in this part of the matrix for their real interest is usually to boost their circulation and they may care little or nothing about the issue itself.

When presented as a whole, an analysis of dozens of potential stakeholders clearly signals to the organisers of a consultation where their attention and their budgets should be focused. Their sights are firmly, though not exclusively, on those with high interest and high influence, and those groups or individuals are usually delighted to receive such attention. Except for politicians.

Consultation organisers are exasperated and perplexed. Why would Members of Parliament, tribunes of the people, not wish to immerse themselves in the issue that will be put to their electorate, whose views will be sought? On so many occasions we have been shown invitations turned down, meetings postponed, papers unread and questions or queries unanswered. 'If only they would tell us that they are not interested,' despairs a consultation officer from a local authority, striving valiantly to sit down with the local MP and consider the options available for that run-down housing estate that needs a facelift. Of course the MP cannot say he or she has no interest. The job requires them to have an interest. But it does not extend to doing the work of councils for them. More often than not, a parliamentarian sees their role more as an advocate for causes that their constituents bring to them – not the other way around. What suits a politician is to monitor the local reaction to various proposals. The experienced among them will be a little careful not to ride the horse that is first out of the starting stalls; politics is subtler than that. The aim will be to 'keep their powder dry' and maintain a position of neutrality for as long as possible before deciding which strand of an argument to support.

180

This pattern of behaviour is far from universal. There will be MPs or even ministers who will willingly co-operate by examining the overall problem and help policy-makers to frame their consultation in a way that would most probably help a council or even a government make a more informed decision. But they are exceptions. Far more common is reluctance by politicians to lift a finger to prepare for a consultation. To be fair to them, their ridiculous parliamentary timetable probably makes it impractical anyway, but the main reason for this reticence is that they see themselves primarily as a consultee – albeit an important one. In his book *The Political Animal,** Jeremy Paxman tries to get underneath the popular image of those who serve in Parliament and concludes that many of them simultaneously display signs of public arrogance and private insecurities. Many of them who are loud in debate or persuasive on television know that they would struggle with the minutiae of a planning consultation or the complexity of health inequality data that might form part of a hospital's reconfiguration project. Why become involved with officials whose job is to do this anyway? For whatever reason, the absence of political input when a consultation is being planned is unfortunate and may be the reason why, from time to time, we come across proposals which are so clearly out of step with the prevailing mood.

Maybe a politician makes an initial suggestion. 'Would it not be a good idea if we asked the public what they think about *XYZ*?' They then leave it to hapless officials to try to interpret what exactly they had in mind. Back in 2006 we remember a slim consultation on no less a subject than eliminating world poverty.†

---

* Jeremy Paxman, *The Political Animal: An Anatomy* (London: Penguin, 2007).

† Department for International Development, *Eliminating World Poverty: A Consultation Document*, January 2006.

We remember being quite impressed when we first saw the front cover, for in the days where the average consultation paper was over 100 pages long, this came out at about 15 and it was thin in every way, not just in the number of pages. Looking back, here was a classic case of politicians persuading themselves that it would be a great idea to consult people but failing to follow through their intentions with the kind of meaningful involvement that might have made the exercise valuable.

Politicians quite like the idea of a public debate and most would pay a considerable amount to be invited on the top-line television programmes, which is why, when they get there, they feel so obliged to toe the party line rather than answer hard questions. Public consultations bring out similar fears and feelings. If it is a controversial subject, most MPs know they have to tread carefully and that there will always be those who object either to having asked the people in the first place or to the way in which the consultation was done. Better then to stay away from any responsibility for organising the exercise. Even better to take the credit for laying down the overall rules. As is often the case, politicians are far better at legislating for others than in undertaking tasks themselves, and this leads us to the history of Consultation Guidance.

The first iteration was published in 2000 by the Blair government, though we suspect it had predecessors gathering dust somewhere in the corridors of power. It was called simply the Code of Practice on Written Consultation but, reflecting years later, we see the clue in the title, for this was around the dawn of the 'internet for everyone' age. In its preface, Tony Blair thanked the National Consumer Council for its help in writing it. And therein lies another clue – the impetus for setting standards came not from those who designed and ran the consultations but from those who were increasingly receiving torrents of inconsistent ministerial gobbledegook and scarcely knew what to make of it.

Looking back, we are impressed that so much sound advice was offered. The Code of Practice ran to nineteen pages and read rather like a management manual. The trouble with such documents is that they assume consultation specialists have enough time and few other priorities, and in their enthusiasm the authors assumed a checklist mentality. The danger was that some of the audience might not see the wood for the trees. There were lots of trees! The standout provision was to insist that consultations last twelve weeks, enough time for a document to be sent to interested parties and for them in turn to discuss its content and prepare a written response. There has never been any particular magic to the figure of twelve weeks; it probably derives from the previous quarterly committee cycle in local government. Yet it has become a totemic standard and a rallying cry for anyone who thinks they are being rushed on an accelerated consultation. Back in 2000, it was scarcely controversial.

By 2004, the e-government programme was in full swing and local councils around the country were being encouraged to build websites. Many preferred not to, thank you very much, thinking that this was yet another Blairite wheeze of little real substance. 'Why should we pander to the geeks?' So they were incentivised by being offered grants or denied projects unless an online channel was established. Few people now remember, but in the earlier days of public sector websites they were mostly one-way communication tools – what the commercial sector referred to as 'brochure-ware'. The potential for these to serve as useful platforms for genuine dialogue was in the dim distance, but far-sighted people in and around the Cabinet Office began to see the possibilities and tried to influence the 2004 update of the Code to reflect the new electronic age. They failed. The new version was shorter and maybe a little clearer, but it mentioned the words 'online' and 'website' precisely once each. In other respects, we still envisaged a world of official paper documents and traditional methods of consulting the public.

Meanwhile the wider public sector embraced these documents and began incorporating them into their own working procedures. Encouraged by an active Audit Commission, local authorities began writing consultation strategies for their own councils and soon other public bodies were finding it useful to copy chunks of the Whitehall document. Wales, Scotland and Northern Ireland published their own codes of practice, and almost all of these documents provided for twelve weeks as the default standard length of a consultation.

By 2008, Blair was gone and senior civil servants started getting queasy about their vulnerability to legal challenge. The catalyst was the Greenpeace case in 2007,* which sent shock waves through government, as officials realised that failure to observe codes of practice could contribute to successful legal challenges. Pressure was on to dismantle many of the safeguards originally sought by the consumer lobby and to soften the requirements for *best practice*. Fortunately, a very able and far-seeing young civil servant, even then destined for higher things, was given the task and set about listening to the views of consultees and other policy specialists rather than just the complaints of ministers and their closest allies. We remember being involved and convening groups of experienced people from local as well as central government. What emerged was a need for minimum standards, alongside a

---

* R (*ex parte* Greenpeace) *v* Secretary of State for Trade & Industry [2007] ECHC 311.

confidence that departments would not cut corners or, following Greenpeace, mislead consultees.

The 2008 Code of Practice was the high-water mark for politicians in government taking the lead in establishing good practice in consulting its public. It still stressed the twelve-week rule but introduced the idea of 'proportionality', indicating that officials needed to weigh up the costs and benefits of each proposed exercise and to think twice if decisions had in practice been all but taken and the consultation was merely a bit of box-ticking. One of the debates raging at the time was whether the Code should set a standard for the whole of the public sector in England, but in the end a compromise was found whereby organisations outside central government could 'opt in' to its provisions. The names of about sixty bodies eventually emerged on the Department of Business website.

We never really understood why responsibility for a key methodology for the way in which government works was transferred from the Cabinet Office to the Trade and Industry Department, or whatever it was called at the time! It seemed to make no sense whatever. Then of course we learnt an important lesson about the politics of consultation. Recession and belt-tightening leads those at the top to wish to be seen as cutting anything that is centralised, and offering to 'devolve' it to somewhere else. Politicians themselves were probably barely consulted. Most likely all they did was to demand headcount reductions from their officials. Suddenly, cutting red tape became flavour of the month and here was a chance to eliminate 'wasteful' and unnecessary bureaucratic niceties such as consultation. Indeed for a time the department was called the Department of Business, Enterprise and Regulatory Reform! Fortunately when the transfer of responsibility took place, the 2008 Code was ready

185

for publication and no one wanted to fight for a further dilution of its provisions.

That had to wait for the coalition, which eventually scrapped the whole thing in a zeal of unthinking machismo. Oliver Letwin asked some clever civil servants (whose consultation expertise was, to say the least, minimal) to draft a set of principles that would replace the 2008 Code, which was now viewed as an encyclopaedic homage to the excesses of New Labour. They produced what we have for some years viewed as the worst-drafted document ever to come out of Whitehall, though colleagues insist that competition has intensified in recent years. To anyone who knew and understood the complexities of the trade, it was clearly an amateur production. The press release accompanying the publication of the Consultation Principles signalled an important switch of emphasis as the government announced that henceforth consultations (and much else) would be 'digital by default'. Eagerly we all looked at the Principles to see what this might mean in practice. We found nothing. It wasn't even mentioned. Instead, we were drawn to the radical twist in the 'twelve-week' story. No longer necessary, said the Principles. Let each consultation last as long as may be appropriate in the circumstances; anything from two weeks to twelve might be okay. That took some digestion, for the duration of a consultation is just about its most visible feature. If it now became a free-for-all, suspicions would grow that controversial issues would be deemed to warrant a short as opposed to a long dialogue. The Principles did not sound like a foolproof set of guidance; we could see disappointed consultees heading straight for the High Court.

Then our attention was drawn to a footnote. This in effect said that nothing in the guidance was meant to overrule the Compact deals with the voluntary and community sector.* Now the Compact prescribed twelve weeks for consultations, and applied to any issues of relevance or concern to the third sector. It does not take long to figure out that that covers 80 per cent of all local consultations and a fair proportion of national ones. So for all the headline-hugging departure from the hallowed twelve weeks, the practical effect was mostly no change.

There were other surprises in this document. Apart from the fact that it was written in a loose narrative style, it announced that it applied to all public bodies and not just to government departments. That would have laid to rest some long-running debates about its relevance to the NHS and others, were it not for the suspicion that the words had crept into the hastily approved draft without being checked. The Principles also dropped any reference to providing feedback. We know that civil servants find this an irksome task, but it is quite vital for *best practice*, and consultees have every right to know what has been said in the consultation. Again, to this day we are uncertain whether this was meant to have happened.

Inevitably, the Principles came in for criticism. No one bothered much in the House of Commons but in the Lords sat experienced administrators, ex-ministers and lawyers who could see at once that this was a clear attempt to dilute consultation standards and tackle the inconvenience of having to consult! Prominent among them was Lord Bichard, who had served as permanent secretary to the Department of Education, so was no one's fool when it came to the intricacies of the Whitehall machine. He sat on one of the more esoteric of Parliament's scrutinising bodies – the House of Lords Secondary Legislation Scrutiny Committee. Its

* See Chapter 2.

remit was to cast an eye on the mass of regulations or orders in council passed by governments increasingly prone to secure primary legislation that bounced many of the difficult issues into a less visible process. Its ire was aroused when it began picking up on regulations that had been published for relatively short consultations, but with a closing date *after* the regulation was slated for approval by Parliament! The committee summoned Oliver Letwin to appear and defend these and other misdemeanours and gave him some uncomfortable moments on several hearings. Ministerial apologies followed with letters explaining the exceptional circumstances and why this would be unlikely to happen again, but that the pressure of business might prevent the government from giving any formal guarantees, blah blah.

Had any of these unhappy cases been legally challenged, the government's case would have collapsed before you could say 'obfuscation', but of course they weren't. For those of us in the business of consultation, it was the latest piece of evidence that the government was paying mere lip service to consultation, just hoping for the best, and that middle-ranking civil servants could make it look as genuine as possible. Complacency, however, turned to concern as a range of other legal challenges emerged. In one of them, the parliamentary horse-trading affectionately known as 'ping-pong' came under the microscope. The case was in fact on a very serious matter as it arose following changes to the legal rules about bringing compensation claims in civil proceedings and it greatly exercised those suffering from the long-delayed onset of asbestosis or mesothelioma. * The government, through its Commons majority, wanted changes that

---

* R (*ex parte* Whitston (Asbestos Victims Support Groups Forum UK)) *v* Secretary of State for Justice [2014] EWHC 3044 (Admin).

many campaigners thought would deter claimants from seeking compensation, but the House of Lords disagreed. Back and forth it went, with neither side backing down. In the end, to enable royal assent, ministers agreed not to implement the provisions to asbestosis sufferers until the Lord Chancellor had conducted a review. The court case turned upon whether he had actually done so properly. For fairly obscure reasons, the department chose to conduct the review by means of a consultation, so that it could consider some other matters as well. It then complicated the situation by drafting the key question with a caveat that asked for responses on the assumption that other related proposals were approved. Unsurprisingly the department lost the case, and it shows, we think, how a cavalier attitude towards consultation standards still prevails in parts of the government machine.

Eventually, we think someone cried, 'Enough!' The Principles were rewritten and tidied up, obviously with help from government lawyers. For the first time they seemed consistent with the Gunning Principles but omitted any reference to the voluntary sector Compact; we think this was a mistake as government departments have recently taken to mentioning it on their own account. On the vexed issue of timing, the revised Principles state that 'consultations should last for a proportionate amount of time' and we think it may only be a matter of time before legal challenges are made to individual consultations. Lying behind all this is a determination to do as much as possible online and to limit the time officials have to spend on the exercise.

To its credit, Whitehall sometimes gets it right. There are examples of excellent government consultations but it is far from clear whether the credit for these goes to the civil service machine or to individual ministers. Ministers are blamed when things go wrong, but do they actually deserve some credit when a consultation they have initiated goes well? Many BBC Radio 4 listeners and the articulate middle class may have been appalled by parts of John Whittingdale's massive consultation on the future of the BBC in 2015,* but from a technical point of view it was well constructed and satisfactorily conducted. We are not sure they had bargained for 190,000 responses, but an astute politician – even one with controversial views on a subject – may have an instinct that it is better to bring the debate into the open through a well-structured consultation than to let it fester.

Around the same time, an unusually comprehensive consultation emerged on sports policy from the same department. What made this unusual was that it was a truly cross-departmental exercise – with involvement and options offered from the Departments of Health, Education, Business and so forth. It is important to acknowledge that highly effective consultations are produced in Whitehall and one of the questions for us is whether ministers who are blamed when things go wrong actually deserve some credit when a consultation they have initiated goes well.

Bringing all these various strands together and trying to understand what influence politics plays in consultation, one is tempted by the conclusion that the office politics that is found well beyond the world of civic affairs plays a big part. Leaders who want to achieve significant change and who wish to carry stakeholder opinion with them, and who are wise enough to resist the temptation to dictate solutions autocratically, find consultation an effective tool to engage with people whilst still retaining room for manoeuvre. Of the many ways in which the technical tasks of organising such exercises can be undertaken, what politicians prefer is to influence where and when they are

---

* BBC Charter Review Public Consultation 2015.

done and maybe to approve sensible guidelines. Only when they make mistakes, as Oliver Letwin may have done in 2011, do they find themselves having to become involved in the detail.

Chapter 9

How political timing affects consultation

Established consensus | volatility | the policy life cycle | the
electoral cycle | 'purdah' problems | the Big Conversation |
serendipity

Timing plays a critical role in politics. Indeed, policy-making owes
much to the accident of timing. So do political careers and the
successes or failures of governments and their creations. To
appreciate the relationship between consultation and the political
process, it is essential to explore the way that timescales impact
upon decision-makers' ability to listen to the cacophony of voices
that may wish to influence them.

We start with the broadest of historical perspectives. Consultation
is inevitably affected by the prevailing consensus and it would be
almost perverse to see such an exercise occur in defiance of the
mood of the moment. Anachronisms emerge, of course,
especially in politics. A distinguished backbench politician, noted
for holding ultra-traditional views, has frequently been called the
'Member of Parliament for the Last Century', and there are those

who claim that elements of Western democracy similarly feel outdated in a modern world.

Worldwide bodies such as Transparency International* and the Open Government Partnership† track the progress of almost a hundred countries as they strive to develop democratic principles, and are finally making headway only because they have recognised that every state is in a different position in its historical evolution. Some are old and tired democracies – politely called 'mature'. Some are freshly minted with enthusiastic campaigners for causes that were previously implausible. Yet others are more hope than reality; the word 'flaky' springs to mind! In all cases, however, the dominant zeitgeist represents what is politically do-able and may set the boundaries of legitimate debate.

We first began drafting this chapter in 2015. We intended to remark that thirty years of broad agreement on neo-liberal market globalisation was a reality that made it very unlikely that the public in Western democracies would be consulted on any radical alternatives. In the UK context, certain ideas had been unfashionable for decades. Instead, a cosy consensus approved of privatising public utilities, low taxation and economic individualism. Until 2008, nearly everyone also favoured light-touch market regulation, though the global financial crash shook public confidence in such certainties.

Had the clock stopped at this point, we would find critics claiming that policies based on this value set had been pushed through without sufficient public consultation. But in truth, politicians

---

* A global anti-corruption movement with an international secretariat in Berlin and chapters in over 100 countries.

† The OGP was launched in 2011 to provide an international platform for domestic reformers committed to making their governments more open, accountable and responsive to citizens.

offering options that went against the grain of that consensus would have experienced severe problems in being taken seriously. The odd one made his mark: Tony Benn from the left, John Redwood from the right. Had they as ministers been overseeing specific issues at particular moments, it is possible that they might have launched consultations that invited the public to consider options outside the mainstream. But they would have been exceptions.

In those days politicians were under more pressure to conform than we sometimes acknowledge. Although, in theory, we had a plurality of media, the reality was that much of our press and considerable elements of our broadcasters had bought into the established consensus. Few were the occasions where views counter to the prevailing orthodoxy were woven into serious dialogues. A whole range of justified consultations would never have happened.

In three short years, the consensus evaporated. It was not due to new academic or political reasoning, or a measured rethink by world leaders or senior politicians. The election of Donald Trump in the USA, and the rise of Corbynism and probably the Brexit referendum in the UK, were a bottom-up revolt from those for whom that consensus no longer worked. The tectonic plates of politics shifted almost everywhere, with major changes in voting behaviour evident in France, Germany and the Netherlands, and separatist aspirations revitalised as far afield as Catalonia, Scotland and Lombardy. Suddenly, issues and causes that would have been denied serious consideration by the previous unanimity became the legitimate subject of debate. Rail renationalisation, public housing investments and price curbs on energy providers are but three examples in the wake of the British general election of 2017.

A more volatile political environment does not of itself invalidate our main conclusion that where a country's polity happens to be in historical terms hugely influences the willingness to engage on specific matters. We can debate whether this decade's experience is a one-off sea-change, or whether it is part of a long-term trend, where the ebb and flow of economic and political ideas can be presented as a historical cycle.

At a level beneath this macro, quasi-philosophical arch of Western Civilisation's progress, it has long been recognised that public policy-making follows a very definite life cycle. For example, until 2011, the National School of Government promoted the idea in a training course called 'Making Policy that Happens'. The previous year, the Department for Environment, Food and Rural Affairs (DEFRA) published a 'policy cycle' intended to demonstrate value for money and that the policy options being offered to ministers were the most effective and efficient. Other models have been suggested. They differ in detail according to whether or not they are part of a legislative process, and if applicable to regulators, local authorities or other public bodies, but are broadly similar.

Usually, the process has five elements: (1) policy scoping and initiation, (2) policy development, (3) approval and communication, (4) policy implementation and monitoring and (5) policy review. The first three distinguish between the difficult tasks of specifying, or 'scoping', the problem being addressed, developing a policy – assembling the evidence and making judgements on its value and relevance as the policy is developed – and submitting it for approval, entailing the need to communicate. The fourth element comes into play at the critical and important transition point where the policy becomes operational and is implemented, usually by other individuals or organisations. Finally there is an on-going task of monitoring its application, and this also covers occasions when the policy has to be reviewed.

It is without doubt a circular process. As with all cycles, much depends upon where and how you enter it. The entry point explains the constraints that impinge upon our politicians and civil servants. It also explains the differing types and characteristics of the various consultations that may be required at different stages of the cycle.

If we assume a potential policy initiative that can truly be seen as a first-time attempt to influence a certain type of behaviour, governments have a great opportunity to throw out a wide-ranging consultation to see how narrowly or how broadly people might favour the scope of possible legislation. In recent years, we have seen new policies for feed-in tariff incentives for renewable energy technologies, cyber-bullying or services for transgender people. In all these cases, there had been no previous definable policy.

Later on in the cycle, consultation can become very specific, where advice may be sought on highly technical aspects of proposed legislation or initiatives. Politicians who enter the cycle at this point will probably be accused of ignoring other solutions – ones that properly should have been considered at the earlier scoping stage. Provided such an exercise has been conducted, a minister will probably defend the position with ease. But if there was no such consultation, it can be a challenge to focus the dialogue on the intended subject matter. At the implementation stage, it often becomes much clearer what may be about to change.

We can take a local example. There have been many like this. In 2013, Lincolnshire County Council decided to reduce its libraries budget by £2 million and instructed its officials to prepare a plan that could then be put to the public through a consultation. The proposal was drastic – to reduce the number of full-time permanent libraries from forty-four to fifteen, and no one was surprised when a vociferous campaign secured an overwhelming response against the county's plan.

Councillors may not have recognised it, but what they had in effect done was enter the policy-making cycle at that point where the initial scope of the policy ('Let's reduce our libraries budget by £2 million') had already been determined and when options had been examined as to how to provide the service with such reduced funding. It would, of course, have been open to elected members to have consulted at that earlier point in the cycle, and indeed we would argue that they should have, but they knowingly or unknowingly failed to do so.

There is another stage of the life cycle when a consultation can be usefully initiated. This is in the fifth element, at the point of policy review. At this juncture, something has triggered a fresh look at a particular policy. Maybe it has been in existence for years and circumstances have changed. Organised groups may be lobbying for changes or improvements. Or possibly an unexpected event or scandal demonstrates that the *status quo* is no longer viable. Dangers lurk in such circumstances, and governments have been known to respond with unseemly haste. It's often called a knee-jerk reaction and for years the textbook example was quoted as being the Dangerous Dogs Act of 1991, where Parliament legislated swiftly following a spate of serious injuries and death from attacks by aggressive animals.

Speed is the enemy of the kind of deliberation that Professors King and Crewe recommend, but politicians rarely have time to linger over comprehensive policy reviews. An oft-quoted weakness of our system is that ministers' stay in one post is too short and this acts as a disincentive to the type of full consultation that the review stage probably merits.

One final point concerning the policy-making life cycle is that it is accelerating. Policies that might have lasted eight or nine years a few decades ago may now whizz around the cycle in half the time. Certainly the climate of austerity, plus the advent of rapid citizen feedback, discourages administrations from giving policies the benefit of the doubt and waiting longer to see if initial teething troubles sort themselves out. In the current climate, policy mistakes can be very swiftly identified, and can be subject to reviews almost before the ink is dry on their commencement orders. Politicians inheriting a policy problem need the time to consider the options. Panic is a poor principle but is not uncommon, and it is rare to find a satisfactory consultation under such circumstances.

Politicians also have to worry about another cycle – the electoral cycle. The weeks before an election are referred to in political circles as a period of 'purdah'. It's a highly inappropriate term but has been adopted to mean a curtain of discretion behind which certain activities can be concealed that would otherwise influence the public before they exercise their democratic right to vote. In a classic British fudge, it mostly relies not on law, but on a conventional wisdom that accepts that it is better to avoid some situations in the period immediately before an election. The textbooks call it a 'self-denying ordinance', though most government departments and local authorities follow official guidance to the effect that during this period, it is best to avoid significant policy announcements or controversial consultations.

The original idea was to avoid giving any incumbent politician an advantage over a candidate who had fewer opportunities to impress the electorate. Over time this has been interpreted in general as avoiding controversy. The 2011 Code of Recommended Practice on Local Authority Publicity has a section entitled 'Care during period of heightened sensitivity', which warns of the dangers of publishing anything controversial that identifies elected members. It even says, 'It may be necessary … to close public forums' – a recommendation we think is well beyond what is necessary and, in an era of social media, unrealistic.

But many experienced politicians disagree with us and adduce some additional reasons why 'purdah' should be applied very tightly. For example, in an election, one wishes to focus the public mind purely on that election, and to discuss or even mention controversial subjects detracts attention from this goal. Secondly, the same politicians argue that even if public bodies are scrupulous in avoiding bias, the media is very prone to personalising any controversy. Finally, we hear that candidates, when faced with contentious issues, are believed by many (especially officials!) to be prone to 'playing politics' and adopting voter-friendly positions just for the election.

For those who worry about these matters, there is probably a case for prudence. It applies particularly in hung councils, or those which change hands politically at regular intervals. The guidance talks of not starting any fresh consultations during the pre-election period, but allowing those that began earlier to finish. Those who argue for a tight interpretation claim that there should be no consultation at all, effectively preventing any from starting for weeks beforehand. Surprisingly, advocates of a tighter approach include the NHS, which technically is not covered at all, as it is not an elected organisation. During the 2010 election, Sir David Nicholson, its then chief executive, even wrote to health trusts suggesting they suspend any focus groups. Total nonsense, in our view!

If there ever was a time when one could discourage public debate – in order, allegedly, to focus on an election – those days have now gone. Social media means that people will debate whatever they want and no one will tolerate the idea that 'Sorry, we can't discuss that because of "purdah"'! Surely in a healthy democracy, difficult issues and controversial decisions are precisely what should be discussed? Is this not the time when candidates should be put on the spot and forced to declare their positions? To those who claim that candidates will say anything just to win votes, isn't the rejoinder that it is time for them to be properly accountable for what they say and do? If they are foolish enough to promise one thing and do another, the media or the ballot box can often extract revenge. Maybe the current rules are there to protect politicians from themselves? Or to save them the discomfort of having to adopt a position on controversial issues in case they want to change their minds later?

From time to time, we hear that a consultation is 'hijacked by politicians'. But what exactly does this mean? For many challenging issues, as we explained earlier, it would be a positive achievement to persuade MPs or councillors to take an active part in constructive dialogue. True, many would take a populist stance and find reasons to oppose various things. But in a well-designed consultation, it is more difficult to be wholly negative, and having elected representatives actively engaged is usually a plus, not a minus.

The conventional wisdom was that the best time to introduce new policies, especially unpopular ones, was in the honeymoon period following an election. On this basis, we confidently expected to see a flood of NHS hospital reconfigurations following David Cameron's election victory in 2015. It did not happen – or at least not to the extent we expected. Honeymoon periods are a thing of the past. Politicians are perpetually in campaign mode and Cameron's administration will probably forever be remembered for the headlong rush towards the EU referendum. We had expected a similar surge in unpopular reorganisations in Scotland. The experts all agreed that the SNP government had been wise to avoid controversy on such emotive matters before the independence referendum in 2014. Would overdue reforms be introduced afterwards? Well, no; there was the small matter of the scheduled 2015 UK general election. Immediately after that hiatus, politicians started to prepare for the 2016 Scottish Parliament election, and scarcely was there time to reflect upon that before the EU referendum and the (unscheduled!) 2017 UK general election.

A more recent phenomenon is the cross-contamination of political nerves as we all vicariously experience the electoral dramas of our neighbours. The British public probably saw and understood more of the French, Dutch and German elections in 2017 than previous iterations. They noted the rise and fall of Marine Le Pen or Geert Wilders and even smiled benignly at the antics of the Italian anti-establishment Beppe Grillo. This is due not just to the advent of 24-hour news, but to an increasing realisation that one's own domestic politics can be affected by others' electoral cycles. If in doubt, ask Brexit negotiators about the impact of Angela Merkel's bid for re-election in 2017 or the consequences of the unforeseen Trump administration. No wonder politicians find themselves increasingly wary of asking people about issues where the public or stakeholder reaction can be influenced by worldwide political destabilisation.

In Britain, there are also frequent local elections. These are generally held at the beginning of May, and many councils rotate their membership every year, so there are annual attempts to steer clear of controversy, just when councils are into the new budgetary year and need to be taking important decisions. Trying to manipulate policy initiatives to coincide with party political interests at an election feels to us like yesterday's thinking. Politicians these days live in a real-time world with social media probably ensuring that there are few if any honeymoon periods.

Neither is there any 'close season' to policy-making. Political leaders preside over internal party mechanisms to review and propose policies. After all, they offer a major motivation for those party activists who wish to exert influence and a challenge for party officials to balance members' aspirations with leaders' views and the realities of electability.

The days when UK party conferences took the big decisions may well be over, but all our parties have machinery to give their members a say on broad policy themes. In many ways, they are themselves consultors of some considerable experience. This machinery can be highly relevant, especially when parties agonise about their stance on an important issue. No better recent example exists than the Labour Party's dilemma in formulating a policy on the single market and a customs union post-Brexit as detailed negotiations got underway in February 2018. Again, the process was tested to its limits as it sought to satisfy a 'Remainer' membership and a leadership whose instincts were those of a 'Leaver'.

Internal party processes have quite a history. Back in 2003, the Labour Party launched the Big Conversation. At the time it was a major innovative attempt to involve party members. They over-cooked it somewhat. An 83-page document in 13 sections asked for views on no fewer than 206 questions. Its other claim to fame was that it was one of the first such exercises to be conducted almost entirely online. The exercise was much derided at the time and to this day, attempts by parties to elicit members' views are roundly criticised in the media as being purely cosmetic. This is the same media, incidentally, that regularly conducts far less robust polls and surveys to prove whatever point suits it. But the Labour Party did engage with tens of thousands of otherwise-uninvolved individuals. A concerted campaign by students opposed to top-up fees dominated the data gathered at that time and much of the rest of it was largely unanalysable. But over the years all the parties have experimented with ways to offer policy-minded members some channel to tell the party hierarchy what they think.

In 2017, the Conservative Party paid a heavy price for having neglected this approach to policy-making. Bounced into an unplanned general election by Prime Minister May, its manifesto was written in a hurry behind closed doors, with even Cabinet ministers, let alone party activists, only discovering its content when they tuned into Radio 4! The party, nominally, had an internal process; it just was not used effectively on this occasion.

So, to what extent are politicians' abilities to consult the public affected by these intermittent in-house processes of dialogue? The most obvious point is that, when they work, all they hear are the views of one subset of the electorate who happen to be their supporters. Or rather, that is the theory. In reality, party members have often been among the sternest critics of party policies; it is one of the reasons for systematic moves to diminish their influence. Consultation, as a process, is far more acceptable to parties than the shared-decision-making of yesteryear. To that extent, the constraints may be somewhat limited.

But they are committed to a process. Whatever party leaders may think of the ideas emerging from the membership, they cannot be seen to be dismissing them without observing the courtesies... and the timetable of those processes. There will be a set calendar, with a major annual conference in the autumn, a secondary spring conference and maybe a subject-specific policy forum or three.

Unlike the electoral calendar, and its over-rigid application of 'purdah', party management traditions in the UK amount to a chaotic free-for-all, seemingly with annual competition for the most outrageous and creative 'leaks' as politicians seek to manipulate their own internal consultative processes! Ritual it may be, but it demonstrates that politicians who feel otherwise constrained usually find a way... when it suits them. This is all because the oldest and wisest know full well the role of serendipity in political timing. Events have a habit of intruding upon consultations and playing havoc with an objective debate.

Some years ago, the Department of Transport decided the time was right to consult on a possible revision of the motorway speed limits, with pressure from the motoring lobby to secure an increase from 70mph to 80mph. A few days after the consultation began, a horrendous pile-up occurred on the M5 and the resulting injuries and deaths received front-page treatment for days thereafter. The cause turned out to be a tragic premature lighting of fireworks, which spread a pall of smoke over the motorway, but the newspapers all concluded that the scale of the carnage was the result of cars and lorries travelling too fast. Politicians were quick to agree and the proposals were dead in the water from that moment onwards. Bad luck for those of one viewpoint. But for the other side of the argument, divine intervention in having an accident that made their case for them.

We have all heard scare stories that happen to favour one side of an argument, and wondered whether the timing was accidental or whether we were being manipulated in some way. Our local NHS hospital is Bedford, and one where both of us have received excellent treatment. But it is small, and in that category where it is increasingly difficult to maintain a full range of services in all departments. Financial constraints have meant that some changes were inevitable, and the local public and patient involvement team rose to the occasion and masterminded some truly best-practice engagement exercises. Slowly but steadily residents, councillors, care organisations and others were persuaded that there might be a case for some sensible rationalisation. Local managers had been careful to base their arguments on future projections of demand, and the benefits of centralising some services. Then, out of the blue, a report was 'leaked' revealing serious quality issues in certain parts of the organisation. Shock, horror! Were services so poor or so dangerous that change was inevitable regardless of public opinion? People suspected bureaucratic skulduggery. In this case and in many others, it had come as a surprise to the managers as well. The public sector is so complicated, it is almost impossible for one part of the system to anticipate in detail what and when another part may publish, and no one can forecast how it might affect a forthcoming public consultation.

Politics is full of what-ifs as careers rise and fall and as issues move up and down the public's agenda. Mass media plays an immense role in determining the political weather, and subjects of comparative obscurity can sometimes rocket into prominence for seemingly trivial reasons. If these happen to be the subject of a consultation, their impact is totally unpredictable. With timing, only so much is manageable, the rest may be down to luck!

Chapter 10

The community's influence on consultation

Parish politics and the willow tree | petitions ancient and modern | petition platforms | analysis treatment | the cardinal's miscalculation | community advocacy | voluntary bodies

In a democracy, power is widely distributed, and politics is not confined to the electoral process. The shifting sands of power and influence are visible in a wide range of institutions and environments and the whole field of public engagement, including consultations, is massively affected by the dynamics of communities and the way in which they behave.

In Bedfordshire, there is an attractive village with the quintessential picture-postcard triangle of church, pub and duck pond. It was made more picturesque by the drooping branches of a weeping willow tree casting its shade over the water, much appreciated on a fine summer's day. Mothers who took their children past this spot on their way to school one day discovered, to their distress and amazement, that seemingly overnight the tree had been surgically removed. There was an instant and hostile reaction of a kind that only a modern interconnected online

209

community can give. Who could have done this? On whose authority? Then a confused and typically disjointed story began to emerge. Some months earlier, it seemed, at a low-key session of the parish council, a representative of the unitary council within which this parish stands had talked about a number of environmental and related issues. The willow tree featured. The unitary council's tree officer, the parish council was told, was getting a little worried that the root structure of the time-honoured willow might start affecting the lining of the pond. A serious investigation would be needed.

So some weeks later at a poorly attended and badly reported meeting of the same parish council, the tree officer duly came along, muttered dark thoughts about the future viability of the willow and said that it might well need to be taken down. When the odd councillor expressed surprise, they were firmly told that whilst the unitary council would consider any representations, this was a technical issue and if the tree was to be felled, so it would be.

Now, a more politically astute parish council might have spotted the danger signals and made people aware. They would, in the jargon, have 'taken soundings'. But this was not a politically aware bunch, so nothing was said to anyone. The people who lived next door to the willow knew nothing; neither did the pub landlord. The vicar was unsuspecting! Only when the tree was felled did all hell break loose. Only 300 people live in this village, but it is said that 100 of them communicated with each other by email on the fateful day; social media was still a novelty. Residents who attended a hastily convened public meeting reported a nasty, aggressive tone that led to resignations from the parish council and almost a public lynching of the hapless tree officer.

For years, we used this as a diversionary case study when teaching the dynamics of *community engagement*, for it illustrates in microcosm the issues that arise when people feel they have been denied an opportunity to influence what happens. All kinds of things went wrong. People knew little and cared less about the representative structure that took decisions on the community's behalf. So they took little interest in what happened. The parish councillors themselves were also at fault. They lacked the kind of political antennae that would have immediately warned them that any threat to the tree would be perceived as a disproportionate challenge to residents' sense of place. They also naïvely accepted a well-meaning officer's insistence that there was no *duty to consult*. More experienced elected members would have known that there does not need to be a legal duty. There are times when it is just sound common sense to talk to those who will be affected by change.

There are 10,000 or so parish councils in England, and in many places their members are almost literally dying on their feet. Councillors are an ageing breed and successive governments have talked about trying to revitalise parish councils. They are not all as tiny as the one in our Bedfordshire village. The most local tier of government includes many settlements with substantial populations, where the councils are often termed town councils: for example Weston-super-Mare, Shrewsbury and Aylesbury.* Right across the spectrum, however, there is a desire to connect local people closer to decision-makers. The bottom-up phenomenon that is common in social media may well not always translate into active parish councils. However, it certainly

---

* Populations according to the 2011 census: Weston-super-Mare 76,000, Shrewsbury 72,000, Aylesbury 59,000.

stimulates local dialogue rather more effectively than anything done by governments top-down.

A good example to look at is the role of petitions. Ever since people could write their names on paper or parchment, the idea of collective demands has been an ingredient in politics. Think right back to the thirteenth century and Magna Carta; what we have there is a reluctant king responding to the demands of the nobles. The concept of petitioning is entrenched in the American constitution and has a most distinguished history in the UK, particularly in the role it played in the abolition of the slave trade and in the Chartist movement.* As a mechanism for indicating the strength of feeling on an issue and placing subjects on a legislative or governmental agenda, it has been remarkably successful. Looking back, we remember how campaigners struggled to obtain signatures, standing in the rain on market-day, clipboard in hand, with a polythene sheet to protect the hard-won names and addresses that would eventually be gathered together and ceremonially carried maybe to the doorway of 10 Downing Street for the obligatory photograph. It did not matter whether the petition was for abolishing or preserving hunting, for or against nuclear weapons or for or against grammar schools, this type of process was a regular feature of post-war politics.

Opinions vary about the effectiveness of petitions. In 2003, the Stop the War Coalition† chose to place its emphasis on public demonstrations. But it held local petitions all over the country. Our view is that on the biggest questions of all, petitions play a

---

* Chartism was a working-class movement for political reform in Britain that existed from 1838 to 1857.

† The Stop the War Coalition was established on 21 September 2001, shortly after the September 11 attacks, to campaign against what it believes are unjust wars. *Per* Wikipedia.

relatively small role in the overall landscape of engagement. But as a tool for bringing narrower or unpopular issues to the attention of a wider public and a means of building coalitions of interest around specific ideas or proposals, they are extremely effective. They can be viewed as the mirror image of a public consultation. Instead of a public body challenging its population with difficult questions, here is the community challenging those in authority to respond to its view. Hence the relationship between top-down consultation and bottom-up petitions is now an established feature of public engagement.

The principle and purpose of petitions may not have changed but technology certainly has. Today the ease with which tens of thousands of signatures can be gathered over social media has transformed the situation; more might mean less, and there may be a danger of their currency being devalued. At local level, they perform a useful function because in many places they have been integrated into the local government culture. Where this happens, a council passes a resolution enabling petitions to be submitted as a routine agenda item for council meetings. Some have rules whereby petitions reaching a particular level, such as a thousand signatures, will be debated in council. It was, and is, a somewhat hit-or-miss tradition, taken seriously by local authorities where councillors have used petitions to secure discussion of particular issues. The theory is that if citizens know that their signatures lead to a consideration process, they are more likely to take an interest and participate.

In 2007, the then Secretary of State for Communities and Local Government, Ruth Kelly, proposed a statutory *duty to respond to petitions*. Every council was to be obliged to publish and consult local residents about a consultation scheme, effectively putting into statutory effect the kind of rules already adopted by the best councils. Echoing existing practice, if a defined percentage of the local population put their names to a petition, then not only would the subject be debated, but councils would need to report on the actions they had taken.

The Conservative opposition argued against this innovation, as it believed that any half-decent authority would see the self-evident benefits of handling petitions responsively. The government of the day, however, forced it through and the Local Democracy and Public Involvement in Health Act brought the relevant provisions into effect in April 2010. A month later, Labour lost the general election, and the subsequent Localism Act repealed the *duty to respond to petitions*, and also the *duty to consult*. No one, except public engagement officials, noticed.

But strangely, whilst this had been going on, there had been some interesting changes of mind at Conservative Central Office. A policy paper published in 2009 (parts of which were said to have been written by a certain Douglas Carswell MP), advocated a strong element of direct democracy for local councils. If five per cent of the residents demanded a particular proposition, there would have to be a referendum. This would have led to hundreds of plebiscites and the idea was soon dropped when Eric Pickles drafted his Localism Bill. Of course, what actually happened was that when the policy paper was written, it was still difficult manual labour to gather signatures. In two short years, it had become ten times easier, thanks to the advent of online petition platforms. Right now the best known are 38 Degrees, Change.org, SumOfUs and, internationally, Avaaz. No doubt, more will come.

38 Degrees really intrigued us. To begin with, the name is tremendous. To those who do not participate in winter sports it may be new information to learn that 38 degrees is the angle of a

slope at which a human can set off an avalanche. We have not tried to put it to the test, but we love the concept. It lies at the heart of the petitions phenomenon — trying to gather enough support for a proposition so that it builds upon its momentum and becomes an unstoppable force. Fundamentally, this is a campaigning organisation and asks its 'members' to propose subjects or causes they wish it to advance. Many people have questioned the basis upon which 38 Degrees decides which issues to pursue and it is not always clear for this, or other petition sites, whether they are paid to secure support for a particular campaign. Its email marketing is sophisticated and those who have ever signed a petition are regularly bombarded with requests to append their signature to others.

These sites claim credit for significant political achievements. They have succeeded in gathering large quantities of signatures on the eve of important parliamentary debates and one of their earliest 'wins' was at Caroline Spelman's expense over the future of Britain's forest estates.* Ministers claim that petitions have negligible influence over anything that matters and officials take an even dimmer view of them. But the fact remains that one of the most useful tools for a campaigner to use is a petition, maybe not as an end in itself but as a mechanism to gain media exposure and to gather more public support.

Governments realised some time ago that petitions do have a role in diffusing political energy and allowing people to express opinions in a public place. The parliamentary equivalent for decades has been the early day motion — a device to register a petition or maybe to draw attention to a particular issue or grievance. It is never intended for debate, just to make an

---

* See Chapter 4.

appearance on the order paper – a short and unsung procedural life. Except that once in a while, a minority interest gathers unexpected traction and instead of being signed by its originators and a few friends, hundreds of MPs (or peers) sign up. Occasionally we get rival motions, just as we get rival petitions – the converse of a consultation offering the public a choice. Here the public offers itself a choice, 'Sign this petition… or the other one'.

When the government set up its own petitions database, it was astonished by the extent to which it was used. Over a thousand petitions were registered in the first year, with environmental issues by far the favourite topic. It became the natural home for campaigners unable to make headway in Parliament, with calls, for example, to reintroduce capital punishment and, prophetically, for a referendum on the European Union. The coalition in 2010 moved the database from the government website to the Parliament one,* and agreed that any petitions achieving 100,000 signatures would be debated in Parliament.

Nowadays, no controversial consultation is free of petitions in favour of one argument or another. For consultation organisers, they muddy the waters. If, after painstaking pre-consultation and delicate negotiations with the prospective decision-makers, the questions are agreed, then your prime task is to gather answers to those questions. How, therefore, to handle the petition that does not directly address any of the questions specifically? Officials and politicians wrestled with this one for years. There are two schools of thought. On the one hand, petitions are welcome indications of interest by citizens, even if one cannot always assume that they are *bona fide* citizens. Little or no information may be available

---

* https://petition.parliament.uk

about who precisely has signed. Despite this, every signatory has a right to be heard. Surely, their opinion matters every bit as much as the professor who submits a fifty-page thesis? On the other hand, it can be argued that signatories to a petition cannot compare with formal respondents to a consultation. The latter can be presumed to have read, or at least looked at, the consultation paper. True, there may be summary publications as well as the full-text version, but again the likelihood is that respondents will have participated in the dialogue in some way. After all, with petitions online, there is no guarantee that the signatories have even bothered to read the text of the petition. Maybe it is a case of 'We must support Amnesty International. If they want our signature, let's give it.'

The established practice is to report as consultation output only the data that arises from an analysis of those who respond to the consultation. This will normally exclude petitions. Ignoring them completely, however, is a mistake. In 2017 the Mayor of London, alongside the Metropolitan Police, launched a consultation into the potential closure of public counters at more than thirty police stations in the capital. It excited much controversy, not least because the Consultation Institute branded it as possibly the worst consultation of 2017. To its credit, the London Mayoral Office sought advice on how to improve its process, but unfortunately not before further antagonising many campaigners by publishing its consultation findings without taking account of the petitions. It emerged that 14,500 people had signed eight different petitions – some in respect of general principle but others to try to retain specific facilities at local police stations. No mention was made in the findings of any of these details and whilst the consultors were perfectly correct in interpreting their analysis brief tightly, it was politically inept.

Wiser consultors will acknowledge any sufficiently relevant petitions. We advise meeting the organisers on the grounds that their prime objective is to be heard. Picture a meeting at which the petition organisers are congratulated for having achieved so much interest in the issue. Then, maybe at that point, it can be explained that, valuable as their contribution may be, the signatories cannot be classified with those who had responded to the full consultation.

On Christmas morning in 2013, Archbishop Vincent Nichols, then head of the Roman Catholic Church in England and Wales, took to the radio to criticise the government for announcing it was proceeding with plans to legalise marriage for same sex couples. Nichols was in rare form, railing against the iniquity of these proposals. What made it worse, he added, was that twice as many people 'voted against it' in the recent consultation as voted in favour. Leaving aside the *faux pas* about consultation ever being a 'vote', some of us knew that the number of respondents announced by the government as being in favour was actually much higher than those against. We could not both be right. The explanation, of course, was that the archbishop included in his figures the number of signatures found on the extensive petitions organised against the proposals by the Catholic Church. It is not the only time that campaigners have sought to influence the public's perception of consultation output by conveniently adding petitions to the equation.

The voluntary and community sector often under-estimates the influence it has had on public discourse, both nationally and through its thousands of local pressure groups. The landmark moment was probably the signing of the Compact for it enshrined in administrative practice, if not specifically in law, the principle of consulting its members on matters affecting the sector. Their

218

interests do not always coincide. With the NHS, for example, condition-specific groups and charities vie with each other for limited funding. But there are also times when they can effectively make common cause. On one thing they have been united and that is to obtain the 'even playing field' that public consultations, in theory, provide.

They have also discovered how important it is to influence the design of the consultation. Only in respect of the NHS is there a specific statutory requirement. In the relevant section of the 2012 Act, as in its predecessors, the NHS is obliged to consult relevant patients/parties and the public in the development and consideration of proposals for service changes. For many years a degree of lip service was paid to this provision, but in terms of local politics, the implications are immense. It means that those individuals or groups who become involved at the early stages of options development get an inside seat on matters which were previously closed to consultees.

Some areas remain out of bounds to them. Early in 2018 the Independent Reconfiguration Panel (IRP)* published its report on proposals for changing NHS services in Stoke-on-Trent. The council's overview and scrutiny committee had complained about the lack of consultation. It had originally been impressed with a programme of change, which NHS managers had called 'My Care My Way: Home First', but clearly local people had not been convinced about proposals to close a number of community beds. No one had involved them in planning these changes. The IRP did not mince its words. In its opinion, three years after initially outlining its new model of care, 'the NHS has not established a

---

* See Chapter 6.

robust programme for change'.* Apparently the programme had experienced a number of false starts. The bed modelling presented to councillors had proved 'entirely incorrect and misleading'. The IRP accused the relevant clinical commissioning group of failing to keep its promises, suggesting that it had been 'overtaken by events and demonstrated a lack of both capacity and capability to implement major change with [its] partners'. Such an indictment would have clearly galvanised the NHS into action and no doubt kick-started a fresh and hopefully more constructive dialogue with local people. However, it should not be left to a convoluted appeal mechanism for local communities to force public servants into constructive engagement. These processes bear the hallmarks of *ex post facto* correction rather than the preferred culture of getting it right first time.

Too many public services rely upon the apathy of local residents. We began the chapter with the sorry tale of the unresponsive parish council that overlooked local affection for its willow tree. Sadly, there are pockets of deprivation and disappointment where few voices are raised when services are withdrawn or curtailed. Carers are a case in point. There are more than 1,500 local organisations supporting over one million carers and seeking to promote or defend services, many of which have been painstakingly developed on a discretionary basis. Many provide respite care which parents of sick children or those looking after the vulnerable elderly find invaluable. Such services are often under the radar. They are provided to small numbers of individuals and are rarely uppermost in people's minds.

In contrast, the provision of essential tasks like refuse collection has always been prominent in residents' perceptions. Changes to

---

* IRP, letter to Rt. Hon Jeremy Hunt MP, 18 October 2017, available at 'IRP: Stoke-on-Trent Initial Assessment', gov.uk, 19 December 2017

these services always attract interest. When government ministers recommended moving from weekly to fortnightly collections in 2010, local angst was universal. There was no need for voluntary and community bodies to sharpen their pencils and start campaigning; the local newspapers, aided by social media, were enough.

Away from the glare of publicity volunteers have needed to become advocates. Charities, churches and community bodies have changed. They can no longer rely much on municipal funding. They have almost all had to fight rearguard actions to defend existing programmes. It has made them alive to dangers lurking in the next public consultation. Many have gone to court and argued that withdrawing support can hurt those least able to defend themselves, and sometimes they have won.* Councils have argued that such changes are essentially contractual matters. The toughening stance of judges and clarification of equality law have worked to make public bodies observe consultation principles when expenditure cuts like these are contemplated.

Whilst all this has taken its toll on Britain's impressive voluntary and community sector, it has made them far more dependent upon the politics of consultation. Wise campaigners now know to look for any suggestion of forthcoming changes of policy. Time is of the essence, early warning critical. Local authorities, being democratic, offer a relatively transparent window into their future plans. Other public service providers are much more opaque. Local campaigners, therefore, need to recruit and mobilise those with skills and aptitude. Fortunately for them, the early retirement of educated, articulate professionals, comfortable with traditional and social media, makes this relatively easy. There

---

* R (*ex parte* Capenhurst) *v* Leicester CC [2004] 7 CCLR 557.

221

are snags. White, middle-class activism is only too visible but in many parts of the country including more multi-cultural cities, it is a struggle to secure the involvement of black and minority ethnic people. Responding to consultation is only one of the core skills they need, but it is becoming vital.

There is a positive angle. As local communities become more self-sufficient in fighting for and funding their projects, they have more opportunity to experience the emerging range of contemporary engagement *best practice*. *Co-production* is the most prominent methodology. Another popular variant is labelled 'asset-based community development'. This places the emphasis on using local resources and facilities. When these work well, they encourage *communities of interest* – a concept that is alive and well among business and commercial groups, which have historically enjoyed easier and swifter access to decision-makers.

Back once more to the willow tree. As events unfolded it became clear that among residents at large there was no apathy. The same probably applies across a broad range of issues and concerns. Our problem lies in the transmission of public will and its ability to be heard when decisions are taken. Our next chapter considers whether business and industry are more successful.

Chapter 11

The influence of business on consultation

Public affairs and lobbying | the water industry | privatised utilities | BBC Charter renewal | West Coast Mainline fiasco | management consultancies | single options | airspace consultations | fracking | Big Tobacco | fixed-odds betting | clientelism

Lobbying has been around for generations and is by no means confined to the business community. No exploration of the way in which power affects how we consult can exclude the dynamics of business and the influence it wields.

Most large companies have public affairs departments. Sometimes they host the media and communications functions; at other times public relations is a separate activity. An even more specialist model is to have a dedicated government affairs department. Whatever the organisation, a company's prime objective will rightly be to protect and advance its interests. In a world of intense regulation, there is no substitute but to develop the capability to engage with governments and their agencies as professionally as possible. For a major commercial business, anything less would be a dereliction of its duty to shareholders.

That said, the approach that companies can take varies enormously. Some prefer a largely covert presence, whispering in the ears of government at the right time rather than openly arguing their case in public. This rather secretive method is struggling to survive in the age of transparency and social media, but it still persists, as does a suspicion among opponents of lobbying that it is more prevalent than is, in fact, the case. Not for nothing is it said that the most successful lobbying operations are the ones you never knew took place.

The growth of public consultation has been a challenge to these traditional forms of wielding influence. There was a time when one hired a lobbying firm principally for its contact book, containing the names and positions of key civil servants, but in the last twenty years this information has become a matter of public record. It was a classic case of who you know rather than what you know. It still occurs, of course, but ministerial diaries have become public and the media is swift to write stories about cash for influence. Members of Parliament, ex-ministers and others have been caught out through various forms of entrapment. Two former Foreign Secretaries, Malcolm Rifkind and Jack Straw, were exonerated of any malpractice following an investigation in 2015, but dozens of ex-ministers and parliamentarians remain vulnerable to allegations as the old methods of seeking influence now increasingly sound like bribery and corruption. That is why they are slowly dying out.

Instead, we greet the arrival of a new generation of public affairs where the emphasis is on policy research and managing the transmission of important messages to key stakeholders. This is on the assumption that there will be, or at the very least may be, a consultation. The same toolkit of *stakeholder identification* and *mapping* can be used, though overlaid with political insight and a lot more homework than public bodies are typically able to do. Excellent illustrations of the new ways of lobbying can be found in heavily regulated privatised utilities.

The water industry in England and Wales is mostly now formed of major corporations, some of them foreign owned. They operate in an environment of strong public interest protection through Ofwat, the industry's economic regulator, which is in turn closely engaged with the sector's monitor, the Water Consumer Council. Together they have made increasing demands upon the water companies not just in commercial and operational terms, but also in the ways in which they engage with the public. Indeed, their relationship with consumers has become a priority issue.

Years ago, the water companies' response to this kind of pressure would have been to campaign against anything they felt might threaten their position. Interestingly, there is today an acceptance that societal changes and the expectations of the informed public leave them with no alternative to the direction of travel signalled by the regulator. For the 2014 price review,* each company was told to establish customer challenge groups (CCGs, not to be confused with the NHS's clinical commissioning groups!). The role of these groups was to check that each company was engaging with its customers, and to verify to Ofwat that they were happy with what took place.

In a sense, this is similar to the mechanisms imposed on the NHS by Parliament, except that in the case of Healthwatch and its predecessors, the quality assurance function is accompanied by an advocacy role. In the water industry, and in other regulatory environments like transport, these panels – for technically that is

---

* Price reviews are carried out every five years.

what they are – are more straightforward. They are there simply to verify that the water companies are genuinely conducting themselves as the regulator requires, thereby saving the regulator from having to undertake the task for itself.

The glaring weakness in the water industry approach is that it is the companies themselves that select the chair and the members of the CCGs. Whilst no one suggests they are packed with yes-men and yes-women, a sceptical observer might be forgiven for wondering how independent they might be, or how robust a critique they might give a company that nominated them in the first place. The CCGs have the power, and in cases were originally encouraged, to commission research into the effectiveness of engagement processes that might have been beyond their immediate visibility. In one case we know the views of a hired consultant were swiftly dismissed as being biased against the company, but we have no evidence that this was widespread. On the contrary, water companies professed themselves satisfied that having an external panel to scrutinise their engagement and consultation was rather helpful.

This particular industry shared with others a difficulty acknowledging the difference between market research and consultation. A good illustration was the decision to build a major part of its 2014 price review around a technique called 'willingness to pay'. It is a complex process, developed in the research industry and designed to measure the value that customers place on different services, and their propensity to pay for them. Its processes rely on focus groups and quantitative techniques for prioritisation, but it had a chequered history when used elsewhere. Back in the 1980s, we remembered, it was briefly popular in the IT industry. At the time one of us worked in that sector and found it critical to discover the answers to two questions: would people pay to telephone a help desk hotline, and might they be prepared to pay a software licence fee year after year? The data suggested 'Yes' in both cases, but experience showed far more market resistance than had been forecast. In short, people had lied.

Market researchers are well aware of this; opinion pollsters even more so. But the use of these methodologies in public engagement is questionable and we are not sure that Ofwat learnt much about those miscellaneous services – over and above supplying clean water and disposing of the dirty water. At best they may have learnt that under *some* circumstances, *some* people might pay *some*thing or more for *some* services. Was it worth millions of pounds to find this out? We doubt it.

For the 2019 price review, the regulator requires even more emphasis on consulting consumers. It has retained the CCGs but is expecting 'a step change in customer engagement'. With operational goals of more affordable bills and much improved customer service, Ofwat says that the quality of customer engagement 'will be central to our assessment of Companies' business plans'.* If marks were awarded for enthusiastic use of participatory language, the water industry would score highly.

For industries with a weaker tradition of customer consultation, to focus their attention on better engagement cannot be bad. Other utilities face some real challenges. They mostly came from the public sector and were privatised at the end of the twentieth century. Despite being 'owned' by the public, their customer service track records had been universally disgraceful and one of the rationales heard to justify their absorption into the

---

* Ofwat, *Delivering Water 2020: Our Final Methodology for the 2019 Price Review*, December 2017, available at https://www.ofwat.gov.uk/wp-content/uploads/2017/12/Final-methodology-1.pdf (accessed 26 March 2018).

commercial sector was that they would treat customers better. Market disciplines were expected to induce them to improve their customer-facing skills; a renewed commitment to customer dialogues could encourage innovation. It has not quite worked out this way, as evidenced by a succession of regulatory fines and reprimands. Far from being high-profile consultors, our largest energy companies have allowed their own regulator to lead on customer consultation. In a random week selected in 2016, Ofgem had fifteen open public consultations, ranging from deeply technical (operating incentives) to public interest issues (the Code of Confidence regarding domestic price comparison services). All regulators have extensive programmes of this kind, and because their businesses are directly affected, firms in the regulated environments have to be involved in the process.

They have to tread carefully. Like banks, energy companies have long-standing reputational problems. It does them no benefit to be seen to be in open disagreement with their own regulators, especially if the people discern that the public interest is given rather less priority than the distribution of dividends. For affected companies, it is far better to hold quiet discussions with the regulator and influence the shape of the consultation than to be seen to challenge or dispute regulatory ideas or proposals once they are published. It is, therefore, rare indeed to see a company, in this or any other sector, openly campaigning for its own interests when the matter is subject to public consultation.

The 2015 consultation on the future of the BBC was something of an exception. Without openly saying so, the Corporation aggressively responded to what it perceived to be a hostile consultation by immediately announcing its own parallel exercise. * It scarcely merited the term, but its initiatives encouraged BBC enthusiasts to respond to an online questionnaire that gave them the opportunity to extol the broadcaster's well-known virtues. It made public a dispute of some substance – but we wonder if it would have been so obvious had this been just another regulated company; after all, the BBC is in a unique position in terms of both its public reputation and its ability to influence the policy agenda.

Maybe a better example is the fiasco that took place in 2012 when the Department of Transport sought to refranchise the West-Coast Main Line service. In a story that would probably be deemed too far-fetched for an episode of *Yes Minister*, civil servants ran a complex process leading to the award of a fifteen-year franchise to the FirstGroup, thereby displacing Richard Branson's Virgin Trains group. Branson immediately sought a judicial review, claiming civil servants had 'got their maths wrong with FirstGroup'.† Meanwhile the department maintained a solid rebuttal stance to the many arguments made by politicians and others that the refranchising process was unfair and technically flawed. Just before the court case was scheduled, the department backed down and admitted that three of its officials had, after all, made mistakes in calculating the costs and the benefits of FirstGroup's bid. They were suspended and the department drafted in the boss of Centrica,‡ Sam Laidlaw, to hold an independent enquiry into what went wrong. He uncovered a litany of mistakes.

---

* 'Tomorrow's BBC', BBC Trust website, http://www.bbc.co.uk

† 'Virgin Trains takes West Coast Main Line court action', BBC News website, 28 August 2012

‡ Centrica is an energy and services company, parent company of British Gas, Direct Energy, Bord Gais, Centrica Energy and Centrica Storage.

But we think something else quite major went wrong. Where was the voice of the customer? Few doubt the need for such a retendering process to look at the financial and operational advantages of one operator over another. But tens of thousands of regular passengers on Virgin's trains had opinions and for many who had experience of both Virgin and the rival FirstGroup there was little doubt that it was the former that tried harder and succeeded mostly to satisfy its customers. The ultimate climb-down by the Department of Transport was as ignominious as it was comprehensive and, in this particular case, it was the commercial interest of Branson's rail company that appeared to be on the side of the public against a more financially driven government. If it had had a significantly worse reputation, however, would it have been so eager to champion the cause of the passenger? Maybe the lesson of the story is not that there is always a case for listening to customers, but that companies can be very skilful at exploiting the situation if their own interests and those of its customers coalesce.

We have identified several different ways in which commercial interests can influence a public consultation. The first, and possibly the most obvious, is in the decision whether or not to have a consultation at all. No one who has a clear pecuniary interest in maintaining the *status quo* will welcome a consultation that may herald significant change. In the same way as a forthcoming general election can create a climate of uncertainty, the realistic fear that there might be adverse impacts as a result of policy changes is a threat which some companies will feel requires intervention. If change is inevitable, they will feel the need to influence its scope and direction, and it is at this point possibly that the most targeted lobbying occurs. For some it is purely a damage limitation project, seeking to curb the more expansive ambitions for change. Some years ago, when successive Conservative administrations attempted to circumscribe the powers of trades unions, the labour movement generally and unions in particular fought well-directed campaigns to limit the scope of proposed changes. From the other end of the political spectrum, we recall the rearguard action fought by supporters of fox-hunting, seriously delaying and diverting the campaign for its abolition.

Whether there is in fact a formal consultation may not always matter. Some issues become the focus of debate with or without the framework of a consultative process. Experienced parliamentary affairs professionals, whether in Edinburgh, London or Brussels, know that for every issue that becomes a formal consultation, there is another of equal importance that is also an argument to be won, albeit on a less visible stage. The ban on smoking in public places, for example, was never consulted upon in England and Wales, though it was bitterly disputed for many months. In Scotland, there was a public consultation attracting 53,473 respondents at which the tobacco industry's interests were visibly represented.

One advantage of the formal process is that the options presented to the public effectively set the agenda. A policy option that fails to make it to the final consultation paper is, in most cases, off the agenda. So, for a commercial body that opposes something outright, the ability to remove certain options from consideration is a worthwhile prize. For years, confectionery manufacturers kept a sugar tax away from active consideration. The banks, similarly, avoided discussion of the consumer issues surrounding payment protection insurance (PPI).

A determined lobbyist can influence the choice of options, either overtly or more indirectly by influencing the methodology of options development. Many of the top management consultancies derive lucrative revenues from guiding clients through the intricacies of identifying, assessing and ultimately selecting which proposals will go to the public as a part of a consultation. In technical areas such as clinical procedures or civil engineering, there are tried and tested ways of evaluation and those are normally the province of specialist firms with advanced modelling capabilities and the experience to match. It was always a problem for the opponents of the HS2 railway that the public consultation proceeded on the basis of a route option that had been selected using such techniques and published in a hundred-page document incomprehensible to most people.

In practice, the choice of options is a hybrid mixture of the technical and the human. For this process a wide variety of methodologies have been developed, many based on one form or another of regression analysis. * Few of these can be used transparently, for the trend in recent years has been to open up the process to build confidence in the decision-making process. If the choice of options is hidden, the argument is that those consulted will feel they have not had a true opportunity to have their say.

In the NHS there is a widespread fear that the use of external management consultants will dilute the traditional ethos of the service. Those holding this view focus attention on the way that

---

* A set of statistical processes in statistical modelling for estimating the relationships among variables. *Per* Wikipedia.

the Top Five management consultant firms* conduct the option appraisal process. Essential to these is the choice of who gets to vote, often called the 'Who's in the room?' question. For the NHS in England, guidelines require the general public and patients to be involved at this stage, though there is less agreement on the form that this involvement should take. What laypeople fear is that a combination of all-knowing management consultants and expert technical specialists will so bias the selection of options that the public interest will be subsumed to commercial or professional self-interest.

It is easy to forget that the top consultancies are not just the agents of their clients; they are multi-billion-pound businesses in their own right. Their influence on public consultation is undeniable, but they come to it with a deep cultural disadvantage. It is what can be described as a predisposition to a single solution. These are the firms that hunt down the cleverest graduates, recruit them and train them in the best they can offer. They do so in the knowledge that clients come to them expecting the finest skills and the brightest people. High fees and high expectations come together to imply that there is no problem so difficult that they cannot point to the solution. For anxious politicians and civil servants run ragged with unattainable objectives, this is manna from managerial heaven. Unfortunately governments are reluctant to pay for these answers; indeed Francis Maude, when at the Cabinet Office in the early 2010s, is reputed to have demanded that initial problem-solving be done by these firms free of charge, surely in the expectation of substantial revenues later on...

---

* There are many different league tables, but the Top Five are generally recognised to be Deloittes, KPMG, McKinsey, PricewaterhouseCoopers & Accenture.

From a public consultation perspective, however, it is the bias towards a single solution that is troublesome. We have described earlier how legal and operational trends have made single-option consultations a high risk. Yet consultancies continue to urge public bodies just to consult on what they have persuaded themselves is the optimum solution. This solution is, of course, even more attractive to them if it proposes a course of action that assures them of continuing business or further client opportunities.

Maybe this is too broad a generalisation as, of course, it is wrong to characterise all assignments by all consultancies as self-serving in this way. Neither does the cloud of suspicion necessarily mean that the favoured options are any worse for having been suggested or supported by a commercial consultancy. A high-integrity consultation should offer stakeholders meaningful choice between viable solutions. A transparent system should make it visible if, under certain circumstances, groups or interests in the pre-consultation stage have wielded undue influence.

Another way of influencing a consultation is in the level of detail it chooses to address. Those who studied the Department of Culture, Media and Sport consultation on the BBC might have scratched their heads about some of the questions asked. They might equally have wondered whether the massive Murdoch business empire had made a contribution towards the scope of the consultation. In fairness to Sky Television and its executives over many years, they had regularly expressed their concerns over what they perceived to be the BBC's privileged market position in the public domain. Speeches at conferences, briefing papers, press releases and the full gamut of public relations techniques had been used to influence the next review of the BBC Charter, and to ensure the agenda switched to the department's preferred vision. Hence some of the questions asked in the consultation!

A trusted colleague, with years of public affairs experience, observed recently that whenever he saw an industry code of practice agreed in preference to legislation, he would expect the invisible hands of lobbyists to have been at work. Making a consultation overtly technical, so that it inhibits those without detailed knowledge from responding, is a recognised way to influence an exercise. In the *stakeholder mapping* methodology we discussed earlier, a normal matrix positions certain stakeholders as having a very high interest and considerable influence. We teach that these are the ones that lie at the heart of the dialogue, but are inevitably those with the greatest technical know-how. Consultor organisations, therefore, have to engage with them on those terms. They cannot send junior managers to talk about matters of such importance to a stakeholder that fields its top experts. The *asymmetry of expertise* noted in *The Blunders of Our Governments** can be a major issue where the technical specificity of consultation questions, as recommended by industry stakeholders, puts a consultor's dialogue team at a disadvantage.

There are dozens of examples where the specialised nature of an issue gives certain stakeholders a clear advantage. This may occur when proven expertise and a technical reputation enable them to hold sway. Alternatively, consultations occur where technology impacts the lives of local communities. A classic illustration is the explosive issue of noise and pollution around airports. For years, there has been a regime under which the Civil Aviation Authority polices a set of rules whereby airports consult near neighbours when controversial changes to flight paths are deemed necessary.

* Anthony King and Ivor Crewe, *The Blunders of Our Governments* (London: Oneworld, 2013).

In 2011 one of those disputes, involving London City Airport, went to the High Court,* but the airport was considered to have consulted satisfactorily. Airports in general face a real challenge in communicating the impact of technical constraints that may prevent them being better neighbours.

Noise-related consultations strike a very human chord and we can all sympathise with residents subject to regular take-offs and landings above their homes. Further away from the runway, opposition may be more muted and decision-makers find themselves mostly influenced by the technical assessment of the air traffic controllers. They, rightly, have the final say on issues of safety. However, they are seldom, if ever, the actual consultor. National Air Traffic Services (NATS) is at one stage removed, but to have technical expertise that can influence the content and conduct of a consultation is an important element in steering the dialogue one way or another.

In an ironic twist, a consultation on marine conservation was held where the weight of respondent opinion came down heavily in favour of strong measures to curb fishing and other commercial activities. When the government came to take a decision, however, it ruled that the science was not sufficiently proven and deferred any further action until the scientific case was stronger. We hear that conservation groups were outraged and detected the hands of the relevant industry bodies at work – this time not hiding behind science and technology but denying it gave a clear message.

A similar 'wait and see' approach has characterised the fracking debate, with governments keen to be seen as striking a balance

---

* R (*ex parte* Griffin) *v* Newham LB and London City Airport [2011] 1 EWHC 53 (Admin).

between the industry's technical arguments and the fears of communities. It may be worth quoting the response of a group called Residents Action on Fylde Fracking. These consultees expressed their reaction to the relevant consultation in the following words:

> A pile of documents, some with over one hundred and twenty pages, all full of jargon, technical drawings and acronyms (DCO, GDA, NPPF, NPS EN-6, NN NPS, LEP, TTWA, AOD, BLF, MOLF, and so many more – most without explanation!) does not, in our opinion, have any resemblance to a consultation. The whole edifice is based on the premise that the proposed construction will inevitably go ahead, and the text is designed to convey only that. Whether the documentation is in any way suitable for a sensible debate with people who are more at home dealing with more mundane things is doubtful.

In the eyes of the action group, the industry was seen to be running rings around a compliant government, which failed to provide the reassurance local people needed to convince them that all was above board.

The environmental lobby is very suspicious of industry tactics in several sectors, but aviation once again provides us with the best illustration of a further way in which big business can influence a consultation: by dominating the debate. At the time of writing there is not a consultation on a new airport runway in south-east England, though there have been several abortive take-offs and near misses. So convinced are the owners of Gatwick and Heathrow, however, that sooner or later there will be such a consultation that they have already spent millions of pounds promoting their causes. Maybe they are acting on the dictum of Carwyn James, a Welsh rugby coach for the British Lions in the 1970s who encouraged his forwards to 'get your retaliation in first', for, without doubt, the money spent has been serious. Their behaviour also acknowledges the importance of winning the battle for public opinion, validating the role of consultation in the system.

Many industries operate in the public space, but none has demonstrated the malign influence of commercial intimidation more than the tobacco industry. Its fall from favour has been well documented and it is now in a thirty-year rearguard action to protect its carcinogenic products from regulation and worse. Possibly the most significant moment was when the US courts found the industry had lied and deceived generations of smokers and politicians,* concealing vital evidence it held about the dangers of its tobacco products.

Undaunted, it continued to campaign against those who sought to control tobacco. Despite the Framework Convention on Tobacco Control with 180 subscribing countries, a full-blown EU directive and a reasonably strong commitment by the British and other national governments to introduce further curbs, the industry fought tooth and nail. The World Health Organization found it necessary to publish guidance to the effect that the tobacco industry should be treated as having adopted a deliberate strategy of subverting public health policy. Enough said.

One of its tactics was to oblige governments to pay a high price if they wanted to pass legislation. This usually meant bombarding civil servants and ministers with studies, research or arguments

* United States of America *v* Philip Morris USA Inc. et al., US District Court for the District Court of Columbia (Civil Action No. 99-2496 (GK)).

opposing whatever was proposed. If a minister went to public consultation, the tobacco firms would individually and collectively respond aggressively, opposing controls on their business. Their whole approach illustrates a feature of the impact of politics on consultation, in that there are some interest groups that are so powerful or so motivated that any government that challenges them has a battle on its hands. Knowing that every step along the policy-making process will be scrutinised has a debilitating effect on some reforms. Politicians willing to embark upon such adventures have to be prepared to spend long hours and much money seeing these groups off.

A favourite trick is to discredit supporters of change. It takes a rare form of arrogance to accuse your opponents of bias without acknowledging in the least that your own advocates are themselves far from independent. The tobacco firms called public health professionals the 'tobacco control lobby', and appeared to insinuate that any evidence adduced by such people was suspect to some degree or another. The object, of course, was to discourage ministers from taking any action inimical to their commercial interests.

There might have been a time when health campaigners were ahead of public opinion. Although the Scottish Government consulted the public on smoking in public places in 2004, the industry's campaign made Whitehall a little more cautious for fear of an English backlash. Remember FOREST? It stood for 'The Freedom Organisation for the Right to Enjoy Smoking Tobacco' and enjoyed close relations with the industry. However, in the last twenty years the public mood has changed. The prospect of widening the debate and involving a potentially limitless constituency of people is deeply threatening to 'Big Tobacco' and so it is the last thing it wants. Change tack, therefore, and do everything to persuade the authorities that a public consultation really is not a good idea.

All this, as it happened, was played out in the High Court over several days' argument in December 2015.* Mr Justice Green had to listen to fourteen barristers, including seven QCs, represent the might of British American Tobacco, Imperial Tobacco, Gallaher and Philip Morris – not forgetting the cigarette tip paper manufacturers – as they argued their case. They claimed that it was unlawful for the Secretary of State for Health, Jeremy Hunt, to introduce regulations they did not like. In dispute was a proposal to force tobacco firms to adopt plain packaging, part of a policy to reduce their appeal to cigarette-smokers, particularly young smokers. It had first been introduced in Australia in 2012 and the tobacco companies had already won a reprieve by aggressively objecting to contemporaneous moves to do something similar in the UK. The government hedged its bets and organised a consultation. So persuasively did the tobacco lobby argue that the results of the Australian experiment could not conceivably be analysed so soon that Hunt ordered a further review before another consultation in 2014.

Having failed to persuade the government to abandon its policy direction, then failed to forestall a public consultation and then been unable to influence the conduct of that consultation to any great degree, what was left? Only to discredit the consultation's findings. The industry's firepower became focused on proving one simple allegation – that those who interpreted the consultation responses had been unfair. In the tobacco firms' language, it was wrong of the government not to take their responses more seriously. Officials had admitted that they had

---

* R (*ex parte* British American Tobacco and other tobacco companies) *v* Secretary of State for Health [2016] EWHC 1169.

240

given only 'limited weight' to the 'expert' witnesses who had sought to prove that the government's proposed regulations were misconceived. This admission was seized upon by the army of tobacco companies' lawyers as proof that Hunt was acting unlawfully and the court action, therefore, became a dispute as to whether the government was right to take the quality of the responses into account.

In the event, the Department of Health had been smart, very smart. Probably anticipating the judicial review, it had prepared a ten-point set of guidance by which it had decided to assess consultation responses. Whoever produced the guidance deserves a medal; it was very good and effectively saw off the tobacco industry's challenge. And in doing so, it has pointed the way for the kind of standards-led future we see for public consultation and which we cover in the final part of the book. The guidance covered such important questions as the true independence of the responder, his or her research, the value of peer review, transparency and consistency with previous external or internal studies or statements. All these were relevant to the tobacco case and when the consultation submissions made by Big Tobacco's friends were ultimately put under the microscope of these tests, the judge ruled that the government was quite right to treat them with a degree of scepticism. Even the prestige of a Nobel Prize-winning scientist did not, of itself, make his evidence convincing.

But in the politics of this particular consultation, there was one overriding factor, on which the significance of this court case will finally rest. Here was a judge confirming that it was lawful for consultation organisers to take into account the *credibility* of those who responded. He recalled the industry's previous misdemeanours in the USA. He took account of the World Health Organization's damning conclusion and alongside the shortcomings of its evidence, when assessed against the published criteria, dismissed Big Tobacco's claims. Every one of them. The Court of Appeal agreed.

We should be cautious in seeing this belated victory for the righteous as the end of the story, for surely the biggest lesson here is the awesome power of determined commercial interests to deter and challenge elected governments and properly constituted public consultations. There may be no equal to the tobacco industry in general public opprobrium, but we know people who regard Big Oil or the motor industry as equally powerful lobbyists against green politics. Then there is the growing battle between multi-national or supra-national companies and host governments over the size and jurisdiction of tax demands. There is an almost endless list of high-profile industries whose interests may, from time to time, be threatened by the questions raised in a public consultation. As we mentioned earlier, at the time of the 2015 consultation about the BBC Charter, there were those who speculated that the Murdoch empire's tell-tale footprints were visible in some of the questions. Recent policy initiatives on obesity have similarly aroused suspicions that the drinks industry has sought to influence the design of consultations and steered successive administrations away from a sugar tax or its equivalents. With the introduction of the tax in 2018, the industry finally lost its battle, but will no doubt continue to lobby to limit the impact on its business.

Meanwhile, another industry has shown itself to be cautious. Furious lobbying by backbench MPs put tremendous pressure on the government to 'do something' about fixed-odds betting terminals. John Humphrys on the BBC Radio 4 *Today* programme called them 'the crack cocaine of gambling'. Punters could, in theory, lose a stake of £100 every few minutes. In autumn 2017 the government chose to consult and as it approached the closing date, leaked to a Sunday newspaper that it might well opt for a radical reduction in the maximum permitted stake, possibly to as little as £2. Howls of protest from bookmakers and racing enthusiasts predicted job losses and withdrawal of support for the sport of kings. Had the government already pre-determined the outcome? Was the consultation therefore lawful? The industry hedged its bets. It valued its access to ministers and stopped short of prematurely threatening a judicial challenge. But it made sure that the Department for Digital, Culture, Media and Sport knew it was there, anxiously watching what happened. In the event, the Government did indeed decide to go with the more radical £2 minimum stake option – a decision we believe made politically possible only by having held a public consultation and built an impressive amount of support for that policy response.

In all these cases and many more, there is ample evidence of the potential susceptibility of democratic governments to a degree of manipulation by big business. It may not be corruption in the traditional meaning of the word; 'clientelism' may be more accurate. It is a term used to describe a subtler idea, a *quid pro quo* whereby politicians trade favours in return for electoral support. Many of the commercial interests are campaigning for a cause which parts of the electorate arguably support. So tobacco companies argue their case in the name of smokers; drinks manufacturers are defending the rights of Coke and Pepsi drinkers, as well as those who prefer a beer or whisky; oil companies portray themselves as the friends of the motorist. Clientelism also extends beyond the business world: older people's charities no doubt see themselves as the champions of the elderly; Greenpeace fights on behalf of environmentally aware citizens; and so on. It works as political parties strive to offer these 'clients' policies which will secure their votes. They do this even when research shows that this group would have voted for them anyway...

Readers may be suppressing a hollow laugh at the thought of powerful interests having to camouflage their commercial self-interest by dressing in their clients' clothes. But as the charity examples show, the representation of voters' preferences is not entirely bogus. There *are* smokers who want their rights defended. Fizzy drink users may well wish to avoid a sugar tax. The motorist may equally wish to escape punitive fuel taxes. What a public consultation obliges Big Business and Big Campaigners to do is to present their arguments in terms of popular utility. They can no longer exert power and influence policy on a narrow platform of economic advantage. A more public, transparent debate obliges them to reach for a more acceptable rationale.

In spite of this, raw commercial pressure is still a factor in the UK and no doubt elsewhere, and it can affect the scope, the conduct and the effectiveness of public consultations.

Part Four

Where next? The Challenges Faced by Consultation

Chapter 12 – Introduction
Revisiting the rationale

Employee consultation | power imbalance | Sciencewise and
the culture of the expert | engaging on badger-culling |
unpopular politicians | challenging direct democracy |
dumbing down debates

Consultation is an imperfect process full of contradictions and
open to political interference, as the preceding chapters illustrate.
In the final part of this book, we consider whether there is
sufficient evidence of its potential value as will sustain it as a
mainstream method of public participation in the coming years.

We might start by asking whether consultation is a mechanism
robust enough to earn its keep, even if we disregard the
complexities of politics. Many people question whether there is
any real proof that decisions are better if more people have been
involved. There is so little academic research, and anecdotal
evidence tends to depend upon who is telling the anecdote! One
of the most pertinent insights, however, comes from the
ambivalence surrounding attempts to inject a more consultative
spirit into the world of employment.

In fact, management gurus in the twentieth century spent a lot of time agonising over whether the active involvement of employees was beneficial. All kinds of hypotheses were advanced to prove causation between a more participative style of decision-making and improved performance, but the results were usually inconclusive. In the UK, forms of industrial democracy were viewed with suspicion by trades unions and actively opposed by private employers. Consensual business practices, such as are found in France and Germany, were dismissed as unworkable in our more adversarial culture. Worker-directors, it was said, would rapidly lose the support of the shop-floor and, as if to prove a point, a 1977 committee of inquiry* under Professor Alan Bullock which proposed methods of worker participation received little support from any part of the political spectrum.

Yet the belief persisted that, all other things being equal, a culture that gave everyone in an enterprise a bigger role in fashioning its fortunes and its future must be positive. Instead of a state-sponsored top-down imposition of structures and rules, participative management has, in fact, evolved quite differently. It may now be over thirty years since Tom Peters popularised some of these themes with *In Search of Excellence*† and its sequels, but American companies towards the end of the twentieth century certainly started to think that their 'human capital' was capable of more than just doing as it was told. The argument was not *whether*, but *how* to do it.

Formal mechanisms such as consultative committees have been a feature of the corporate landscape for a long time. They suit

---

* *Report of the Committee of Inquiry on Industrial Democracy*, Cmnd 6706, January 1977.

† Thomas J. Peters and Robert H. Waterman, Jr, *In Search of Excellence: Lessons from America's Best-Run Companies* (New York: Harper & Row, 1982).

both sides. Managers have the benefit of discussing their ideas and their problems in a reasonably safe space and can indulge in a degree of kite-flying without being over-committed to a course of action. Employees can get a better understanding of the business environment and promote their ideas without having to be signatories to a formal agreement. As in all truly genuine processes for dialogue, there are huge advantages, not least of which are the creation and maintenance of long-term relationships. These can be helpful when times get tough. But there are also drawbacks, such as the image of ineffectual talking shops. Having unrepresentative staff in discussion with middle managers far removed from the true locus of power in a company looks good but achieves little.

More promising has been the growing popularity of *co-production*. We noted its use in the NHS,* but manufacturing industry had much earlier adopted forms of involvement such as 'quality circles' as a means to harness the ingenuity and know-how of factory workers in a shared endeavour. These are normally led by supervisory-level managers and are credited with motivating otherwise-sceptical and uninvolved workers with a desire to participate. Nowadays they are mostly found in the tiger economies of south-east Asia, but that is because our change-obsessive business communities can't wait to move on to the latest fad. In a sense, it does not matter what the most recent formulation may be. What so many of these techniques share is an attempt to hear from the front line and a recognition that bosses do not always know best.

That simple truth is what lies at the heart of a consultative culture. It avoids the hugely difficult task of finding legitimacy in any

---

* See Chapter 6.

alternative way of taking decisions. Power remains firmly in the hands of those who own the process. But it forces those in charge to listen to arguments and counter-arguments and creates a more competitive space for ideas. Free of political interference, a pure form of consultation gives a decision-maker a broader canvas upon which to draw by ensuring a degree of externalisation to what might otherwise be a rather narrow debate.

Employee consultation may be a fair illustration of relationships where political power in the sense of public policy is absent, but of course it is far from immune to the influence of 'politics with a small "p"'. The ability to hire and fire is about as potent a weapon as any party to a relationship may have and consultation can be conducted *under duress* in situations where a strong employer sees it as a convenient communications tool, rather than a genuine exchange of views. When one side of the dialogue has demonstrably far more clout than the other, this lopsidedness makes for a very unbalanced relationship. The best-known example would be the provisions inserted long ago in early employment legislation requiring an employer seeking to make someone redundant to consult the individual before proceeding. This was originally intended to force reluctant managers to explain their thinking to trades unions, who previously were powerless to challenge large-scale job losses. The consultation was to be an opportunity for them to advance constructive proposals that might avoid or mitigate the bad news. It is still relevant. When TATA Steel closed plants and threatened to pull out of the UK altogether in 2016, the ensuing discussions were part of the consultative effort that the law requires. In that particular case, a worried government was lured into the discussion, with largely positive results.

Not all redundancies are in large multi-billion-pound corporates. Where a small business has to reduce its staff and remove a specific job, the individuals at threat have to be 'consulted' too, which in effect means given an opportunity to plead for their jobs. Generations of people who have lost jobs in this way have found the experience demeaning and divisive. They see it as forcing them to argue that one of their colleagues should be made redundant instead. The manager that says 'Have you got any counter-proposals?' is almost always merely going through the motions recommended by the HR department. Although we are told examples exist of staff successfully identifying measures that had been overlooked and saving their jobs, the more common experience is that the whole process is a charade. Managers have almost always made up their minds and were the standards now expected of public policy consultations applied to cases of redundancy, seldom would they comply. Few applications of the term 'consultation' have caused more damage to its reputation.

The reason is not hard to find. As mentioned above, where there is a massive imbalance in the relationship between consultor and consultee, consultation is very difficult. But it is not necessarily a question of conventional power. When a government seeks our views on a matter of public policy, the legal authority rests in its hands. Therein, theoretically, lies the power. But key stakeholders also have influence. In education, for example, the Secretary of State may hold the reins of power. But teachers, individually and collectively, are absolutely vital and wise politicians know that changes in policy pushed through in the teeth of their opposition stand a lesser chance of successful implementation.

Not all stakeholders have that pivotal role. They may have nothing more than a passing interest in the subject. Collectively, however, the general public have a bigger source of power – that indefinable, almost mystical authority we can call 'legitimacy'. It is what makes it so difficult for politicians to proceed with unpopular policies where the weight of public opinion opposes them. If, maybe, knowledge is power, we have to accept that there are competing sources of power and that modern democracy is increasingly acknowledging the weight of (arguably less knowledgeable) numbers. A widespread consensus now sees the Brexit vote in 2016 as the moment when a majority of the British electorate turned against the culture of the expert. Institutions that would previously have been revered as wholly trustworthy and truth-telling were viewed as partial and self-serving. What would have been a lopsided dialogue twenty years ago, with power on one side and critics on the other, became a much more even contest as a scepticism of those in authority became itself a source of political muscle.

Changes in the balance of power can be traced back some years. Earlier we referred to the debate surrounding genetically modified foods and we believe it was this, in part, that inspired a government initiative called Sciencewise.* Its stated purpose is 'to improve government policy-making involving science and technology by increasing the effectiveness with which public dialogue is used, and encouraging its wider use'. Although now reduced in scope, and with reduced financing, it has notable achievements. In more than a decade of excellent work it has explored public attitudes, and has developed and experimented with a wide range of techniques for talking to people about the kind of issues most of us struggle to understand. Back in 2005 it had organised a dialogue about nanotechnology. In 2008 it explored in detail the public's views on stem cell research, the

---

* 'Sciencewise: Public Dialogue on Science and Technology', gov.uk, 4 April 2016, http://www.sciencewise-erc.org.uk (accessed 27 March 2018).

possibilities that were emerging and those issues about which people are anxious. In 2011 it offered us workshops to explore attitudes to major geo-engineering options; giving politicians a public steer as to whether to invest in carbon dioxide reduction techniques, which aim to reduce greenhouse gases in the atmosphere directly by removing carbon dioxide from the air, and solar radiation management techniques, which seek to limit the amount of sunlight reaching the planet by reflecting more of the sun's energy back into space.

On this particular issue, we have no view. Neither of us is an engineer, though we have an active citizen's healthy interest in the world around us. Like many others we are concerned about climate change, though it is not an area on which we have read widely or thought deeply. Had there been a more widely publicised public consultation on the subject, there is no reason whatever why we would have taken the slightest interest and we certainly would not have participated. Any consultation on such a technical subject would probably have secured the involvement of experienced scientists and academics. Had it offered a choice of policy positions or directions on future research investment, for example, this should have stimulated a meaningful and balanced debate. There would have been a reasonable equivalence of power, status and legitimacy between consultor and consultee. The debate remains one held largely in an informed bubble. There are no visible public campaigns and no apparent strong feelings in the wider society. That is why Sciencewise rightly sought to construct a mechanism to tease out the public's attitudes.

But let us take another example. In 2013, the government started organising a programme of dialogue on a far higher-profile issue, bovine tuberculosis. This had been a growing problem for years and with 28,000 animals slaughtered in 2012, it was visible in the public eye. The government knew full well that its strategy aroused strong feelings among farmers, countryside residents and wildlife protection groups. It had drafted a strategy and held a consultation in 2013 to seek public views on that strategy. What the Department of the Environment and Rural Affairs (DEFRA) now wanted was a better understanding of what shaped those views. So it organised a series of six public dialogue workshops, carefully selecting participants so that they reflected key demographic and diversity characteristics. They also held ten stakeholder workshops; these included local farmers, vets, conservation and wildlife groups, county councils and supply chain representatives, and were held in both high and low-risk areas to seek to understand how opinions were affected by locality and closeness to the problem.

All this was to recognise the limitations of the consultation. We can ask as many questions as we like but very seldom is it possible for surveys to tell us what has led people to certain views and how they will react when presented with inconvenient facts or counter-arguments. This is particularly important when there are matters of genuine controversy around, and in this case it was the policy of selective badger-culling that aroused strong feelings. Predictably, the stakeholder groups divided according to their established positions: farmers approved the culling, environmental and wildlife groups disagreed. But the organisers felt they learnt more from seeing areas of consensus emerge. People wanted better explanation of scientific evidence; they wanted different groups to work together. And, tellingly, they wanted to keep politicians and 'political interests' well out of the picture.

So much depends upon the information provided. In these workshops, participants were given authoritative presentations

254

and provided with far more data than is usually available. It clearly shaped their conclusions, though the organisers admitted to having real difficulty setting out a wholly neutral, unbiased picture. They sought academics or scientists who could contribute objectively, but found that every external stakeholder with the right amount of specialist knowledge about the subject already had a view and could therefore no longer be considered truly independent. Attempts to create an even playing field and to equalise the power of information between opposing sides in a controversy is genuinely difficult, as is the objective of influencing the key decisions.

This public dialogue cost almost £400,000, found useful common ground on some aspects but totally failed to resolve the dispute about badger-culling. Disappointingly, DEFRA, though commendably supportive of the exercise, found little in it to affect their strategy or its implementation. At least they obtained a better understanding of people's attitudes. To no one's surprise, they discovered that participants demanded that policy should reflect evidence. They just could not be sure who was right. It is precisely this problem that affects most issues of a technical nature and makes it difficult for ordinary citizens to participate. *Which scientist to believe? Which clinician is being realistic? Which engineer is right?* And, famously perhaps for the 2016 EU referendum, *Which economist do we trust?* This was hard enough in an age of deference when the advocates on either side of an argument were respected. What happens if the social mores have tilted against experience and expertise and if sheer weight of numbers is suddenly to be the prime determinant of policy?

Supporters of direct democracy have always believed in the numbers game. Referendums are to them the obvious way to take decisions that matter, with one-person, one-vote a clearly more egalitarian principle than letting educated elites take decisions. Critics of this approach prefer our representative democracy because it encourages the pursuit of principled, consistent policy-making whereas the general public is perfectly capable of taking wholly contradictory decisions. What direct democracy advocates share is a palpable and consistent dislike of politicians. The general public may be unsure which scientist to believe, but it is sure about one thing and that is that it does not trust politicians.

Pollsters have been tracking public opinion about key professions for years, but few surveys have produced a more clear-cut trend than a poll question that was first asked by Gallup in July 1944: 'Do you think that British politicians are out merely for themselves, for their party, or to do their best for their country?' Ideally we would hope that the interests of the country were seen to come first, but sadly they never were. In 1944, 36 per cent of those asked felt that this was a politician's prime motivation. By 1972 the figure had dropped to 28 per cent; in 2015 it stood at 10 per cent. Academics refer to an 'anti-politics' culture, and research shows that it is particularly prevalent among the young. What this tells us is that public engagement is so much harder if politicians are seen to be anywhere near it. One of the conclusions of the bovine TB public dialogue was that information provided by the government should be balanced; evidence should not be interpreted or communicated through a political lens – a classic rebuke to the system where information and research seems contaminated in the eyes of those who see it.

There is, therefore, something of a crisis in public involvement. It faces pressure from the direct democracy lobby, which is so disenchanted with conventional, routine politics that it wants to bypass the whole parliamentary pantomime and let the public make its choices based upon radio, television and the media – old and new, of course. To make matters worse, decision-makers are confronted by ever-more difficult decisions and are desperate to involve the public, so as not to be seen to be imposing their views regardless. The harder the questions asked, the greater is the chance that the politicians who happen to be in charge will be blamed, no matter how approachable they are.

Their response to this is to rely increasingly on consultation as a way of saying, 'We would like to do this, but of course, we will consult first...' When delivered from a conference podium or announced on prime-time television, this can be a useful fudge. It provides a degree of flexibility and avoids having to answer for the difficult details of policy too early. It buys time for reflection and refinement and even signals to the direct democracy fan club that there will be a quantitative element by counting how many in the consultation agree and how many disagree. An example of this ploy was the unexpected move by the new Theresa May administration to abandon the ban on building new grammar schools. Immediately a Green Paper was published, though this was in fact a public consultation. One look at the questions would, however, have disabused the direct democrats of any idea that this was a simple yes/no argument. Rightly, officials had persuaded ministers that the aspects upon which a wider range of views were needed covered such matters as the proportion of pupils in new selective schools that ought to come from lower-income families – a level of detail considered too much for those who just want a vote on the general direction of policy.

What consultation does, therefore, is to introduce a level of complexity which our anti-politics culture prefers to ignore. In many ways it challenges the fashionable view that public policy debate is being dumbed down. This, after all, is largely based on the theory that most people have a short attention span for anything that sounds serious. The principle of consultation therefore stands firm against the dilution of public debate, and to assess its chances of continued success, it is necessary to look closely at the forces that bring us to this juncture.

Chapter 13

What consultation must combat

Three drivers of dumbing down debate | disappointment with democracy | failure of political careers | looser language and lies | social media | echo chambers | fake news | trust

There are many reasons for the dumbing down of debate and not all of them are pernicious. Any objective analysis of Western democracy's traditional style of political and social discourse would find it elitist and based upon comfortable assumptions of consensus that have long since ceased to be valid. We often see short clips of post-war television interviews in which a politician is asked a question along the lines of 'Have you anything to say to our viewers, Prime Minister?' and we smile at the obsequiousness and, on one occasion, Clem Attlee's wonderfully dismissive answer, 'No, nothing at all'. Of course, that has all changed; indeed the pendulum has swung completely in the other direction. As we noted earlier, people's opinions of politicians have declined in public esteem to an alarming degree.

This, however, may signal an even more serious malaise, the first discernible driver of dumbed-down debate: a disappointment with democracy. We sometimes forget that electorates vote not for processes, but for outcomes. Eighty years ago, in the early days of the motor car, you needed an oily-shirted mechanic to explain and express the difference between a Triumph and a Daimler. By the end of the century, relatively few drivers cared much about what was under the bonnet, as long its looks and status on the road accorded with their self-image. In short, we had moved away from decision-making based upon a technical understanding to an obsession with outcomes and performance. Today, with so much taken for granted, as one takes the internal combustion engine for granted, when they enter the voting booth, people rarely think about that engine; their minds are elsewhere. Some may think they are placing their cross for a member to represent them in Parliament, or indeed a political party that they want to support. But, in reality, the choice is about outcomes and it has become progressively more difficult to distinguish one set of promises from another.

Mario Cuomo's famous quote that politicians 'campaign in poetry' but have to 'govern in prose'* reflects the lurch to managerialism. It is easy to get wound up by uplifting rhetoric on the need to reduce child poverty, but hard to get excited about the details of universal tax credits when the route to policy delivery gets deep into the detail. The voting public can so easily will the ends without a care about the means, leaving the hapless politician to fine-tune the details. To continue the automotive analogy, there is a move away from any wish to understand what goes on under the political bonnet.

It helps us to understand the anxiety of the US political establishment at the advent of a Trump presidency. Here was the

* *New York Republic*, 4 April 1985. Mario Cuomo was governor of New York from 1983 to 1994.

one candidate who cared very little about what was under that bonnet. Those who hoped that Trump would follow Cuomo's advice only had to wait for his Inauguration speech. Instead of the traditional consensual mantras, out came the campaigning rhetoric of his Twitter-speak style that relied on short, pithy optimistic promises he knew his supporters wanted to hear. Those who wanted to hear him restate a commitment to 'build a wall' were perfectly happy. Only the technocrats inside the Washington bubble worried about how he would deliver.

Donald Trump epitomised a response to the public's comfortable indifference to the mechanics of policy-making. It is probably a characteristic only of mature democracies with a long history. When people fought for basic education and health services, or when fundamental human rights were still unheeded, it was relatively easy to garner mass support and to unite all shades of opinion behind worthy causes. Once achieved, they retreat into distant memory and social historians may be right to worry that we do not teach our children about the struggles that occupied previous generations. An affluent economy and a cradle-to-grave welfare system has given rise to a form of complacency that makes it genuinely difficult to excite any enthusiasm for what are, at best, incremental changes to a benign *status quo*.

What seems to work instead is to offer radical solutions around an *oppositionist* credo. This was undoubtedly Nigel Farage's success in the twenty years before achieving his goal of a British decision to leave the EU. Being against something big, especially if it is seen as an unsympathetic, unresponsive monolith, like the European Commission, resonates with those who have no wish to grasp the details of how it works. In France, Marine Le Pen offered a similar vision and in the Netherlands, Geert Wilders likewise stoked the fires of anti-immigrant sentiment. Ditto

Trump in respect of Mexicans, Muslims, climate-changers, the Washington establishment and much else.

If democracy is struggling to maintain people's interest in the incremental minutiae of positive changes, it certainly thrives on opposition. Organising a protest group against any large-scale project has never been easier, whether it is high-speed rail, new airport runways or major housing developments. The same zeal can be witnessed in those who want to preserve current patterns of public services. There is probably a campaigning template using the words 'Save our…' into which you can insert 'Hospital', 'Library', 'Day Centre', 'Fire Station' or even 'Countryside' as you like! Politicians looking for a round of applause find it easier to align themselves to such causes than to sweat over the risky business of painting a realistic vision of the future.

To their credit, many of them try. In the field of social policy the UK has seen some remarkable progress in some areas. The Conservative Party would claim that the Right to Buy gave council tenants an unprecedented route onto the property ladder; no doubt the Labour Party would make a strong claim that a minimum wage revolutionised employment practices. Gay rights may be the best example. Indeed, it must be difficult for some to acknowledge that despite the ignominious ending of his premiership, David Cameron may be most generously remembered for championing equal marriage and passing the necessary legislation. He did it in the face of considerable opposition, but it is a rare example in a world where it is easier to oppose than to propose.

Enoch Powell's quote that 'all political lives, unless they are cut off in midstream at a happy juncture, end in failure, because that is the nature of politics and of human affairs"* is a gross over-simplification. There are many examples of those with more limited ambitions, and a reading of political biographies finds many who are supremely satisfied with their achievements. There are also what some might see as high-profile successes too, like Martin McGuinness in Northern Ireland, Rhodri Morgan in Wales or most famously, Nelson Mandela. Yet the prevailing view is that politicians rarely achieve their goals and this has enabled the media to undermine the idea that democracy can be an effective tool for outcomes that people want.

A climate of pessimism has thus been produced in which there is felt to be little point in debate, as nothing will change. A consultation, like other tools of engagement, is the Establishment going through its own motions and has little to offer those who are outside. No wonder the anti-politics culture has flourished!

The second driver of change is language. Politicians and policy-makers appear to many to possess a vocabulary and style of speaking and writing that is now totally alien to the general public. Rehearsed sound bites probably make it worse. Despite trying to dispense with the technocratic lexicon with which they are familiar, they find themselves losing that all-important authenticity which has been the hallmark of the more successful populists such as Trump, Le Pen and Farage.

The most impressive review of this complex subject is Mark Thompson's 2016 book *Enough Said*, subtitled *What's Gone Wrong with the Language of Politics?*† As a previous director general of the BBC, he makes a strong case for recognising the pivotal role of

---

* Enoch Powell, *Joseph Chamberlain* (London: Thames & Hudson, 1977), p. 151.

† London: Bodley Head.

language in the changing landscape of public debate. As a broadcaster, he traces the key moments in the evolution of language and notes the influence of American-style political coverage and its adoption on this side of the Atlantic. For Radio 4-type listeners, the shorter, punchier style of the USA public service broadcasters has always sounded like a dumbing down of debate, but the depth and intensity of argument over there is not necessarily inferior. Thompson describes how time pressures caused the US networks to assume a rapid, urgent style with a strong emphasis on actuality, in many ways providing a greatly intensified experience for the listener or viewer. The price for this is that everything is condensed. Time slots are shorter, and if there is a debate, there is never space or time for more than two sides of an argument. There is no place for nuance. Shades of grey are seldom heard.

None of this would have shocked the spin-doctors of the 1990s. Alastair Campbell* was vilified for having sought discipline from Tony Blair's Parliamentary colleagues in the run-up to and after the 1997 Labour landslide, but he was not the first of his kind to appreciate the need for politicians to be on message. A generation earlier, Margaret Thatcher had hired a bluff, gruff Yorkshireman called Bernard Ingham† who on occasions acted as a lightning-conductor to soak up some of the odium otherwise directed at the PM. All this offers a reflection that politics has, over time, acquired a great many of the hallmarks of marketing, with political parties investing heavily in focus groups and deliberative polling

---

* Tony Blair's spokesman and campaign director, also Downing Street press secretary.

† Bernard Ingham, a journalist and civil servant, was Margaret Thatcher's chief press secretary from 1979 to 1990.

in order to find the best ways of communicating ideas and politics to the wider electorate.

The result is that there is now a disconnect between the language used to sell a policy and the stark reality of the subject itself. In the 2016 EU referendum, the sheer brilliance of the Leave campaign's battle bus and its much-criticised slogan, 'We send the EU £350m a week; let's fund our NHS instead', was that its disputed veracity guaranteed it infinitely greater coverage than it would have attracted had it been true. It may well have happened by accident, as rumour has it that those who originated the slogan knew little or nothing about the arithmetical arguments it unleashed. The point is that reducing complex issues to simple – if contested – statements becomes astonishingly important and is a major factor in the dumbing down of debate.

Midway through the EU referendum campaign, a lady from the audience of the BBC's *Question Time* uttered the words 'I want my country back' and sparked off a long debate among the commentariat. *What did she mean? Who had taken it away? Had she taken the tabloid press seriously? Or Boris Johnson?* What she had done, of course, was absorbed one of a number of formulations used by anti-EU campaigners, and almost certainly gave it a huge boost. For her fellow travellers, it instinctively encapsulated what the Leavers wanted and played to the claim that this was not really about who made laws or what we paid; it was about identity. For Remainers, it equally highlighted what they saw as nonsensical, irrational nostalgia that was unattainable and incoherent.

When a single pregnant phrase can, almost unintentionally, spark off the deepest of debates, who has need of a White Paper... or a consultation document? The shorthand seems to work. Can the same not also be said of Trump's formulation 'Make America great again'? What works is not just the skill of the slogan-writer, but also the ability of whoever uses the slogans to make them symbolise a whole range of policy positions that can be internalised by individuals according to their personal prejudices. We may well have arrived at the politician's dream destination where such phrases can mean all things to all people and there is little that anyone can disagree with.

This brings us to the third driver of dumbing down debate. If the actors in the democratic drama have disappointed us, and if language has substituted slogans for substance, there is also the challenge of the channels we use.

Social media brings us so many benefits. In theory, a better-informed citizenry should be good news for democratic discourse. The trouble is, as every user knows, the sheer volume of messages, even from those we regard as friends, exceeds our capacity to read and absorb. We all naturally search for ways to prioritise or filter what we see. The result is that we screen out those opinions we have no appetite to hear and ultimately only see views with which we broadly agree. At the same time the application provider, keen to sell us advertising, tries to find ways to show us only those offers that might interest us. As a result, the breadth of information we are shown online is being technologically narrowed, filtered by algorithms and tailored by our increasing power to shape the news we see.

The conclusion is that some people only hear the news that they want to hear. Their existing perceptions are reinforced. Their information base is less likely to be broadened by anything that challenges their assumptions. This is known as the echo chamber. Talk to your online community of friends or acquaintances and if they respond, you will hear much the same views as your own.

That is the echo. Experience shows that we are much more inclined to believe what our self-defined community tells us, *even if it might not be true.*

Very solid US research from the Pew Research Center in 2016 told us that a majority of the public found political content on Facebook or Twitter very stressful and disliked it.[*] Many people found the tone of the social media debate uniquely angry and disrespectful. At the time, Pew said that about one-third of its user sample had changed their Facebook settings in order to see fewer posts from someone in their feed because of something related to politics, and a quarter had blocked or 'unfriended' someone for that same reason. Around the same time, UK researchers from Demos discovered that people with more polarised political affiliations tended to be more inward-facing than those with more moderate political leanings and that therefore the further their group was from the centre, the more pronounced was the echo chamber effect.[†]

Despite this, for all the tensions and annoyances that accompany political debates via social media, other users see a good side to these interactions, particularly those who have a high level of interest and involvement in the political process as a whole. But how many such people are there? Research evidence is thin, but a fair estimate is that roughly 20 per cent of social media users would be classed as interested in current affairs and would be happy and willing to engage in the online debate. That is a huge number and far exceeds the three to five per cent traditionally thought of as active citizens. It also dwarfs the one per cent who

[*] Maeve Duggan and Aaron Smith, *The Political Environment on Social Media*, Pew Research Center, October 2016.

[†] Alex Krasodomski-Jones, *Talking to Ourselves? Political Debate Online and the Echo Chamber Effect*, Demos, September 2016.

might actually participate in public consultations. It is this group, maybe one-fifth of the population, who take part in debate. It is these people that are beginning to be deaf to the views of others.

All this has been confidently predicted and will come as no surprise. For years, the internet was compared to the Wild West, as being totally beyond regulation. In 2012, one of the biggest headaches for the Leveson inquiry* was how to justify even a modest degree of press regulation if online bloggers and publishers were not equally covered. More recently the outcry about 'fake news' and the unrestricted availability of anti-social, dangerous or pornographic material have changed the mood, and have made the major application platforms more willing to police their content. But this should fool no one. Social media allows all manner of misrepresentations, lies and half-truths to become viral within minutes and completely overwhelm attempts to correct or rebut.

If that is all a given, it is problematic, to say the least, that the government's clear policy for communicating with citizens is *digital by default*. Obviously there are cost advantages and the evident rise in the proportion of people who have access to mobile technologies helps make it a viable proposition. But there is a world of difference between using the internet for transactional purposes like, for example, the renewal of the vehicle excise duty, and doing so to offer your views to a public body on a controversial subject. If the percentage of people having access to online services hovers between 80 per cent and 90 per cent, it is unlikely that more than one in five has ever

---

* The Leveson inquiry was a judicial public inquiry, chaired by Brian Leveson, into the culture, practices and ethics of the British press following a phone-hacking scandal at News International, publisher of *The Times* and *The Sun*. The Leveson report was published in November 2012.

entered into an opinion-based dialogue with a local council or another governmental institution.

If we acknowledge that social media polarises debate and has difficulty distinguishing fact from fiction, over-reliance on this channel is likely to weaken the cause of evidence-based policy-making. Note the surge of sentiment on Twitter following a news story. Or even a fake news story. Social media can form a view on political developments remarkably quickly and tends to be mutually reinforcing. In other words, initial reactions can rapidly become fixed as orthodoxy, often before the facts have been established. It is particularly vulnerable to the impact of well-known personalities. Such is the culture of celebrity that politicians and campaigners are equally determined to secure the endorsement of anyone featured in the pages of *Hello!* or *OK!* magazines. The world of social media can disseminate news of their support with amazing speed and sycophancy. Seldom has this anything to do with rational debate or objective evaluation of evidence. It is the antithesis of the reasoned debate that the establishment elite has promoted in the last fifty years, and is a clear challenge to many mechanisms and structures built or adopted before the world changed.

Public engagement has already started to change in response to these powerful forces. To accommodate the declining reputation of politicians and the democratic process, complementary machinery has emerged that compensates for their failures. A range of participative tools offering variants of *co-production, co-decision-making* and *empowerment* have found favour, particularly with those who wish to dismantle current power structures and for whom consultation is too weak as it reinforces the *status quo*. To compensate for the problem of language, there has been a move away from the big-fat-document style of consultation and imaginative new tools are in use to present complex situations to a wider audience. Social media, however, changes everything and very few have yet come to terms with its full implications. For certain, those who genuinely wish to consult the public would be foolish to rely solely upon it.

At heart, the three destroyers of decent debate amount to an issue of trust. If our politicians are held to be liars and cheats, if their language misleads or deceives people and if social media dialogue becomes an unprincipled shouting match, what is at stake is nothing less than the integrity of the system. For those who believe that processes like consultation are beneficial, there is only one response. It is to avoid being contaminated by this virus and to establish and maintain standards that will counter these damaging trends.

As noted earlier, consultation is highly susceptible to manipulation by unscrupulous, or even just careless, politicians and officials. Only if steps can be taken to eliminate the more obvious abuses can the reputation of a consultation exercise be restored to the point where it will be taken seriously by the public at large.

So are there standards available and can they work?

Chapter 14

Improving consultations: three duties for consultors

Winners and losers | parliamentary posturing | too many standards? | duty to define | duty to explain | duty to engage

We once listened to a debate in the Scottish Parliament. Edinburgh airport was being castigated for having run what the carnaptious * Labour MSP Neil Findlay described as a 'fundamentally flawed' consultation. The proposal was to make changes to the use of airspace above Scotland's capital city, so it was properly and legitimately a matter of great concern to local residents. Findlay wanted the proposal scrapped because it 'set community against community', and we have little doubt that many people agreed with him. After all, in many difficult decisions, there are perceived winners and losers.

An open, transparent consultation is one way to make such judgements, but it is not the only way. A handful of civil servants could, for example, take a decision far more quickly, but we doubt whether Findlay would be any happier if they did. In the event,

---

* Scottish word for grumpy.

that particular consultation was not handled too badly, despite some mistakes and a few glitches on the way. But the vehemence of Findlay's attack, echoed by many colleagues, raises important questions about how to judge the quality of such exercises.

Less than a year earlier in the House of Commons, English Members of Parliament had queued up to complain about NHS England's controversial Sustainability and Transformation plans (STPs).* They were mostly concerned to ensure that there would be consultation. Here is a flavour of their arguments:

> 'People are so suspicious of consultation processes that they simply do not believe that they are being properly engaged in them.'
>
> Norman Lamb (Liberal Democrat), North Norfolk.

> 'Often the word "consultation" is used when what is meant is "information", and scenarios are not put forward. The public are not stupid. They need to know what happens here if they choose this option, and what happens there if they choose that option.'
>
> Simon Hoare (Conservative), North Dorset.

> 'Consultation with the public does not mean presenting them with a completed plan as a *fait accompli* and asking them whether they support it. It means involving them from day one.'
>
> Justin Madders (Labour), Ellesmere Port & Neston.

Over the years we have logged hundreds of similar comments expressing anxieties of this kind. Some politicians are undoubtedly mischief-making, and searching for any weakness, anything at all, upon which to criticise a policy they oppose. No

---

* See Chapter 6.

doubt they are expressing the views of most of their constituents. Their parliamentary firepower is, however, seldom well directed. Busy MPs either focus on whatever critique was brought to them by their campaigning electors, or they target what's most likely to be well covered by the local newspaper or television station.

Here is the sad truth. For many politicians an acceptable consultation is one that produces the right answer. Only those with a wider perspective or with a keen interest in the machinery of decision-making are willing to acknowledge that the process of listening to people's views is an essential tool of the process. They may be in a minority, but in their hands is the hope that the widespread scepticism expressed by so many politicians can be tackled. We need Findlay and his friends somehow to be reassured that, whatever they think of the *substance* of the issue, the *process* would itself be sound. Then there would be a chance of a more honest debate.

To do this, we need more consensus on what makes a satisfactory public consultation. Do we know what the standards of *best practice* ought to be?

In one sense, we have too many standards. We earlier chronicled the successive sets of guidance and principles published by Whitehall. In Scotland, there has been a widely acknowledged set of *community engagement* standards for years. They include a wonderfully optimistic requirement that 'communication between all participants [be] open, honest and clear'. Similarly, the administrations in Wales and Northern Ireland have also, from time to time, published guidance of one sort or another. In the case of the NHS in Wales, it adopted what we thought was by far the most ambitious process for consultation and engagement. Even this excellent set of standards became unpopular with ministers due to a succession of judicial reviews, and those were mostly unrelated to the guidance. Local authorities have also developed and published their own sets of standards, if only to ensure a degree of consistency between one department and another; other public bodies have done the same. And, thanks to the courts, we also have the Gunning Principles, and on equality three further sets of legal tests from the Brown, Branwood and Bracking cases.* But these, like all judicial pronouncements, are prone to idiosyncratic interpretation from case to case.

The trouble with having too many standards is that we might as well have none. This is why there is a reluctance to call them 'standards'. 'Guidance' is a bit softer. 'Principles' sounds even better. No wonder MPs are unsure how to challenge a consultation. Before they can identify any provision upon which to focus, there will be an argument as to whether or not it applies. There is also the reasonable objection that consultation occurs in such a range of situations and environments that it is difficult to devise a set of standards that might make sense across the board. That is also to ignore the inevitable issue of how to apply and, whisper it very softly, enforce them. If they were easy to articulate and if anyone could design a framework within which they applied, it would have been done before now.

On the other hand, we have argued that public engagement is at crisis point, and either we do it properly or maybe we should abandon the pretence. The previous chapter claims that the challenges facing rational, transparent debate are considerable, so our task is to propose precisely the kind of measures that might make a difference. We start with the idea that there should be three straightforward but demanding duties on all consultors.

---

* See Chapter 3.

There should then be three equally clear rights for consultees. They are symbiotic, reflecting the crucial inter-dependence one on the other. It is, after all, a unified concept. Looking at some public consultations, one might imagine that the two parties are poles apart. They never meet. They never have a proper dialogue. They just shout at each other from a safe distance. True consultation requires a recognition that upon those who have the responsibility for consulting, there is the burden of important duties. The whole point is that effective consultation confers concomitant rights for those whose views are sought. This is not to deny that consultors have some rights too, or that consultees also have some duties. In the main, however, the duties are on the one party, and the rights are with the other. Taken together, we think they might provide a clear and sufficiently simple framework.

In short, consultors have duties to define, to explain and to engage. Consultees have rights to know, to be heard and to influence.

The duty to define

The scope of a public consultation goes to the heart of its fundamental purpose. Over the years many tears have been shed over the ambiguities and evasions of managers and ministers as they have wrestled with this. When the Consultation Institute conducts its exhaustive Quality Assurance on a controversial consultation, its starting point is to discover precisely and then document what decisions have already been taken. What remains to be discovered is where the consulting organisation is willing and able to be influenced. Ironically, it is strange to find that public bodies are unsure how to define the exercise; surely that is obvious when one embarks upon the process? Trouble arises

275

when decisions taken higher up the policy chain create uncertainty. 'Are we allowed to consider such-and-such? Or will that be against our sponsoring department's policy? Or preference?'

In our experience, managers are genuinely unsure of the extent to which they can use their discretion. Fear of falling foul of powerful masters is a huge constraint for NHS managers, civil servants and anyone below director level in local authorities. A clear *duty to define* then obliges them to confront the powers-that-be, possibly an uncomfortable task given that managers often feel squeezed. They know that they dare not have made up their minds before launching a consultation. But their bosses may well have a perfectly formed view of the desired outcome and see the ability to deliver to this agenda as a key performance indicator.

Such have been the inconsistencies and ambivalence that surround too many public consultations. They have contaminated the process because consultees are aware of strings pulled by hidden hands. The consultees question the integrity of the exercise, suspicious that whatever they say, the consultor will be heavily leant on to reach a pre-ordained conclusion. They fear that everyone will be careful enough not to leave any tell-tale evidence such as would support a legal challenge based upon *pre-determination*. There will be no embarrassing emails, no reports or planning documents that give the game away. Everyone will be able to declare, hand on heart, that no decisions have been taken. Only in the small print might one discover that simultaneously, managers have to achieve financial savings that are all but impossible without a certain consultation outcome.

Of course this is an extreme scenario, but it happens. One clue is to examine the governance structure of the decision. Who exactly

276

takes the decision? We know of many consultations when this was far from clear – a real problem where legally independent and accountable bodies join forces to take tough decisions. It happened when the NHS in south Wales sought to rationalise hospital services across four health boards. These boards had their own governance arrangements, making them wholly responsible for delivering services to many hundreds of thousands of people.

Decisions to move services, no matter how well intentioned or executed, can be deeply unpopular and place stress on local managers, who are vulnerable to charges that they are disadvantaging those whom they are statutorily required to serve. Once the consultation was over and hard decisions were needed, the governance arrangements put in place for the purpose became critical, but at least that was in the open. In general, however, there is a lack of transparency about who gets to take decisions. In central government, the fiction is that the minister decides. In practice, it can be very different and even powerful politicians end up being a rubber stamp.

No one should pretend that defining what lies within and what lies outside the consultation is easy. In the airspace consultation in Edinburgh, one of the complaints of objectors was that the whole exercise proceeded on an assumption that the airport should expand and the aviation industry would grow substantially in the coming years. Environmental campaigners and the Green Party, with six seats in the Scottish Parliament, did not share that vision. The airport, having been told by the SNP government to assume aggressive aviation growth, excluded such issues from its consultation. Had it in fact included such a major policy item within the exercise, it would have been deluged with submissions but would have been powerless to act upon what people said. The issue, after all, is owned by the Scottish Government. Insisting on total clarity at the outset would not have assuaged those who wanted to argue about the policy, but it would have helped to clarify who is responsible for what. Such clarification could trigger further policy reviews or consultations elsewhere. Certainly it would form a better basis for the current exercise.

The *duty to define* goes even deeper. Having defined the issue, a consultor must then work within that specification. The information provided, the dialogue methods selected, the questions asked and the decision-making process all have to work around that project definition. We must avoid last-minute adjustments, after-the-event changes of mind or changes to the scope. Of course that can sound unrealistic, but to change tack late in the process, without sufficient agreement from affected stakeholders, is to risk a breach of trust between the parties if consultation is to work well. All the more reason, therefore, to think it through properly at the start.

The duty to explain

The second Gunning Principle states that the consultor should publish sufficient information about proposals as would enable consultees to give them *intelligent consideration*. We love that last phrase but, in many ways, this is a somewhat imprecise formulation. After all, what one person might require to apply his or her intelligence to the subject may be very different from what another might. The courts have also found it troublesome; witness the long list of cases where claimants said that important information was denied them. Cases have gone both ways and it would be a brave lawyer who could predict with certainty the extent to which a judge would be impressed by what's been published.

The classic case on this concerned the planned reorganisation of local government in East Anglia. Breckland District Council in Norfolk challenged a consultation run by the Boundary Committee, which had sought views on a move to unitary councils, replacing the current two-tier system. First time around, the judge found in favour of the committee. The case turned on whether the complex financial consequences of reorganisation had been properly explained. Judge Cranston had to decide whether the consultation had provided enough information for local people and others to respond. In doing this, he made one of the most insightful comments we have ever seen in a court judgment*. His point was that the council was just being too idealistic. It made disproportionate demands upon the committee. He struck us as having understood something that has eluded many judges, namely that:

> consultation may be tangled and untidy – a standard which the appellants criticise as insufficient. It encompasses a multitude of parties with a range of expertise and interest. Ideas are mediated through opinion leaders, typically councils and the local press. The mediation process will usually result in a 'bottom line', possibly a figure such as the £29 million which [another] council had initially attached to their proposal. It will be to that stripped-down version of what is in fact a complex issue that the general public will react.

He went on to say that 'the law must recognise the realities and imperfections of our democratic process'. What we think he meant was that, provided the macro-picture was understood, then the Boundary Committee was in the clear. Unfortunately, it

---

* R (*ex parte* Breckland DC) v Boundary Committee for England [2009] EWHC Civ 239.

wasn't in the clear. What the Court of Appeal described as 'complex and indigestible' financial analysis could only be found in consultants' reports and workbooks (yes, workbooks!) placed on the Boundary Committee's website. In a telling indictment of the whole story, their Lordships were unequivocal: 'The need to explain the financial side of the draft proposals to the public in an understandable way was lost sight of or not understood.'

And here is the nub of the issue. The strict legal formulation of the second Gunning Principle is all about providing information, but what is really needed is a *mission to explain*. That phrase is a retread from thirty-five years ago, when John Birt at London Weekend Television and the celebrities who launched the ill-fated TV-am channel argued that broadcast journalism needed to accept a bigger responsibility for the audience's absorption of complex issues. The same applies to consultations, in that there is surely a similar type of responsibility for ensuring that target audiences appreciate what is going on.

In 2007, Frank Luntz, a US pollster for the Republican Party, wrote a best-selling management book whose title included the phrase *It's Not What You Say, It's What People Hear,*[*] and we think the key message from the Breckland case is that the courts have decided that, however comprehensive may be the information that you have provided in a consultation, ultimately the test is what people have actually absorbed. If, therefore, their understanding of the issues underlying the consultation is inadequate, then it will fail. Much as Judge Cranston commended the approach, relying upon 'opinion leaders' or the media to learn

---

[*] Frank Luntz, *Words That Work: It's Not What You Say, It's What People Hear* (New York: Hyperion, 2007). Luntz offers a behind-the-scenes look at how the tactical use of words and phrases affects what we buy, who we vote for, and even what we believe in.

about the whys and wherefores of various proposals will not do. In short, organisations cannot sub-contract this requirement to explain, or leave it to luck as to whether someone else will do the job for them. The buck stops with them and it is their job to be certain that consultees have heard enough. Being inundated with information is no substitute for honest communication that properly explains the issues.

Here, of course, lies an ever-present danger. Whilst some stakeholders will be thoroughly familiar with the subject matter, others will literally know nothing. Somewhere in the middle are those who may know a little but will need to approach the issues afresh and in whose case a little knowledge is often a dangerous thing. In the case of airspace changes, considered earlier, there are consultees with considerable knowledge of the aviation world; there are clinicians with expertise in the adverse effects of noise on vulnerable people. There are probably also environmental bodies or anti-aviation groups that have accumulated a substantial amount of specialised know-how. What they need is so different from local residents who may never have given the subject the first thought until the moment they realise that the tranquillity of their neighbourhood is threatened by the unwelcome roar of jet engines.

Consultation has long had a supplementary role in educating wider society in the complexities of decisions that might affect it. But educationalists are often conscious of the bias that can sometimes inadvertently creep into any elucidation of controversial issues. Religion is often a lightning-conductor for such disputes. In 2011, the pro-life lobby were insistent that a consultation by the Royal College of Obstetricians and Gynaecologists provided biased information. Similar cries of outrage were heard when David Cameron launched his consultation on same-sex marriage. Environmental disputes have also lead to allegations that misleading information was used to sway the argument on major projects like HS2 or the Hinkley Point nuclear power station.

Protest groups will routinely accuse public bodies of lying, but in our experience, what goes wrong with their attempts to explain is more screw-up than strategy. Mistakes arise from a mixture of over-enthusiastic communications teams and staff who are too anxious to please their political masters. Two London examples may suffice. In his book on 'post-truth',* Evan Davis describes the time when Transport for London (TfL) reconfigured a part of the Underground and made changes to the Circle line. Instead of being a complete circle, it was now going to be integrated with the Hammersmith and City line, with Edgware Road tube station acting as a terminus. As Davis notes, this was not a big deal as the timetable changes were sensible and almost unnoticeable; on TfL's calculations, where there had been seven trains an hour, in future there would be six. They decided to proceed with the change and then people started noticing and went back to check what they had been told. They found the poster. It made three simple points: the change would mean fewer delays; Londoners would enjoy a more reliable service; and there would be more trains to Hammersmith. Nothing about the reduction in service. A classic case of being at sixes and sevens... literally.

Some years afterwards, a south London MP, whose constituents were highly exercised by the redesign of a local bus station, contacted us. TfL had helpfully provided artists' impressions of the two competing layouts and although our recollections may be a little faulty, what we remember is seeing one brightly lit drawing

---

* Evan Davis: *Post-Truth: Why We Have Reached Peak Bullshit and What We Can Do about It* (London: Little, Brown, 2017).

depicting the newest London buses with happy-looking people alighting beneath a canopy of sun-dappled lime trees over gaily painted ultra-smart bus stops. The artist of the other picture had presumably been to the location in poor visibility. The pouring rain affected the body language of those trying in vain to dodge the spray from roadside puddles whilst older-looking buses prowled around in convoy. Guess which was the preferred option? Okay, we probably exaggerate, but a picture can, of course, easily mislead. In both cases, critics can rightly accuse the authorities of being 'economical with the truth'.

A *duty to explain* must resist all temptations to gild the consultation lily and to mislead whilst ostensibly explaining. It must also overcome the mind-numbing reliance on jargon, which infests public bodies like fleas on a dog. 'TMA' has long been amusingly said to stand for 'too many acronyms', but surely it is time to call a halt when consultation papers have to publish a multi-page appendix to list all the abbreviations contained in the body of the document. Maybe in a predominantly specialist consultation, there may be a case for more technical terminology but most of what we see merely obscures key messages and stands between the authors and their audiences. Without doubt, there is a need for a layered approach to explaining. We need better use of audio-visual and modern communications techniques aimed at stakeholders with different levels of understanding, pitched in language and tone that's appropriate for each one.

Across the spectrum, however, there is one way to explain that continues to work – the ancient art of storytelling. Supporters of a technique known as 'appreciative inquiry' * rely heavily on

---

* A model that seeks to engage stakeholders in self-determined change. According to the management academic Dr G. R. Bushe, it 'revolutionised the field of organisation development and was a precursor to the rise of

participants recalling instances where a particular problem or situation arose. The idea is that together, shared stories stimulate the identification of solutions to difficult issues; if one can learn from successful outcomes, maybe there are pointers towards effective strategies. This is why some of the better consultations find it useful to illustrate proposals for change with case studies. New patient pathways in health, for example, are so much better explained by referencing a real live person and his or her journey through the labyrinthine corridors that make up the NHS. The *duty to explain* in public consultation requires the best skills of communications professionals, working with a political sensitivity that is not always their strength. This is because they have to tread a fine line, making it easy for consultees to form a thorough understanding of the subject and what is proposed, without leaving them feeling they are being steered towards an inevitable outcome.

The duty to engage

This most obvious of requirements is strangely absent from the common-law principles as they have evolved. We might view it as a Gunning Gap. It was not an issue in the original Gunning *v* Brent LB* case and no court has yet added a fifth Gunning Principle. We, however, think it is necessary, for without a clear need to identify and engage with the right people, one might easily satisfy every one of the other Gunning Principles and conduct a consultation that is perfectly lawful, but deeply flawed in terms of *best practice*. Were we to draft the fifth Gunning Principle, we would declare: 'A reasonable and proportionate attempt should

---

positive organisation studies and the strengths-based movement in American management'. *Per* Wikipedia.

* See Chapter 3.

have been made to engage with and obtain the views of stakeholders with a significant interest in the issue.'

The small matter of proportionality is important here. Were a government to consult on a question that affected every one of the UK's 66.4 million people,* there is no suggestion that it would have to find ways of engaging with all of them. What is needed is either a properly managed commitment to talk to a representative sample of that broader whole, or an identification of those who are most affected and an effort to have a dialogue with them. In both cases, it begs the question: what, in this context, is meant by *engage*? Also, in contrast to consultation, are there rules that apply to *engagement*?

The answers are in some ways unsatisfactory. *Engagement* is the softer notion, and is very attractive to organisations that find the process of consultation, and the rules that apply to it, rather demanding. In practice it means having to establish some form of meaningful relationship with individuals or groups. If all that a planning officer does to consult a village about a planning application is to put up incomprehensible statutory notices on trees and lamp-posts in the time-honoured way, we are reluctant to see this as the local authority having engaged with that community. If a public exhibition is arranged with opportunities to meet a building developer or a local councillor and hold conversations about a likely project, then we would concede that *engagement* has indeed happened.

Our challenge is that there are no hard and fast rules that can help us determine whether *engagement* is adequate. Unlike the strict and specific rules of engagement that authorise the military to fire on the enemy, the civilian concept is rather warm and woolly. It

* 2018 estimate.

would be far too narrow a view just to include those who have read, or even just seen, the relevant consultation paper, but neither is it enough to count everyone who may have heard that a consultation exercise is going ahead. If we ask corporate communications directors if they have engaged with the local population, they will proudly point to the print run of the monthly magazine they distribute to every household. Or even the television advertisement. Or the billboard next to the supermarket. Or the number of hits that they have had on their Facebook page. That may indeed be their reach but they have scarcely engaged unless there is some reciprocal action. Liking a social media page, or better still sharing it, may be closer to the mark, but still falls short of the kind of obvious interaction that might lead us to think that genuine *engagement* has occurred.

So why not look at it from the stakeholders' viewpoint? Might it be better to regard the question of whether there has been *engagement* as a subjective test? Might we therefore ask 'Did the council engage you in this consultation?' Or 'Did the government find enough people like you to engage with?' That would bring us back to the reality that some stakeholders are more equal than others. There are consultations where, to borrow again from *stakeholder mapping,* the failure to have a dialogue with certain high-interest, high-influence players would cast serious doubt on the exercise. Not only would it be sensible to have engaged with them, it would be essential and the nature of that engagement would need to have been at a suitably appropriate level. If the subject matter is, for example, police recruitment and the Association of Chief Police Officers (ACPO) are viewed as key stakeholders, then it would not be wise for the Home Office to send to a meeting with ACPO only their youngest, least experienced graduate trainee.

The *duty to engage* is therefore a multi-layered obligation. It requires consultation organisers to have carefully analysed the relevant stakeholder base and found ways to offer and establish the kind of dialogue that befits the status of those stakeholders. It is particularly critical with those groups or individuals that are mapped as having a considerable stake in the issue but little or no influence. The term 'seldom heard' is now preferred to the outdated 'hard to reach' (they weren't hard to reach at all; rather, it was public bodies that were hard to contact). But whatever they are called, these stakeholders quite definitely need special attention, what the Americans call 'affirmative action' and we term 'positive discrimination': a deliberate policy to allocate more resources, spend more and take more time and trouble to engage with them. This might mean training up specialist staff to work with groups like Gypsies and Travellers. It means investment in the skills to interact with and involve those with mental or physical disabilities. It almost certainly means seeking out and working with ethnic or religious minorities in their places of worship or community centres. Where a significant number of people lack adequate English language skills and where consultation proposals might seriously affect them, written or oral translation services are probably needed. Without taking such steps, the likelihood is that a range of important voices will not be heard.

How far can we go in insisting that consultors engage with sufficient people? When is enough enough?

One of the earliest Quality Assurance projects undertaken by the Consultation Institute took place in 2010. It resulted from the sad case where a German national with limited English language skills provided an out-of-hours service to an NHS primary care trust in East Anglia and unfortunately a patient died. It obliged the NHS to reconsider the provision of out-of-hours services and the resulting consultation covered about 200,000 people in a large rural area. Quite correctly, efforts were made to identify key stakeholders. Unsurprisingly, one of the groups deemed particularly vulnerable were families with very young children, especially new mothers coping with their first baby. These were to be a priority group, but were proving unexpectedly difficult to contact. Midway through the consultation, there was still no effective engagement. Local managers had asked GPs to mention the consultation to the relevant patients and now letters had been sent to mother-and-toddler groups in the area. Come the closing date, there still had been no response. The NHS always has an immense communications workload, and this was one of several consultations running simultaneously. Skilled staff were over-worked. What were they to do? They argued that they had done all that could reasonably be expected of them. If people did not want to respond, they claimed, so be it; at least they had been given a chance.

We disagreed. NHS officers were being passive, waiting for consultees to come to them. There are times when consultors have to be proactive. It would have been perfectly possible to convene a few focus groups, or even to identify individual patients and conduct one-to-one interviews with them. In fact, there were a dozen things that could have been done, but they all took time and some of them cost money. Imagine, however, that nothing more was done and that the views of such mothers were omitted from in the consultation. What might have been lost? Might they have contributed some insight, or argued for a policy that might have had an important bearing upon the way the out-of-hours service should be provided? In practice, the absence of certain voices can be accommodated by diligent homework, and experienced officers trying to guess what the silent voices might have said. But officers can be wrong. Without the authentic voice of stakeholders, there is a risk that new arrangements or policies may be put in place without fully appreciating how they might affect certain groups.

Getting the right balance of voices is far more important than securing a reassuringly high volume of responses. In fact, the whole obsession with response rates misses the point. Consultation is about hearing all the relevant arguments – not about counting votes. There can, however, be occasions when the numbers participating are so derisory as to invalidate any conclusions whatever. At other times, those responding have been glaringly unrepresentative. Over the years, we have been constantly urged to recommend a target percentage of the population, whose responses would confirm the validity of a local consultation. There is no single correct answer but if a council achieves one per cent on an issue that really matters, that is about par for the course. As a number, however, it is pretty meaningless. Double it, and we still only have the view of one in fifty residents. If they reflect the demographics of the area quite closely, then that is a bonus, but most public consultations attract older, whiter professionals, with young people definitely in short supply. Even if we have a respondent profile that closely matches the reality on the ground, the fact that these respondents are self-selected means that we cannot be sure that their views would be the same as a structured sample.

The truth is that in a public consultation, those that are resistant to proposals for change are likely to be far more motivated to participate. Consultation reports are therefore bound to be full of the anxieties, concerns and objections of the critics, and very useful they should be to decision-makers. What they do not do is give a comprehensive picture of the wider public response – unless specific research has been done to ascertain their opinions. That is why councils throughout the UK have wrestled with cuts to library services, informed by a persuasive set of consultation responses from an articulate middle class whose campaigns have spurred one per cent of the residents to respond – whilst unsure what the other 99 per cent of the population might think.

The *duty to engage* is, in part, an attempt to move away from that model and to oblige those who run a consultation to seek out sufficient stakeholders from as wide a range of perspectives as possible and to enter into dialogue with them. This is not about swelling the ranks of consultation participants. It is about ensuring that relevant information is gathered, relevant attitudes are captured and that all the relevant arguments are heard.

The three duties – to *define*, to *explain* and to *engage* – do not amount to a radical agenda for changing the behaviour of consultors. They are not meant to be legally enforceable. Rather they are offered as a means of setting new norms for *best practice*. In essence they are designed to simplify, demystify and clear away the cloud of complexity that has often obscured the consultative atmosphere. Only when set alongside what we propose for consultees does the scale of the challenge emerge...

Chapter 15

Improving dialogue: three rights for consultees

Consultee entitlements | right to know | right to be heard |
public consultation hearings | right to influence | notional
framework

Before considering the rights and expectations of consultees, it is
worth noting that the entire discussion and literature on public
consultations seems geared to the perspective of the consultors –
mostly organisations or government agencies who have to run the
process. Little is known and even less has been written about the
issues that affect those who participate in or might respond to a
consultation.

This is strange. A few years ago, we attempted to measure the full
cost of a consultation, and in Chapter 2, we told the story of an
aborted Labour policy, consultation for which we estimated cost
£10 millions. That was in 2003 and the calculation took account
of the true cost of officers' time in 400 local authorities, using
established methods of activity-based costing. However, it is
symptomatic of the traditional lack of rigour in these matters that
such 'internal' costs were rarely considered by those who

examined public engagement. With austerity economics, consultors are suddenly only too well aware of the resources required. But they are still too dismissive of the burden their consultations impose on consultees.

Most of the cost of consultation falls upon consultees. As we have moved to the digital-by-default principle, it can, superficially, appear quite cheap for organisations to mount a consultation. Responding online can, of course, save money for consultees, but not to the same extent. Anything that is serious enough to warrant consultation requires some thought.

Stakeholder groups are actually reasonably democratic. Unless they are blessed with a research department, a policy expert or policy-making machinery of some kind, they will need to ask their members, or their regional committees, or their topic-specific working groups, and bring together a range of views in order to formulate a response. We call this *secondary consultation*, and for trade associations, major charities and national or regional campaigning groups, it is an immensely important, though neglected, activity. It is one of the main drivers for retaining the twelve-week duration for consultations involving the third sector. It is also a major aspect of sustaining membership – giving members a voice in matters that affect them.

The salient feature of consultees in general is the range of individuals and groupings that are found. The term 'heterogeneity' may be appropriate, and this makes a difference to any attempt to develop standards that are useful to all types. Civil society, as well as the business community, consists of thousands of organisations, which keep the economic and social life of the nation ticking over. An average-sized local authority has probably between 5,000 and 10,000 organisations, which might, at some stage or another, wish to take part in dialogue with the council. An average NHS clinical commissioning group may need to deal with about 150 condition-specific charities or affinity groups operating in its area, and about 500 other bodies who would expect to have a say on aspects of health and social care.

A distinction must be drawn between these groupings of various kinds and individuals. Movers and shakers in many communities tend to be the same few people. An individual can run the bowls club and the local amateur dramatics society, sit on the parish council, support the Royal British Legion on poppy-selling and be active in her local church. These community activists are the salt-of-the-earth types who find themselves sometimes labelled the 'usual suspects', for they are the ones that appear at public meetings and ask the awkward questions. They would love to take part in more public consultations, as they are not often reticent with their opinions. However, they are chronically short of time and would much prefer it if the groups to which they belonged could organise themselves better and represent their views with greater fervour and skill.

To these individuals and organisations, we offer the prospect of three important rights. These are indicative entitlements. They are not to be compared with all-important human rights, but if consultation is to work as a mechanism to strengthen a modern democracy, it needs a better sense of what potential and actual responders to a consultation have a right to expect. Although the shorthand labels are kept succinct, it follows that their application will differ between individuals and organisations. As with the duties proposed for consultors, they are suggested as indicators of *best practice* rather than as legally enforceable obligations.

The right to know

First, a statement of the glaringly obvious. Unless people know about a consultation, it is highly unlikely they will participate. The consultee's *right to know* is complementary to the consultor's *duty to engage*, but it raises interesting questions about the way in which it works in practice.

A local resident who is directly affected by spatial planning is almost certainly likely to be notified by the council. If someone wants to build a leisure centre at the end of your road, you will be told. The same goes for a housing development, a waste management plant, a new factory or a new road. In these contexts, the *right to know* is really not an issue.

If the same council, however, wants to change the boundaries of its controlled parking zones, revise its green spaces strategy or even ask for views on the thirty-five proposals in its budget consultation, we are less sure how you might know. And what if the local academy decides to change its admissions criteria? Or the NHS suggests reducing the cycle of IVF interventions it is willing to offer couples? Or the police and crime commissioner wants to merge two police stations and relocate the fire station? How on earth can we keep abreast of all of these? Oh, and simultaneously the Ministry of Housing, Communities and Local Government would like to know what we think of a radically new approach to domiciliary care in our old age. And the Home Office is seeking views on its proposed treatment of overstayers from the EU in order to meet its aggressive net migration targets. Give us a break!

A decade ago, we thought that technology might offer a solution to some of this. 'Create a local portal,' we said. 'For any area, build a comprehensive consultation directory that contains every proposed and current consultation that affects local people.' It would be regularly updated by all local service providers and might even feature national consultations where they had particular local implications.

It did not work. Despite the efforts of a few enthusiastic technophile authorities, such consultation websites as were built struggled to secure support from within their own organisations, let alone external bodies. Then the reorganisation of the NHS occurred in England and primary care trusts disappeared, along with half the public engagement staff whose skills and know-how would have been needed to make this work. On a national level, the government, to its credit, has created a single point of contact* for central departments; at the time of writing it hosts more than 4000 documents.

The fundamental flaw in our thinking was believing that a comprehensive directory actually helped consultees. It may well be valuable to have a resource where one can check to see if one has missed something of interest. It may also be useful to use a standard methodology to search for relevant documents and discover what happened at the end of the exercise. But it does little to help consultees and stakeholders find out about something that affects them in time to do anything about it.

If you are a serious campaigning body and hold strong views about a particular subject, our assumption would be that you are already plugged into policy discussions. For these organisations, close to the top of the consultee food chain, anything less would be a failure of their *raison d'être*. If the British Medical Association

---

* In the multi-purpose Gov.uk portal, one of the nine top level options is called Consultations, and is fully searchable by keyword, publication type, policy area, department, document status, location and date.

(BMA), for example, does not know that the Department of Health is considering a relevant issue and is preparing to hold a consultation, it is simply not doing its job. Similarly, if the Royal Society for the Protection of Birds (RSPB) is unaware that a government department is seeking changes to the Habitats Directive and that a consultation is contemplated, something is wrong. One more example: if a local authority is worried that proposed changes to health and safety regulations might imperil some of its council tenants and suspects changes will be made with insufficient consultation, but fails to act on its suspicions, again it is probably a dereliction of duty. That is because bodies such as this are there to represent views and be heard. BMA members, RSPB members and councillors would deem it a failure if their respective organisations were not fully aware of the likelihood of a forthcoming consultation. The more astute ones would no doubt seek to influence its scope and methodology, as we discussed in Part Three.

For every well-equipped representative body with a permanent, full-time commitment to respond to relevant consultations, there are thousands of others which we could characterise as part-time, opportunist consultees, who will only stir themselves to participate when it matters to them. Many will either have a single research or policy person, but far more will employ public affairs specialists to advise them. This can be big business and the biggest consultancies will see their role as holding a watching brief on the policy landscape as it affects their client. If they do their jobs properly, they will see a consultation coming from a distance and hopefully, will advise accordingly. It is not an easy task, especially on behalf of clients who may have a broad range of legitimate interests. There are comparatively few short cuts. By definition there can be no database of possible, but not confirmed, consultations. They are as speculative as potential transfer deals between football clubs. For most of us, intelligence on such matters is best gleaned by going onto social media and reading the various 'football gossip' websites. For most major matters of public policy, there are equivalents of varying provenance and it takes experts to monitor them. That is where and why public affairs firms earn their keep.

One approach is always to make sure you are registered with the online communities used by organisations to keep their stakeholder information up to date. With the best stakeholder portals, it should be possible to indicate which aspects of an organisation's policy portfolio excites your interest, a little like social media seeks your interests for the purposes of unleashing its advertisers upon you. Ideally, it can then offer you a range of involvement opportunities, one of which might be to take part in a consultation. In this way, the best policy-makers surround themselves with a range of potential stakeholders who have registered their interest in the topic.

The other advice we proffer campaigning groups and community organisations is never to wait until a consultation is imminent, but to articulate their views and take them to the relevant authorities whenever they wish. The drip-drip of persuasive arguments may fall on deaf ears whilst policy seems fixed and settled and where there is little appetite to open up a subject for review. But in politics, business and civic society, things change. Who in 2015 would have anticipated that long-avoided, *wicked issues* such as fisheries policy or agricultural subsidies might be open to debate as a result of Brexit? Long-standing campaigners such as those advocating liberal end-of-life options recognise that they are in it for the long haul. They will be fully aware of forthcoming consultations even if they are only tentatively related to their cause. Persistence and patience pay off over a longer period, and in all probability, part of their campaign will be to seek a public consultation specifically on their cause.

For individuals who merely wish to exercise their rights as citizens, and to express their views, we need a mass media that does a better job of promoting consultation. We also need innovative use of social media. Looking first at traditional media, we might start with local newspapers. In our part of Bedfordshire, we appear to have been blessed with a local paper that always makes a point of covering consultation rather well. If the local council has asked for views on something of interest, we might read a story such as 'Deadline looms for views on Draycott Lane' or 'Councillor attacks sham consultation'. Naïvely we imagined that all papers did the same. So, when travelling on Institute business, we made a point of analysing the local paper. To our dismay we found major cities with evening papers selling in tens of thousands and with little or no coverage of municipal matters at all, and rarely a story – good or bad – about a public consultation. This probably results from years of custom and practice, and culturally there are different approaches in various parts of the country. But we think that consultors could do better to make their consultations more newsworthy. Too many of them are slipped into the public domain *sotto voce*, as if one of the objectives was to avoid, rather than to attract, a large number of responses. Until Eric Pickles did his best to circumscribe them, council newspapers were a great way to promote 'your council wants to listen to you'-type stories. Today they are fewer and thinner and less effective at that kind of communication.

Broadcasting is a better option. One of the best examples of effectively promoting a consultation was a video we found on the local breakfast television programme in Ottawa, Canada.

Controversy had surrounded plans for an extension to the existing tramline and the scheme's promoters were holding a public consultation by means of a drop-in session at the local council offices. In that type of jaunty morning-time bonhomie that divides any nation into those who can tolerate it and those who cannot abide the thought, the presenter encouraged a councillor to extol the virtues of his scheme. Vivid artists' impressions showed how scything through green spaces had been accommodated by putting the new route in a trench and how the environmental critics had clearly misunderstood the plan. The three-minute advertorial concluded with the presenter admitting that, personally, he was much in favour of the scheme and that he would certainly be coming along in the afternoon – and so should his viewers. When we show this video to British local government officers in training courses, it usually divides the room. For everyone who recognises a superb piece of television promotion, there is someone who finds it a little too brazen and not quite British. One thing is for certain, though. A fair proportion of Ottawa's citizens knew about the consultation!

Looking ahead, however, the *right to know* is largely going to depend upon social media. In fact, savvy consultors will publish in traditional ways, issue a press release but then rely on a Facebook page and other local social media sites to spread the word. We sense that we are only beginning to see applications being developed that make best use of mobile technology. Has anyone, we wonder, yet developed an app which, as we walk down a street, alerts us to the fact that as we come across a particular building, there are six days left to give our views on the planning application that may double its size? If we visit an Area of Outstanding Natural Beauty, can we receive a prompt that tells us that the view we are witnessing will change if plans are approved to build a wind farm on top of the hill? And this is what it will look like...

If you stay at a hotel, it has for years been the norm that you are invited to give your views of the experience, usually in the form of a satisfaction survey. More recently, public services have adopted similar practices so our stay in hospital or even the online renewal of a driving licence is followed by an invitation to provide feedback on the experience. Some of these mechanisms are better than others. When the NHS introduced its Friends and Family test, it was discovered that patients were being double-counted, both giving an instant physical response ('Please place your token in one of these boxes') and later responding to an online survey. In a sense that doesn't matter. The good news is that people are increasingly being exposed to requests for their views; we are just not yet good at integrating the operational 'how was it for you?' stuff with the broader themes we tend to cover in a formal consultation.

Taking all these things together, consultees are slowly but surely becoming more aware of the opportunities to express their views. To be consulted. Our concern has always been that this is not enough. Unless we make progress on the next two issues, that greater awareness will do little to induce people to participate.

The right to be heard

Current consultation practice has one big weakness. It leaves consultees totally unsure of whether their arguments have been heard by anyone. They send in their responses, which then seem to disappear into a big black hole, never to emerge again. If you are a key stakeholder, there might be some hope for a dialogue of some sort, but there is no guarantee. Individuals may be a different matter, but people are not unreasonable. If they know that they were one of thousands who submitted their views, they do not necessarily expect personal treatment. And yet...

Everyone who takes the time and trouble to participate in a consultation does so for a reason. Not everyone expects their contribution to make a difference, but those who take part expect something. What? Is it just a recognition that they have contributed to the debate? Is it a wish to be counted alongside others of a like mind so as to increase the numbers supporting a particular line of argument? Or have they, perhaps, invented a totally original, unique perspective that will not have been offered elsewhere? All these are subtly different forms of motivation.

Consultee expectations will reflect their motivation. Similarly, the consultor's ability to react effectively will need to take account of the many reasons that inspired responders to take part. Being heard is important to them all, but in different ways. For some, what surely matters is that the argument they support is properly considered. If the sheer volume of support for such arguments is likely to be important, then consultors need to appreciate the weight of numbers. For those with a more individualised contribution, it is likely that nothing short of a direct dialogue on their proposition or an acknowledgement of it in a feedback report will do the trick.

The number of responses is indeed a problem for many of the more popular consultations. Over 60,000 took part in the HS2 consultation; three times as many gave their views on the BBC Charter.* No one is suggesting that a single contributor from among such thousands should have access to decision-makers. Yet the logic of consultation is that those who decide should be

* See Chapters 6 and 11 respectively.

fully aware of the views expressed. The problem is that, short of including her particular response in a large analysis report, the contributor may well be unconvinced that it was worth her while bothering.

Social media makes matters worse, for it has created a culture of 'publish and be damned', with contributors fully aware that those who read their words will probably be friends or those sympathetic to their views. If we tweet, we know that the chance of being given a modicum of attention is slim; effectively, we are in competition with everyone else to be noticed. This may possibly be one reason why people strive for creativity, originality or just cussedness. The level of ambient noise in the ether is unimaginable, so we all tend to shout ever louder in order to be heard. Far from there being a *right to be heard* on the internet, what we have is a disorderly cacophony where our shouting for attention distorts our judgement, perverts our language and almost always loses us focus and friends.

If we respond to a consultation and then announce on Facebook that we have given our views, say to the local council or maybe to the local NHS trust, most of our friends will think we are behaving abnormally. Or showing off. If we say we have responded to a government consultation, many will think we have ideas above our station. Only among those with whom we make common cause is there a hint that this is may be a wise and responsible thing to do. We worry about our democracy when consultation is treated with such disdain, but the truth, of course, is that we have brought the situation upon ourselves by conducting these exercises in a way that no one ever knows if anyone really considers their arguments.

All this is to explain why we favour the return of public consultation hearings. We say 'return' because early consultation was almost entirely oral. If an organisation wanted to know someone's views, it convened some kind of meeting where different perspectives could be aired. In the modern world, we are losing, and in many ways have already lost, the face-to-face element that is at the heart of personal relationships. If consultation is merely a one-off transaction, maybe we can rely solely on a here-today, gone-tomorrow online questionnaire. If it is more about building *communities of interest* and learning how to devise solutions that accommodate different interests, then we need to reach for mechanisms that incorporate a closer dialogue.

It is wrong of course to suggest that public hearings are making a comeback; they never went away. Our judicial system is founded on the principle of public hearings, and for good reason. Nothing is more sacred to a democracy than having total transparency over the way that guilt, innocence and punishment are established. In a mature democracy, the credibility of the system requires that rather more than the justice system secures this level of transparency. Courts of inquiry or royal commissions, when addressing matters of heightened public interest, are always now held in public. Councils used to discuss many items behind the veil of secrecy that allowed them to exclude the press; today this happens far less frequently. Any body established by statute in recent years has found itself bound to hold at least its annual meeting, but sometimes all its meetings, in public. We also have the precedent of multi-party parliamentary select committees.

Because they are now televised, far more of the public are familiar with the select committee format than used to be the case. The normal procedure is for a committee to issue a 'call for evidence', accompanied by some questions which it would like answered. It will then often publish the submitted evidence but usually in narrative form, not as an analysis. Working through supporting officials, it will then invite a small number of key stakeholders to appear before it in person, and it is invariably these events that attract publicity. Even the absence of an invited witness can make the news – Mark Zuckerberg of Facebook will confirm this.* The committee chairpersons have become famous for aggressive cross-examination of witnesses, and civil servants have been known to fare badly when confronted by angry MPs or peers. Although select committees have been established for years, it is the advent of television that has given them a wider audience. Similarly, it is this ability to video-stream public consultation hearings that will enhance their appeal and emphasise the transparency of the process.

At a stroke, we can counter some of consultees' scepticism that nothing happens when they offer their views. Holding public hearings sends a powerful signal that something *is* happening, especially if key decision-makers are there in the room. It involves creating a situation where such people physically meet consultees. This matters because, except for the odd public meeting, the likelihood is that many a consultation is held without those who decide ever meeting anyone who has responded to the exercise. We suspect that there are senior executives or board members of public bodies who have spent a lifetime avoiding direct contact with a consultee, and it often shows.

Public hearings are a transparent form of evidence-gathering. As such they offer a good riposte to anyone who suspects that

---

* In March 2018, following revelations that Facebook data had been inappropriately used for political purposes, the site's founder, Mark Zuckerberg, was asked to appear before the Digital, Culture, Media and Sport Select Committee.

decisions are taken in ignorance of that evidence. A hearing records precisely which arguments have been tabled and which have not. It can reveal how seriously the evidence is being considered, and does much to clarify what are the most important issues. Formal dialogue like this does more than any number of written submissions to identify whether there is common ground between consultor and consultee. It will highlight more visibly where the real fault lines may be. It can identify those matters that must be addressed by those who propose change, if they are to carry people with them.

In fact, there are a legion of practical advantages why hearings might strengthen a public consultation:

- It can be difficult sometimes to generate interest in a consultation; a public hearing provides a symbolic occasion around which can be built the other forms of dialogue.

- Written submissions by consultees frequently make claims and assertions and decision-makers have few opportunities to question, clarify and challenge such statements. Public hearings provide that opportunity.

- If a multi-faceted consultation is undertaken, it may be important to some stakeholders to be sure that a particular aspect has been properly considered. A public hearing, especially if focused on that aspect, can prove the point.

- Representative bodies, expressing collective views of members or supporters, often need to be seen to be communicating their messages. Public hearings are excellent occasions for demonstrating that they are doing so.

- Issues which, in the past, may have justified calling a public meeting might be better considered in a public hearing. This is because public meetings are rarely balanced debates and are less effective as a mechanism for evaluating evidence.

- Specialist, 'expert' witnesses or academics can be called and help those on all sides of an important issue have a more informed debate. A public hearing can be a good environment to consider new ideas.

- Decision-makers who are anxious to be seen to be taking evidence seriously can use public hearings to make a visible commitment to listen to people's views.

- The media sometimes has difficulty finding meaningful news stories from a consultation – but they can use a public hearing as a hook on which to build coverage.

The *right to be heard* is not individually exercisable. What we have in mind is that every significant argument should be heard. This places a premium on careful selection of those aspects of a consultation upon which to focus. The consultor should not do this, as it may be accused of bias or worse. This, and selecting which witnesses should give evidence, is a task for an independent person or organisation; so is the role of facilitator or chair. Our preference would be for hearings to be held just as the consultation comes to the end of the dialogue phase. As consultees respond, they can be asked if they are interested in taking part in a hearing and if so to indicate on the questionnaire or in some other way. Those who collect and analyse the incoming responses should be able to discern the main lines of argument and consider them with the independent facilitator, and together select who should be invited to speak. The logistics of these hearings are important to get right. There are dozens of YouTube videos showing hearings like this in different parts of the world. We particularly liked watching the council in Toronto taking evidence as part of its Budget consultation. It takes four hours with pressure groups, community organisations and major non-governmental organisations (NGOs) from the city covering a vast array of issues in half-hour and quarter-hour slots.

Sadly, we don't believe such hearings will necessarily be popular with all decision-makers. Some will insist they do not have the time and that many of the arguments they will hear have been rehearsed internally *ad nauseam*. But in many ways that is precisely why they should attend. We would urge a 'substitutes not allowed' policy and challenge decision-makers to live up to their promises to listen and be influenced. Delegating the listening to subordinates or contracted consultants merely reinforces consultees' doubts that the powers-that-be are truly genuine.

There may be more to this reluctance. Decision-makers may be unsure that they want to place themselves in a position where they could be embarrassed. Many are scarred by bad experiences in public meetings and may see hearings as further opportunities for implacable opponents to have a platform to harangue them. It should be possible, however, to assure the decision-makers that a well-structured hearing is a more controllable environment and will show them in a favourable light, willing to assess evidence objectively. Remember that all sides of the argument can be heard – not just objections or criticisms.

For some campaigners and objectors, there is a downside... but only for some. A public hearing places you and your arguments under scrutiny. Your evidence will need to be well prepared and your manner must be constructive. This is no place for bluster and bullshit, and if knowledgeable decision-makers are likely to cross-question you about your assertions, you will need them to be accurate and based upon something real. Public consultation hearings should not be too legalistic; the last thing anyone wants is an overtly inquisitorial process. So there is a fine line to be drawn between providing an accessible, visible process to show what happens to arguments advanced in a consultation, and degenerating into gladiatorial reality-show entertainment for either side to strut around showing off their egos.

Checks and balances are provided by transparency and the knowledge that the process can be witnessed online. Smart applications can now allow viewers to comment on what they hear or to submit suggested questions. One or more parallel dialogues can be organised alongside the main event; they may spontaneously arise anyway. So, subject to the caveats we have already discussed, public consultation hearings can provide a complementary benefit by intensifying and broadening debate through social media. If the participants perform or behave badly, there is, of course, collateral damage to their reputation and possibly to the arguments they advance.

Set-piece events like public consultation hearings face a real challenge when they have to manage the unrealistic expectations of those whose sense of entitlement leads to a demand to give evidence but whom, for reasons of capacity or balance, it is not always possible to accommodate. Some groups can be very persistent and will not wish to be knowingly under-represented. They would not like their rivals or opponents to be offered privileged access to the decision-makers, if they themselves were denied. Yet for seldom-heard or chronically disadvantaged consultees, these hearings provide an excellent opportunity to remedy any imbalance. A clear aim of the exercise should be to assemble a diverse range of voices so that the nuances of argument can be properly discerned and appreciated. It is one of several reasons why selecting those to give evidence is a sensitive task and best done by someone independent.

Regardless of whether we are right in forecasting that such hearings will become an integral part of public consultations, there remains much that consultors can do to persuade those who respond that they are more than a number in a data analysis spreadsheet. A pro-forma acknowledgement does little, but a meaningful response to an original line of argument, or a request for more information or more evidence, shows that someone is taking an interest in their view. Town planners routinely provide individualised responses, but for higher volumes it becomes impractical. Skilled communications teams can, however, find ways to categorise submissions so that semi-personalised responses are possible. What matters is that the consultees are recognised for having done what was asked and expressed a view. It is their right to expect that effort to be acknowledged and examined properly – a *right to be heard.*

The right to influence

This is the nub of the entire argument. To what extent do consultation responders have any right to influence? And if they do, does that emanate from their status as consultees? Or is it, and should it be, but a function of the quality of their arguments and the skill with which they are expressed? In this respect, we are in Marshall McLuhan* territory. He pointed out half a century ago that 'the medium is the message' and that it is difficult to disentangle the one from the other. Thirty years earlier, Dale Carnegie published his self-help book *How to Win Friends and*

---

* Marshall McLuhan was a Canadian professor, philosopher and public intellectual. He is known for coining the expression 'the medium is the message' in 1964 and the term 'global village', and for predicting the World Wide Web almost thirty years before it was invented. *Per* Wikipedia.

Influence People,* and popularised the idea that by amending one's personal behaviour, it becomes so much easier to persuade people. A legacy of such thinking probably leads us to accept as a starting point that many consultees will concede that, all other things being equal, their influence will depend on the quality of their contribution. If their arguments are strong and they are presented with brilliance, it should make a difference. And conversely, if they half-heartedly go through the motions with under-developed responses, then maybe they won't be surprised if they have no noticeable effect on what happens.

Despite this, we think every prospective contributor is entitled to some measure of consideration – simply because of the process. The obligation is very clearly on those organising the consultation. Common sense suggests, and the courts have confirmed, that anybody who claims to be running a consultation must be presumed to be open to influence. This is a real problem for those who never meant it. It is also problematic for those who consult primarily because government has told them to. Legislation has often encumbered public bodies with a requirement to consult in circumstances when elected members or managers would otherwise feel perfectly able and competent to take decisions. Very likely, these are occasions when Parliament does not quite wish to vest those in office with absolute power and feels the need to fetter their discretion somewhat. The message seems to be 'Go ahead and decide, but make sure you have listened to people first'. Another way to accomplish this would be to go to the town square and read out a proclamation that effectively says, 'Because we don't quite trust those people in the town hall, feel free to influence their decision.'

---

* Dale Carnegie, *How to Win Friends and Influence People* (New York: Simon & Schuster, 1936) and many subsequent editions.

310

We are sure there are times when governments have really thought this through and concluded that this subject or that decision point genuinely needs public or stakeholder input. But we also suspect that it is an easy concession to make when opposition parties patently dislike a proposal and ministers are able to soften its impact by giving assurances that local voices will be heard before certain actions are taken. When it came to the creation of local schemes for council tax benefit under the Welfare Reform Bill 2012, we are a little unsure how seriously the government meant its consultation requirements to be taken. One has to remember the political context. The coalition was trying to introduce universal credit as a purported cure-all for much of the duplication and bureaucracy of the social security system. There were fierce parliamentary battles on the abolition of the disability living allowance, the introduction of a benefits cap and a whole range of other important changes. In twenty-six sittings of the Commons committee that scrutinised the Bill as it meandered through Parliament, there is no reference to the nature of the consultation that was to be imposed on about 300 councils. So, we have only guesswork as to the true intentions of ministers and their advisers.

However, the Supreme Court had no doubts, and when this became a test case that sought to clarify the law of consultation in 2014, it became obvious that the default position is that if a consultation happens, then consultees are expected to have an influence. Lord Reid delivered a judgment that has since become a key pillar of the law of consultation. He was addressing the admitted facts that the London Borough of Haringey* had presented its residents with a single option for its new, local council tax benefit scheme – literally a *fait accompli*.

---

* R (*ex parte* Moseley) *v* Haringey LB [2014] UKSC 56.

In the most quoted passage, his Lordship said:

> In the present case … it is difficult to see how ordinary members of the public could express an intelligent view on the proposed scheme, so as to participate in a meaningful way in the decision-making process, unless they had an idea of how the loss of income by the local authority might otherwise be replaced or absorbed.

Ever since this judgment, any organisation that goes to its public with but one option runs a risk that the consultation will be declared unlawful. The rationale is that when only one choice is offered, then the scope to influence is necessarily absent. More pertinently, the judge assumed that the government had intended 'members of the public … to participate in a meaningful way in the decision-making process'.

Now is that truly what ministers intended? If yes, then it is to their credit. Or might it have slipped into the Bill unnoticed because the parliamentary draftsman happened to use the device of the earlier 1992 Local Government Finance Act to give effect to its provisions? We may never know, but the case, because it was the first time a consultation case had been heard at the Supreme Court, established a vitally important precedent and in effect created the *right to influence*.

It is a collective right, not an individual one. Taken as a whole, the sum total of the exercise needs to impact the decision. So, whereas every single contribution has a right to be heard and to be counted, influence is generated by the overall output of a consultation. And influence is not quite what people think it might be. Dictionary definitions may refer to changes in behaviour brought about by your efforts, but that is too narrow. Indeed, Dale Carnegie's version is about building better relationships and establishing credibility. Influence is not instant; it can be a slow process, gradually creating a powerful source of leverage which may or may not be called upon.

There is another sense in which influence is absorbed. A stock question for journalists interviewing a celebrity is to ask, 'Who has influenced you?' They might then hear recited a list of luminaries in the star's fields of endeavour, and sometimes beyond. Few of these, however, could be perceived to have directly changed the celebrity's behaviour, but they may have affected his thinking or her self-image. Influence is more amorphous than we imagine and is often more likely to affect future behaviour than anything in the immediate situation.

Apply this to the world of public consultation and we see some real contradictions. For years, we have clung to the definition of consultation as being a *dialogue… with a view to influencing* and it is still the best around. It rightly suggests the immediate application of influence, directed specifically at the decision in question. Even though we know that influence is more diffuse and might take time, we focus on the here-and-now and expect those who commissioned the consultation to be wide open to the views of those who have responded.

It does not always feel like that. Those with power to decide can appear reluctant to embrace the wise counsel of consultees. We often see a sullen realisation by some of these consultors that perhaps they should have paid more attention to the design of the consultation. At the outset they might have been more specific about the precise aspects where they were open to ideas and influence. Once it is over, it is too late. The *right to influence* is aligned exactly to the questions that sought respondent views. If there are clear options and the questions ask for a preference, it is assumed that what people express as their preference is meant to be a factor. What is less reasonable is for decision-makers then to base their decision on something else entirely.

This becomes a minefield. If you tell consultees that you intend to base your decision on certain factors and that their views will influence your choice, the courts will forbid you from subsequently relying on other factors. So much was decided when the HS2 consultation asked for views on the competing criteria to be used in establishing a compensation scheme.* Note that if a consultation results in a landslide of support for one particular option, it is perfectly legitimate, even if not always wise, to take a decision to the contrary. However, such a decision had better be based upon alternatives that were clearly explained to consultees.

Consultation is not normally a vote. Only as a referendum specifically given decision-taking power might it be considered as such. Influence is not necessarily numerical. Obviously in that landslide example, sensible organisations weigh up the extent of support as evidenced by the consultation. But they have to bear in mind how few in number and self-selected respondents might be. The classic scenario in recent years has been the rationalisation and closure of many of the nation's libraries. Invariably, councils do this at great risk of controversy as the literate middle class mount the municipal barricades in defence of establishments many of them have long deserted.

One of our earliest experiences of a full-blown public consultation on such plans was when Warwickshire rationalised its libraries in 2011. We remember helping the council prepare the consultation by designing questions that went beyond the

---

* R (*ex parte* HS2 Action Alliance) *v* Secretary of State for Transport [2013] EWHC 481 (Admin).

straightforward and traditional 'Should we or should we not close Bedworth Library?' There is nothing inherently wrong with that question, nor with parallel ones about others on the target list. It is just that the answers generally will not help hard-pressed councillors take the required decisions, because they are entirely predictable. No one opts for a closure, unless it is to keep open a library closer to themselves. Knowing that everyone would like to retain the library of their choice is not especially helpful. Any influence brought to bear on the decision in such circumstances will be of limited value.

But Warwickshire pointed the way to a more constructive approach. It tried to identify current or potential users rather than supporters or interested citizens. It asked questions about users' priority needs and preferences and sought to build a picture of the alternative services that could be developed. They found that many people liked the idea of 'community hubs' able to provide some of the more conventional services. By asking consultees about some of these ideas, it was possible to influence the shape of the future services.

Much the most impressive feature of the Warwickshire consultation is how it stimulated high-quality face-to-face dialogues and it was rightly heralded as something of a triumph. Instead of the customary mass picketing by protestors with placards and the ritual rubbishing of the council, a form of peace broke out, confounding the fears of councillors and officers alike. It emerged that in several communities, there was real enthusiasm to find different ways of supplying a replacement service. What was conceived as a consultation, in essence, became a *co-production* exercise. If you really want to have an impact on something that is being built, become a builder. That, in a nutshell, is why *co-production* is growing in popularity.

Where the *right to influence* breaks down is in pretending to ask a question, but framing it in such a way as to limit its effect. It offers consultees a tantalising glimpse of what ought to have been consulted upon, but in fact wasn't. The best example we know arose in 2016 when the city of Sheffield and the surrounding area sought to become one of the new mayoral combined authorities and needed to satisfy a statutory requirement to consult. Immediately south of the city lies the town of Chesterfield and as the borough council was keen to join with Barnsley, Doncaster and others to form the new entity, plans were being made accordingly. The difficulty was that Chesterfield lies in Derbyshire, whilst the other places are unitary authorities in South Yorkshire – and Derbyshire County Council was far from convinced that this was a good idea. One of its most important constituent districts was to be hived off and become part of another top-tier council. It could think of a hundred and one reasons to oppose the plans, but when it went to court, it failed on most of them.*

But then the judge's attention was drawn to the relevant question in the survey – upon which, no doubt, Sheffield was perfectly willing to be influenced. He was not impressed, because he found that the public were never asked about the core issue – whether Chesterfield should or should not be part of the new combined authority. In short (and unlike that year's EU referendum) there was no in/out question.

Instead the consultation asked, 'To what extent, if at all, do you agree or disagree that local authorities should work together formally where there are strong economic links with

* R (*ex parte* Derbyshire CC) *v* Barnsley, Doncaster, Rotherham & Sheffield CA, the Secretary of State for Communities & Local Government and Chesterfield BC [2016] EWHC 3355.

neighbouring areas?' The judge called the question 'tendentious', suggesting it was leading respondents to say 'Yes'. He went on to say, 'A "No" to the general concept seems distinctly odd, yet "Noes" there were.' In fact, there were 6,000 of them. He rightly concluded that the question had been designed to act as a proxy for the real question – which was, of course, 'In/Out'.

Over the years, we have seen many similar consultations. Instead of asking residents whether they approve of wind turbines or a solar farm, consultors have asked people whether they support the principle of renewable energy. Rather than seek views on the closure of local health services, patients have been asked if they are in favour of securing better health outcomes. We might as well ask if it rains in west Wales!

There is, of course, a reason why this type of practice persists. It is because consultors try to disguise the fact that certain decisions have, to all intents and purposes, already been taken. Councillors in Chesterfield had apparently agreed to join in with Sheffield and were legally entitled to so. But they had not consulted local people. And they certainly had not consulted the wider population of Derbyshire, who the county council felt would lose power and influence if the planned expansion of the combined authority took place. The key question went unasked because it should have been tabled much earlier, but wasn't. This analysis holds good also for the renewables example.

All this leaves consultees unsure about the influence they can wield, and we would urge them to demand greater clarity. Creating the *right to influence* is about emboldening and empowering them to search for those areas where the consultor is open to persuasion. It might mean that the consultor, in turn, has to exercise its *duty to define* more clearly and to explain and engage better so that ambiguity is reduced to a minimum.

★

This notional framework of duties and rights is intentionally but loosely symbiotic. Clearly, they are inter-related. If the *right to influence* is clearly related to the *duty to define*, so also is the *right to be heard* but a corollary of the *duty to engage*. Similarly, the consultor's *duty to explain* is, in part, a mirror image of the consultee's *right to know*. But by adopting what are essentially simple, but not simplistic, notions, we hope to have gone beyond the ubiquitous sets of principles that public bodies and others routinely adopt and publish as their *modus operandi*.

In one important respect, we have tried to go beyond the legally adopted Gunning Principles. The *duty to engage* fills what we consider to be an important gap, for it might be possible to comply with the four established rules without a single meaningful dialogue with key stakeholders. The *duty to explain* also takes us beyond the requirement that the proposals are well enough articulated to enable people to give them *intelligent consideration*. Above all, we need to give those involved in dialogue a sense of what is needed without being encumbered by the niceties of legal language and the lure of management jargon.

Consultees, in particular, need to feel able to question and put pressure on those who wish to consult them. Many of the current problems arise because consultees have lacked the confidence to make a fuss. Alternatively, those who know the ropes and can pinpoint consultation failures do not wish to compromise their relationship with consultors through criticism just at the point when they need to influence them. We are reminded of the caricature of the patient–doctor relationship where a dissatisfied customer (the patient) fears that if he expresses his displeasure, the supplier (the doctor) will provide an inferior service. It is never quite the right time. As we all know, hospital consultants, even today, carry the aura of clinical omnipotence and, as the tragedy of Mid-Staffordshire revealed, can sometimes be untouchable, even within their own profession. The culture of the expert – at least in this respect – remains.

Less of this deference applies at local levels, but we see it with national and devolved governments and also, sometimes, with regulators. When it matters, however, key stakeholders rush to the courts: in recent years we have seen a challenge by the British Dental Association against a fee increase by the General Dental Council* and an attempt by a clinic that disliked the Human Fertilisation and Embryology Authority's (HFEA) new headline metric to publicise each IVF clinic's performance on its website.† In the dental case, the regulator was clearly at fault and its consultation deservedly lost a challenge that should never have been needed. In the IVF case, the HFEA had observed excellent consultation practice and rightly won its case.

What is wrong is that for those consultees without the resources and the motivation to go to the courts, there is little that they can do bring a poor consultor to heel. Our challenge is to find an alternative to the current unsatisfactory position and a way of embedding good consultation practice into the body politic so that it enhances (some would say 'restores') its reputation whilst delivering a flexible support tool for decision-making.

* R (*ex parte* British Dental Association) *v* General Dental Council [2014] EWHC 4311 (Admin).

† R (*ex parte* Assisted Reproduction and Gynaecology Centre) *v* Human Fertilisation and Embryology Authority [2017] EWHC 659 (Admin).

Chapter 16

Is there a better way?

Judicial review, the disadvantages | adversarial legalism |
dredging Oakland Harbour | fluoride in drinking water |
Public Consultation Act | an Office of Public Engagement |
conciliation, mediation and arbitration | participative
environment | fixing democracy | influence | notional
framework

Throughout this book, we have had to make frequent references to court cases where a consultation process has been challenged. In one way, this is entirely helpful for it illustrates so well the range of situations where consultation is used to support decisions. In another sense, though, it shows the inadequacy of a system whereby the only option available to those who are unhappy with the process is to use the blunderbuss of the law. This is not a trivial problem. We noted earlier that the Geneva-based secretariat of the Aarhus convention* had ruled that the UK did not have sufficiently cost-effective access to justice for environmental campaigners wishing to challenge a consultation on infrastructure projects.

In an attempt to facilitate such cases, groups can now ask the court for an Aarhus cost protection order, which will limit the

---

* See Chapter 3.

liability of claimants. It was used when Friends of the Earth brought a claim against the Welsh Government to challenge its choice of a route whereby the M4 motorway can bypass the notorious and congested Brynglas tunnels at Newport.[*] It was also used to challenge a consultation to support designating the Norfolk Broads as a national park[†] and even in a case involving a housing development in Eastleigh, Hampshire.[‡] The government has since tried to tighten up the rules, but in essence they still enable individuals who wish to mount environment-related claims to do so for as little as £5,000.

For everything else, however, there is an ever-tightening squeeze on judicial reviews. Alarmed at the inexorable rise in numbers, successive law officers have scratched their heads and looked for ways to reduce the incentive to rush to the courts. Actually, the increase is due mainly to immigration cases, but the number of consultation cases has also grown. In 2013, Chris Grayling when Secretary of State for Justice proposed a range of measures that included a prohibition of one public body taking another to judicial review. It was politically maladroit and sank without trace. He got further with a bid to force litigants to disclose their sources of funding, though why this would embarrass those unhappy with a consultation baffled us. Mostly, he relied upon increased fees. When cases are held to be in the public interest, judges have historically had discretion to cap the costs incurred by claimants. The government has now made this subject to statutory

---

[*] R (*ex parte* Friends of the Earth) *v* Welsh Ministers [2015] EWHC 776 (Admin).

[†] R (*ex parte* Harris) *v* Broads Authority [2016] EWHC 799 (Admin).

[‡] R (*ex parte* Botley Parish Action Group) *v* Eastleigh BC [2014] EWHC 4388 (Admin).

provisions, probably in the hope that fewer claimants will benefit and more will be deterred.

In the field of public consultation, the idea of public interest is an interesting concept. In principle, anything that helps us understand what is and is not fair when people are consulted strengthens our democracy. In practice, most of the cases that have gone to court have little to do with public interest. They have been predominantly about the specific interests of a group which disliked a decision or a policy where there happened to have been a consultation. Under the Criminal Justice and Courts Act 2015, cost-capping orders – or the removal of the financial disincentive – can be obtained where there is a strong whiff of public interest. But this is not the only requirement. Firstly, there has to be an *arguable point of law of general public importance*. Secondly, there must be a *public interest in resolving the dispute*. Thirdly, the court must be satisfied that it can be an *appropriate means of resolving* it.

We have looked at dozens of legal challenges, and it is hard to be sure that these tests are being met. There is legal precedent dating from a 2008 ruling* that groups complaining about the closure of hospitals are raising an issue that is wider in scope than their own self-interest. And even the celebrated case on the reburial of King Richard III† was found to be of *general public importance*. But as for the requirement of seeing the court case as an *appropriate means of resolving* the matter? Forget it. Remember that for experienced campaigners, recourse to judges in their wigs and listening to erudite barristers in a court of law is in reality but a sideshow, whilst they focus on winning in the court of public opinion. The law is useful, not necessarily as an arbiter of right or wrong, but

---

* R (*ex parte* Compton) *v* Wiltshire Primary Care Trust [2008] EWCA Civ 749.

† R (*ex parte* Plantagenet Alliance Ltd) *v* Secretary of State for Justice and University of Leicester [2014] EWCA 1662 (QB).

as a theatre in which to expose the inadequacies, if any, of a consultor.

In fact, we can make a case that our courts are probably one of the last places where we should look to settle disputes on consultation. It is a question not just of cost, but also of the nature of the proceedings. Lawyers are able to concoct *ex post facto* arguments that bear little relation to the practical world as the participants knew it when a consultation was planned and implemented. We see cases where the first consultees ever heard that they had expected something was when their barrister argued that they had harboured *a legitimate expectation* of a particular element of process.

Now we understand, of course, that the law quite deliberately seeks to place a citizen's gut feeling of justice into some kind of coherent framework. But we invite readers to plough through some of the more convoluted judgments that have appeared in recent years as judges indulge in semantic somersaults and gyrate verbally to find a formulation that enables them to distinguish one case from another. They rightly loathe inconsistency and will strain every strand of horsehair to demonstrate how their decision in any particular case can be squared with another where the facts were similar – but different. They have no choice; they must work like this for fear that they just provide the next clever barrister with the arguments to show that they created an unintended precedent. It is only too easy to make this an exaggerated critique of the courts, for it probably applies to many branches of the law. But we think it is particularly unhelpful in the field of public consultation.

Besides, the formalities of going to court are themselves a difficulty. For a disgruntled consultee, as much as for a challenged consultor, the timetable of the High Court is a problem. Claimants have to issue their challenge within three months and by the time solicitors are briefed, a letter before action is issued and counsel becomes involved this really means a couple of weeks. But, within three months of what? Mrs Nash lost her case against the London Borough of Barnet* because she had waited for Capita to be granted a contract for outsourcing services, which she claimed should have been consulted upon. The court said that the real decision had been subject to a long implementation phase. On any layperson's interpretation, she was hard done by.

More recently, the London Borough of Haringey was challenged† on its decision to establish a joint venture for housing regeneration. In the teeth of growing political opposition from its own supporters, the Labour administration had ploughed on, and the longer it ploughed the more its opponents turned up unwelcome details it disliked. The financial risk became clearer, the problems of democratic accountability grew, and judicial review became inevitable. The challenge failed. As with Mrs Nash in the neighbouring borough, the challengers were held to be out of time. Had they wished to go to court, the judge declared, they should have done so two years earlier, when the project was first agreed.

Consultees with good arguments feel frustrated. Yet there are reasons for the reluctance to entertain claims in the later stages of projects. Consultors face the debilitating stasis that arises when a decision they believe they have taken quite properly has to be held up pending a court case. It can cost public bodies a fortune. For

---

* See Chapter 7.

† Gordon Peters *v* Haringey LB and Lendlease Europe Ltd [2018] EWHC 192.

developers and promoters of large infrastructure projects, there are eye-watering sums involved. Both sides squander resources they would not have dreamt of devoting to the consultation itself, beavering away, searching for and preparing the evidence they hope will convince the court. No wonder lawyers love it.

Yet courts there must be. They are still the gold standard for dispute resolution in civil or public cases. Their limitations have been recognised for decades and this is why we have had a plethora of tribunals or almost-courts to handle everything from employment grievances to rent assessments. Courts are particularly ill equipped to provide remedies in the 24-hour instant-news culture that is the context for controversial consultations. That a hallful of concerned residents were lied to in a public meeting about their local hospital last night is not a matter that our legal system is easily able to handle. And neither should it be. The system's strengths lie elsewhere, as in its ability to process and consider voluminous and complex evidence.

Nor should there be a legal vacuum. Ours is not an argument to remove courts from the landscape, but instead to devise a framework where other solutions can make recourse to them less necessary. We do so in part because of the cogent arguments of Francis Fukuyama in his seminal work *Political Order and Political Decay*.* His critique of democracy in the United States of America includes reflections on the inexorable rise of litigation: in his words, 'the increasing judicialisation of functions that in other developed democracies are handled by administrative bureaucracies'. He paints a picture of state and federal agencies hamstrung by often-conflicting mandates and procedural requirements that hobble most attempts to do their jobs.

---

* Francis Fukuyama, *Political Order and Political Decay* (London: Profile, 2014).

Another American scholar, Robert Kagan,[*] has coined the phrase 'adversarial legalism' to describe this headlong rush to the courts. He points out that one of the main drivers has been the laudable aim of improving access to justice for previously excluded or disadvantaged groups. In a classic example of unforeseen consequences, granting new rights on a major scale has led to a huge proliferation of legal actions, as, understandably, people seek to exercise these rights. It has led to a system characterised, according to Sean Farhang,[†] by 'uncertainty, procedural complexity, redundancy, lack of finality and high transaction costs'.

As an example, Kagan tells the story of the twenty years it took for the Port of Oakland in California to dredge its harbour ready for the new generation of container ships. Successive plans were challenged and rechallenged. As soon as one interest group was assuaged, another, possibly diametrically opposed to the previous litigant, found the subsequent iteration of the plan objectionable. This kind of beggar-my-neighbour politics predictably results in frustrated, over-cautious bureaucrats desperate to play safe and avoid being the target of the next legal challenge. The Oakland fiasco is, in part, a reflection of the decentralised, fragmented nature of US institutions, notably in the environmental field, but it is also a perfect case study of the perils lying in wait for many decision-making bodies trying to balance conflicting pressures.

---

[*] Professor of Law and Political Science at the University of California, Berkeley.

[†] Attributed to Farhang and quoted in R. Shep Melnick, 'Adversarial Legalism, Civil Rights and The Exceptional American State', in Thomas F. Burke and Jeb Barnes (eds), *Varieties of Legal Order: The Politics of Adversarial and Bureaucratic Legalism* (New York: Routledge, 2017).

In Kagan's case study, these were, on the one hand, the pressing need to accommodate larger ships and to dredge the harbour, and on the other, the growing unacceptability of disturbing and redistributing toxic waste that had accumulated underwater in San Francisco Bay. Or anywhere else. Once the environmental impacts were assessed, water-users in the harbour itself obviously complained. When the harbour board proposed taking the waste out to the ocean, the fishermen and oceanographers objected. When it changed tack again and opted for an inland disposal site, the local water quality panel took issue. That the ultimate decision involved dumping the offending material next to the island of Alcatraz is one of those perfect metaphors whereby the bureaucrats of Oakland were held prisoner by the forces of adversarial legalism and from where there seemed no escape.

That the US malaise is so well understood and documented should provide succour that informed opinion is aware of the dangers, but we see similar trends in the UK. We British are prone to assume that we are immune to the worst excesses of American culture and politics, but the combination of an efficient and socially supported civil society, effective equality legislation and a highly developed law of consultation may propel us towards a similar fate. British bureaucrats and politicians also face strikingly similar conflicts. We want airport runways, but we have simultaneously committed to improving air quality, noise reduction and a cap on carbon dioxide emissions. This has been an almost impossible circle to square; hence an impasse that makes the Oakland Harbour case look reasonably rapid.

Mixed messages handed down from legislators and governments abound. In the NHS, reduced funding is obliging local doctors to weigh up the efficacy of one treatment practice against another, even though they are urged by the National Institute for Health and Care Excellence (NICE) to adopt the more expensive option. In a classic case in the south of England, Hampshire County Council and the city of Southampton were on opposite sides in a row about adding fluoride to drinking water.* The area's health authority found itself trapped by regulations that required them simultaneously to balance the best scientific assessment – add fluoride – with the preference of the local people. This was expressed in a consultation where the majority view was 'We believe in "pure water"'. Not very helpful. One more example. It has taken several decades to seek to find and inaugurate a satisfactory site to dispose of nuclear waste. Again, the hapless managers given this nightmare of a task have to balance scientific evidence against the opinions of local people. Difficult.

It all boils down to how these trade-offs are made and how the socio-political environments in different countries operate in practice. Overt legalism is not a conscious policy choice for the Americans. Its origins lie deep in the US fear of an over-centralised state and the reluctance of the Founding Fathers to impose federal solutions and federal laws. Some might add that individuals with money have become adept at spending it to further their own interests with characteristic enthusiasm. Fundamentally, however, it is the dysfunctional structure of routine policy-making, and the institutional weaknesses that this produces, that leads to the lawyers' tails wagging the decision-making dog.

This analysis makes a powerful case for having strong institutions. Strong enough to have confidence in their processes and methods, so as not to have to defend them every five minutes when a litigant invents or alleges some new inadequacy. It also

---

* R (*ex parte* Milner) *v* South Central Strategic Health Authority [2011] EWHC 218 (Admin).

provides an incentive to find a constitutional and institutional basis for consultation that will make it a more stable part of democracy.

We can accomplish this in different ways. One option is to legislate. This means creating a statutory framework within which formal consultations have to be held. After all, the British system has legislated about public and stakeholder consultations for decades. Just bring them all together. It is not an entirely new concept. Some of the Canadian states have flirted with it and Thailand actually enacted it during its democratic phase before the 2006 *coup d'état*. In 2013, a north African regime, anxious about the Arab Spring, decided it would draft a comprehensive law to organise public participation and sought help from the international agencies and the Consultation Institute. Colleagues who advised them told us that, starting from scratch, an all-embracing statute had many attractions and was probably the only way to ensure a degree of enforcement. There was much interest in the proposals, but it was far from clear how they might work in practice as there was no tradition of public involvement.

Legislation cannot, however, make a society participative overnight. A regular refrain from this book has been the inevitable risks when people consult for the wrong reasons. Doing so simply because a law tells you that you should will soon expose the reality that politicians can usually find a way of corrupting the process or discrediting it. We advised the international client to be modest in its aims for such a new law.

But in Britain, we are not starting with a clean sheet. The plethora of statutory requirements to consult has indeed created a patchwork quilt that could benefit from consolidation. Although many of them, such as successive Planning Acts, cover the duration of consultations, and others empower ministers or departments to make regulations, in general they add little to the quality control of consultations. Unless challenged in a court, most public bodies organising a statutorily prescribed consultation can get away with a perfunctory exercise that does rather little to bring about a truly consultative situation. The case for a Public Consultation Act is, therefore, largely one of standard-setting.

There is little doubt that some of the duties and rights we discussed earlier at length might lend themselves to statutory guidance supported by an Act of Parliament. Consultees would jump at the chance of having a statutory *right to be heard*, or *to influence*. The best among consultors would also be relaxed about the duties we suggested for them, arguing that they were observing these rules anyway. They might well point to the ill-fated statutory *duty to involve* that the Labour administration introduced, only for the Localism Act to repeal. It was a total non-event and a Public Consultation Act could go the same way. We are not quite sure about that, but we acknowledge that it would do little to stem the drift towards legalism; in fact, it might accelerate it.

Imagine therefore, if, instead of just promulgating standards, the Act were to establish a regulatory framework. Let us suppose there was an independent Office of Public Consultation – not unlike the Office of Budgetary Responsibility. The latter came about because of public scepticism and mistrust of economic and financial forecasts from within the Treasury and other government departments. Public engagement faces a similar credibility problem. No matter how hard civil servants, NHS managers or local government officers try, they are viewed as being too close to a preferred solution to organise a consultation that lends itself to a fully open debate. They need a regulator that champions the process and acts as a completely independent rule-maker and problem-solver.

The problem-solving is, of course, quite central to our argument against excessive legalism. In theory, therefore, the Ombudsman process should have addressed this long ago. Originally introduced into the UK in 1967, this long-established Nordic concept has spawned a range of applications. The Parliamentary Commissioner for Administration, to give it its original title, now handles over 6,000 complaints a year – and mounts over 650 investigations, 80 per cent of which are about health. There is also a Local Government Ombudsman with three times the caseload. Very occasionally it is called upon to adjudicate upon issues involving consultations. In 2017, its records show compensation payments being recommended for tenants of Fylde Council, who, declared the Ombudsman, had been deprived of being consulted before their housing complex was sold to a property developer. In 2013, a consultation was ruled inadequate by the Ombudsman on a plan by North East Lincolnshire Council to replace a local swimming pool; a few months earlier, it ruled on Isle of Wight Council's consultation on a management plan for beach huts.

It may be disrespectful to users of pools or beaches to suggest that in terms of public engagement, this is fairly low-level stuff. And the Ombudsman's declaration that these consultations were unsatisfactory did not make the front pages of our national newspapers. But it was a remedy... of sorts. Is this not precisely the form of problem-solving we are seeking? And is not the emphasis that all such Ombudsmen place on mediation exactly what the consultation world needs?

Not quite. Cases such as those we mention are few and far between. Much of this is because a last-resort process cannot meet the need for speed. The Ombudsman process seems primarily geared for clearing the mess after the damage has been done. So many of the issues that arise on consultation are time-critical. Consultees need a form of dispute resolution that takes hours, not months. So much revolves around the terms of a debate and the scope for people or stakeholders to participate. The Local Government Ombudsman does sterling work in seeking to train council officers in the wake of adverse decisions, but again, this is after the event.

So why not widen it? Instead, call it an Office of Public Engagement. It could do much to promote the concept of public participation and involvement, starting in our schools, and also influence the use of social media in consultation practice. It should become the custodian of consultation standards and a disseminator of *best practice*, and should provide recourse for those who complain that a consultation breaches those standards.

Maybe a reasonable model is the Advisory, Conciliation and Arbitration Service or ACAS. In the parallel aspect of its brief, it promotes itself as 'an independent impartial third party to help parties discuss, consider and reflect on their respective positions with a view to reaching an agreement' and typically operates in the areas of individual employment-related grievance-handling or collective disputes on pay or terms and conditions of employment.

There are subtle but important differences in the various approaches ACAS and other equivalent bodies outside the UK can take. *Conciliation* is all about helping parties to a potential or actual dispute explore areas of common ground and test the scope for reaching agreement. *Mediation* is where the independent third party actively engages in an attempt to devise a solution acceptable to the parties. *Arbitration* is where the parties decide in advance to accept a decision taken by an experienced arbitrator, who then makes an 'award'. We are all familiar with the use of these words in the fields of collective bargaining or trade disputes, but there are many disputes and disagreements about a consultation which lend themselves to a similar approach.

Take, for example, the perennial problem of how best to handle the consultation aspects of a major infrastructure project. The law requires a project promoter to sit down with a local authority and hammer out a mutually agreed engagement plan. The developer is usually driven by the need for speed and reasonable cost. Councils are more concerned about public opinion and the need to give people fair representation. A *conciliation* service might indeed have spared those trying to build a major offshore wind farm in the North Sea. There, we saw a long-running failure to agree an engagement plan with the county council, which disagreed with the proposed onshore transmission lines and facilities required to support the farm. There was plenty of controversy, but *conciliation* was nowhere to be found.

In another example, we know of a bitter row between an airport seeking to change the local flight paths and campaigners who did not accept the population forecasts published by the airport to calculate the numbers of people affected by different route options. A skilled mediator might have been very useful in helping the parties work towards a common understanding. As for *arbitration*, we know of cases where a consultation has polarised opinion – on the location of new housing or on the rationalisation of health or other important public services, and where decision-makers could benefit from an expert weighing up the arguments and making a judgement. None of these remedies are easily available today and it is maybe a failure of imagination, courage or both that explains this.

A regulated environment might work like this. First it would be necessary to establish which public consultations would be regulated and which would not. In the event of a consolidating Public Consultation Act, any legislative references to consultation, unless explicitly excluded, would be deemed to fall under the new statute. If no such legislation were passed, then the new independent body would have the power to designate any consultation, whether statutory or otherwise, as a 'regulated' consultation. For certainty, it might be wise to have specified that consultations undertaken pursuant to some of the more obvious statutory provisions would always be designated. Examples might include the relevant parts of the Health and Social Care Act of 2012, or the Planning Act of 2008.

A regulated consultation would have to be registered and properly featured on the Government website. There would also no doubt be a demanding set of regulations as to the publicity and the processes required to ensure that *best practice* is observed. As with all regulation, however, enforcement is the real issue and as many of the difficulties arise 'in flight', so to speak, retaining a sanction for use at the end of a consultation process would be of limited value. It might be an improvement upon a judicial review, which typically happens months after the decision, but a regulator needs a range of tools that can address a sub-standard consultation quickly. In addition to offering *conciliation, mediation* or *arbitration*, an effective regulator would need to be able to arrest the on-going journey to non-compliance and find ways to steer a consultation back onto a defensible path.

The goal, after all, would be to restore consultee confidence, to persuade them that the consultation is not a sham and that it is worth their while to participate. In that sense, this would be similar to consumer protection regulation. The state, through an arm's-length independent body, would ensure that people are not taken for a ride. Its most important attribute, therefore, is credibility and this is why being independent of government would be essential. Some have suggested locating this activity in the experienced, well-insulated arms of the National Audit Office (NAO), but as the NAO has to take a position on controversial issues following an investigation, this may not be the best answer. It would be better to equip the new, powerful Office of Public Engagement with an ability to call ministers to account and interrupt an inadequate exercise. It would be the guardian of the wider public interest, namely the right to be consulted.

There are many advantages to this arrangement. The Office would, for the first time, accord consultation a proper and official status in the democratic process: consultation would no longer be just an administrative device of convenience used in a miscellany of contexts and vaguely undefined. It would replace the spectre of governments publishing and reinventing their own guidance whenever they thought fit and using such changes to make political points to try to differentiate themselves from their predecessors. It would provide a better focus for *best practice*, able to work with industry sectors and relevant institutes to strengthen and improve day-to-day consultations. Alongside universities, it could commission or undertake research into the effectiveness of public consultations. This offers the hope that it could, over time, find more cost-effective instruments for capturing and exploring stakeholder views and public opinion. It would own the definitive consultation database; it would insist on deadlines for feedback.

It would provide a single point of contact and a mechanism for processing complaints against a consultation. It would secure improvements in regulated consultations, but would probably influence non-regulated ones also to get better. If successful, it could de-politicise those consultations seen by some elected representatives as undermining their roles as the conduit of the public will on key policy issues. It might reduce the instances where parliamentarians and others quarrel with the process, if not the substance, of consultation. In short, an Office of Public Engagement could inspire trust in a process that struggles with its credibility. Who could possibly object?

Attractive as this may be, there are some major drawbacks. Regulation's ability to change behaviour depends upon many factors and for all the positive benefits, this might be seen as a bureaucratic burden stifling innovation, an only-too-easy recipient of blame when standards are felt to be inconvenient. 'Oh, we are only engaging you in this way because the regulator tells us that we have to!' Hopefully, common sense would deter anyone with such tendencies but the danger remains.

We once saw proposals from the Civil Aviation Authority (CAA) to overhaul and standardise the process for consulting residents about airspace and flight paths, a subject notorious for the controversy it arouses. The regulator recognised the inevitable inconsistencies in allowing each airport to run its own locally tailored engagement exercises, and wanted to introduce a single online portal to capture and publish citizen responses. Technically, this was perfectly possible, but in terms of local identification with residents, it was a less attractive idea. This is not because one could not configure web pages to look and feel local; of course one could. The problem was in the control exerted from the centre as to what could and what could not be shown. The CAA would have needed to approve the consultation paper, adding another layer of sign-off and delay to the drafting of these complex documents. It would also have deemed what feedback would be disseminated and when. From the centre it seemed perfectly sensible and administratively tidy. From the other end of the telescope, it was seen as a power grab.

Then one thing struck us. These proposals actually enjoyed a degree of support from the airports which might have to consult local people. Why? Because if the plan became truly controversial and if local politicians kicked over the traces, they would have someone else to blame. Never under-estimate the instinct to bask in the good news but point the finger at others when life gets tougher.

That cautionary tale illustrates the perils of centralised regulation and its capacity to make things worse rather than better. One of the benefits of the deregulated consultation environment is that accountability is largely clear. The organisation that consults is normally seen to be in charge, and that is the case even in situations that we have described when others are, most likely, pulling the strings. The Office for Public Engagement would need to be sure that it avoided being a whipping boy for controversies initiated by others; that is doable. What might be less easy is handling mass objections if thousands of complaints were made about a consultation that was contentious. Might the existence of a regulator act like a lightning-conductor and attract to it massive volumes of complaints, as people try to clog up the system as a tactic to force a consultation to be abandoned? How long before public bodies without a clear statutory requirement start ducking and weaving or devise new ways to avoid having to consult? If the standards threshold is too high, might it lead to a retreat from consultation? None of these situations are inevitable, nor unmanageable. They are just risks.

A more regulated environment could well be the way forward and is probably preferable to rampant legalism, or a set of statutory standards. Most attractive of all, however, might be a revolution in the way our political culture views engagement and consultation. Instead of scepticism, might we create a genuine desire for involvement and a positive acceptance that, of the many ways in which it can be undertaken, a formal consultation is one of them? We might call this a *participative environment* and we think there may already be signs that it could happen.

The first thing to note is that unlike the statutory or regulated approaches, a *participative environment* cannot be imposed top-down. It has to be a bottom-up development as it depends upon those who might respond to consultation feeling confident that their efforts are worthwhile. This takes us back to the territory we discussed in suggesting the three rights for consultees. To bring about a sustained change in attitudes towards public consultation, we need a far more extensive programme of education. We probably need a more extensive set of rights, but enclosed within a wider agenda of actions to deepen, enhance and, some would say, rescue our democracy.

Consultation is just one of a range of improvements that are urgently needed everywhere. Fortunately, there are campaigners who are alive to this. We like the work being done by the Democratic Society (Demsoc).* Among its aims are promoting a culture of openness and participation in public services, delivering

---

* Demsoc works for more and better democracy, where people and institutions have the desire, opportunity and confidence to participate together. See http://www.demsoc.org

practical and empowering participatory projects and advocating new and innovative methods of participation. * A parallel movement in Canada, called Democracy Watch,† promotes an agenda that includes '20 Steps towards a Modern, Working Democracy', one of which speaks of creating 'meaningful mechanisms for citizen participation'. ‡ Worldwide, there are dozens of non-governmental organisations (NGOs) pursuing similar ideas and making common cause with thematic campaigns on topics such as the environment or international development, although not all of them are as altruistic as might be supposed and it would be unwise to lump them all together, especially where they are advocating particular ideological, partisan or sectarian solutions.

Bearing that in mind and being cautious about one's fellow travellers, our conclusion is that the enhancement of consultation as a tool of participation is inextricably bound up with the progress of democracy in its many forms. The agenda of the moment will, therefore, differ from country to country. In the UK, many are seriously worried about key aspects of our system, not least the trend towards anti-politics. This is fuelled by the instinct of many people that the 2016 EU referendum result dealt a deserved rebuke to those in power. The disconnect between politicians and the public has already been considered, but maybe we haven't fully recognised an important truth. Consultation will never work well if the public's view of those who will ultimately

---

* 'Better Democracy, Everywhere', Democratic Society website

† Democracy Watch is a national non-profit, non-partisan organisation; Canada's leading citizen group advocating democratic reform, government accountability and corporate responsibility. See htttp://democracywatch.ca

‡ 'Mandate', Democracy Watch website, http://democracywatch.ca/mandate/

340

decide is so jaundiced that they refuse to devote their time and treasure to seek to influence them. Because consultation is about ensuring that decision-makers are better informed of people's views and evidence, it is inextricably linked to the credibility of those decision-makers. Where consultors are agencies with little directly-elected representation, maintaining credibility is a task of managing expectations and demonstrating a consistent track record of responding to stakeholder or public preferences. But where politicians are seen to be those who ultimately decide, the public's attitudes are critical to any chance we have of instilling a degree of confidence in consultation.

Two examples will illustrate the challenge. The EU headquarters in Brussels has a public consultation unit with a remit to open up for popular debate an amazingly wide range of potential or forthcoming policies that the European Commission is pursuing. It faces an almost impossible task. The half-billion population of the EU is so vast that the potential volume of traffic would be immense. Nevertheless it has some success. For example, almost 800,000 people responded to the consultation on the future of the Habitats Directive. The unit is looking for ways to make public participation on policy a less geeky activity and more appealing to the EU's citizens. What it acknowledges, though, is that the impenetrable nature of the Brussels bureaucracy makes it difficult for responders to relate to the decision-making progress, leaving the consultee profile to be dominated by the massive lobbying industry, whose main attribute is, of course, knowing its way around the EU's endless corridors of power.

In contrast, where elected members are ostensibly in charge, it is so easy to blame them for everything. A poignant case in point is the aftermath of the tragic Grenfell Tower fire in June 2017, and the way that pent-up frustrations, and feelings of exclusion and alienation, led to a breakdown of relations between survivors, their supporters and the council. Had the Royal Borough of Kensington and Chelsea suggested a consultation, it would have been told to forget it – but in less polite terms. The fire has, quite rightly, spread alarm through many *communities of interest* and raises questions of technical as well as political importance. What it shows is that there is in Britain an underclass ill served not just by our economy but also by our political system. Formal mechanisms that work well for public bodies to hear the views of educated, organised, articulate stakeholders are hopeless in this environment. In fact there are other excellent ways to hear people and to consult them. However, they are in the toolbox labelled 'political engagement'. If we cannot mobilise them and heal the broken bits of democracy, the vision of that participative environment remains a distant dream.

For the immediate future and without prejudice to a proper continuing debate about the options of legalism, statutory intervention and regulation, we have to turn back to the politicians themselves.

Chapter 17

Dear politician...

Hurrah for public administration | pride in process | help citizens participate | champion public involvement | leverage parliament | saying no | care with referendums | better consultative instincts

Were we writing to politicians, we would probably start by apologising for disturbing them and acknowledging that they probably receive a very large postbag. We might then seek to explain why our particular missive was important and warranted their personal attention, knowing, of course, that in many cases, the exigencies of time and space might oblige them to delegate to someone else in the office.

This is, of course, a significant part of the problem. The pressures on elected members, be it in councils or in Parliament, make the kind of slow-paced deliberation we advocate almost impossible to happen. The helter-skelter race to achieve or to accomplish things in a hurry is responsible for so many of the stories we have described in this book. In any attempt to chart a positive course for public and stakeholder consultations in the future, something has to change.

Politics is not immune from the curse of instant gratification. Maybe it is not a curse? The concept that those who stand for office should deliver on what they promised, within a reasonable time, is perfectly sound. Much of the distaste that follows politicians around stems from a suspicion that perennial procrastination is the stock-in-trade of those who do not wish to take difficult decisions.

What too many of them are yet to discover is the essential skill of making haste slowly. In part, this is due to the pattern of rewards and penalties that currently governs the profession of politics. Securing positive media coverage in a local paper that's credible with a large slice of your electorate is seen by MPs as a 'win'. Earning a reputation as a doughty fighter against the evil intentions of cost-cutting service-reducers will also be a 'win'. Being second best in a television debate with an opponent is a 'lose'. Having an open mind and encouraging consultations on largely unpalatable options sounds like another 'lose'.

In theory, this pattern should only manifest itself if the MP in question has a marginal seat. A thumping parliamentary majority that would be safe from anything short of an electoral earthquake should serve to embolden MPs to work with their consciences rather than with their polling advisers. And since most constituencies in England and Wales are perfectly secure from election to election, surely the win–lose pattern should only apply to a minority. But strange things happen to politicians. Whether through a form of groupthink, or a collective compulsion to seek favourable review for every act of every play they perform on the political stage, they seem to find calm reason and detached thinking so hard. Add to the mix the public relations disaster that was the expenses scandal and one sees why so many believe that politicians talk of the public good, but act on what is in their private interests.

All this may be grossly unfair. In the politicians' defence, we can argue that the reason they behave as they do is to make the changes and achieve the goals they have set. Delays and diversions cost them precious time and arouse suspicions that their words will not translate into deeds. One sees their dilemma, especially if they view a period of consultation as an unnecessary procedural hurdle to overcome. This applies as much to the chair of a local planning committee, wanting to meet that target for new housing build, as to the backbencher determined to turn a Private Member's Bill into law. It cascades to key positions in the civil service, or to senior managers in the public services; they are all *outcome* driven.

If the world was as simple as this and if outcomes were all that ever mattered, life would indeed be straightforward. Shoot for the outcomes; ignore the sniping from the sides and the critics making objections. Just focus on decisive actions, and be prepared to stand or fall by their perceived results when the time comes. A world without public consultation would be honest: no fudges, no concessions, unless they were dictated top-down. It must sound an attractive scenario for some in public life, but of course it cannot be realistic. Seasoned politicians know full well that policy-making and public administration are full of messy compromises and solutions that have to accommodate factors they would prefer to ignore. If you don't consult those who have an interest, they will beat a path to your door anyway. Ultimately, those with power have learnt that they need some form of dialogue. Our question in this last chapter is: what can they do to make that process better?

A reasonable starting point is to acknowledge the inevitability of consultation.

We all benefit from having a system that delays decisions until relevant views have been heard. Those who are most directly impacted obviously benefit. They need reassurance that there are good reasons to take decisions that affect their lives or their interests. The general public also benefit, for they need some way to be sure that competing interests can be assessed and considered. They may also need protection from the power of majorities; a safeguard that assures society at large that important minority interests cannot be disregarded by a legitimate majority. Given their conduct from time to time, some may doubt if politicians perceive these benefits particularly clearly, but we argue that a healthy democracy needs the constant of a sufficiently shared set of values to guarantee stability and command continuing support. In the UK, institutions such as the monarchy, the law, our courts and until recently the Church provided solid pillars of genuine community consensus; they acted as enablers for all manner of legislative, administrative and political initiatives.

As some of these decline in influence, their views can no longer be seen as in-built and part of the system. Rather, their stance on an issue must be deliberately sought, and once that happens, there will be countless others who also feel entitled to be heard. Consultation provides the mechanism for that entitlement. It is part of the sensitive balancing act that enables those within the system and those without to contribute their opinions and argue their case. So, as some of the shared-value consensus weakens or withers, that process of hearing more voices assumes far greater importance.

Politicians understand that a key part of their role is to interpret the mood of the public and to translate it into policy. That is why some will regard consultation as a non-issue. They do it anyway. We have yet to meet an experienced politician who does not claim to know the broad sentiment of their constituents on any matter of importance. They point to weekly visits to their constituency, the procession of people through their surgery and on-going relationships with voluntary and community bodies of all shapes and sizes. A few will also refer to the occasional conviviality in a local pub. Divining public sentiment, however, is a complex process. In the same way that social media now creates highly distorted echo chambers to shield us from ideas we may not wish to hear, there are those who argue that politicians also live in such a 'bubble', which no amount of constituency activism can overcome. Whilst some MPs claim to meet their political opponents on a regular basis, the evidence for this is slight. Moreover, such is the powerful effect of mass media and the internet, one is never quite sure of the extent to which the views you hear at ground level are merely the product of what people have seen or heard. If you loudly proclaim that the widget industry is doing really well, then in the absence of direct personal experience to the contrary, do not be surprised if, when asked, local people will simply confirm the same message.

This means that to the list of institutions that may be declining in public esteem, and here we exclude the monarchy, we should add the traditional assumption that the gut feel of the general public is right on most things. There may be wisdom in crowds, but it is no longer a reliable indicator of how they might behave in a given situation. Depending upon one's point of view, there is a case for saying that both the 2016 EU referendum and the 2017 general election results, not to mention the last decade of performance by the opinion pollsters, testify to greater volatility among the electorate. Politicians who thought they read the runes quite accurately have been taken by surprise at regular intervals.

One explanation is the unpredictability of the political agenda. The exam question changes and devices such as referendums are notorious for asking one question, only for it to be interpreted as something else. Politicians have connived at this. In the Sheffield Combined Authority case we discussed, the question that rightly lost the authority the judicial review was a thinly disguised attempt to avoid asking the real question. Where politicians worry that they may not in fact know what people will say, it is tempting to ask them but steer them towards something palatable. Hence the frequency with which consultees are asked 'Do you agree with us that...?' To this day, we are amazed how few people take offence at this condescending formula. We think it demonstrates an arrogance that is ill suited to a genuine consultative culture.

Politicians can do much to help us towards a more effective culture of consultation. Here are our recommendations.

Help your citizens to participate

The UK, for good or ill, enjoyed a fine reputation for public administration for at least two centuries. Hurrah. To this day there is a continuing procession of politicians, civil servants and officials from across the globe who travel to London for training on our civic institutions and the lessons we have learnt from their operation. A brief look at the website of one of many providers to this international business reveals the immense range of issues which attracts over 160 countries to the UK as a source of advice and learning. Our experience of devolution means that there is also considerable interest in visits to Edinburgh and Cardiff, whilst those wishing to learn about conflict resolution and its application in a power-sharing administration obviously find Belfast a fertile learning environment.

More detailed examination of the courses and workshops that sell well tells us rather more about the UK's perceived USP or 'unique selling point'. People look to the UK for governance models, experience in regulation, our legal system and forms of political accountability. This is mirrored by a well-established two-way interchange of parliamentarians interested in country-specific or issue-based dialogues across international boundaries. The UK universities have almost a hundred departments of politics. Our academics feature prominently in the world rankings. Based on an analysis of European politics departments, Oxford, Cambridge and the London School of Economics and Political Science (LSE) took three of the top four places according to one league table; the UK and Ireland together amounted to 21 of the top 50.* To what extent the UK's prominence as a role-model for mature democratic public administration following Brexit is itself an interesting question, but as things stand, whatever we may think of ourselves, the rest of the world, we can be sure, finds us, shall we say... interesting.

Against this background, it is perhaps a little surprising to find some ambivalence among our politicians towards some of the process elements of our constitution. Everyone is so busy concentrating on the issues that the way we take decisions and the activities that impinge upon policy-making are overlooked. Very few universities have studied our consultative practices. In Parliament, there are all-party groups focused on every conceivable subject, but not, as yet, on public consultation. It is

---

* QS World University Rankings by Subject 2018.

as if our politicians see consultation as an occasionally useful transactional device but not as a key component of a modern democracy; we think that has to change.

It is part of a wider change that affects the relationship between ministers and civil servants, or between councillors and local government officers. The last decades have seen a number of 'big picture' politicians, happy to bask in the publicity their more popular ideas generate, but eager to delegate the interminable details to officials in the hope that no great catastrophe occurs in their implementation. No better example exists maybe, than the laudable wish to remove red tape. It is a plea made to every new Member of Parliament and robustly advocated by influential think tanks like the TaxPayers' Alliance. Embracing such policies is one thing, but devising revised, less onerous forms of administration to cope with this aim is difficult. In time, maybe the Grenfell Tower tragedy will become the definitive case study. Anthony King and Ivor Crewe's study in *The Blunders of Our Governments* has, in any event catalogued a number of relevant examples. There is more than a whiff of 'We're too important to bother with the minutiae of administration; you guys just get on with it'.

Not all politicians have such a disdain for the intricacies of public administration; indeed, many of them come from a background of public service, and take pride in their mastery of bureaucratic processes. However, too few of them have this approach, and most have never bothered to delve into the practical details. We guess that most politicians would struggle as much as judges to run an effective workshop with disabled people affected by consultation proposals to change elements of their care. Might they be better at devising a survey that gave us meaningful insights that would inform and influence a decision? Possibly. Almost everyone we know in public service would profess some proficiency in these tasks. Politicians would make improved use of consultation if they understood it better.

Many in politics would claim to consult well already. They might say it is an instinctive response. Someone comes into your weekly surgery worrying about a new housing development and the classic response is to urge him or her to respond to the relevant consultation. Doubtless, this happens regularly, but we wonder whether the advice comes too late. The housing example is a case in point. The consultation that the constituent probably should have responded to would have been about the overall plan for the local area – possibly two years before. Waiting until a particular planning application arrives may not necessarily be too late, but reduces the chance of having an influence.

We would love to see elected members consciously act as advocates of greater civic participation. They need to act as human conduits to convert the less human, depersonalised forms of involvement that now pervade social media into deeper modes of engagement. Some have claimed that the increased percentage of women in the House of Commons might have accelerated a trend towards greater public involvement. We know of many women, and a few men, who genuinely believe that gender makes a difference in political style, and frequently also in substance. Public engagement has become a predominantly female profession, and the suggestion is that women are temperamentally more consensual in approach, and more willing to absorb and be influenced by the views of others.

We look forward to the day when there might be some robust academic research to support or deny this hypothesis, but, looking back, few would doubt that there have been changes in the political dynamic. Harriet Harman, the former deputy Prime Minister, widely regarded as a trailblazer and campaigner for more women in politics, points out repeatedly that when she entered Parliament, only three per cent of MPs were women, and that male values and male methods predominated. That presumably meant a macho-style 'strong leadership' model, less amenable to the listening and assessing *modus operandi* which women are mostly inclined to favour. The trouble with such generalisations is that cultural shifts occur slowly. Supporters of the Fawcett Society and other branches of the women's movement insist that it is still a man's world and that the UK's two female Prime Ministers reached the top by demonstrating proficiency at the old-style politics, rather than the new female-influenced variety.

For us, the male/female dichotomy – if it exists – seems irrelevant, for the case in favour of politicians championing greater public involvement seems unanswerable whatever gender you are. Would it not be good, for example, if, on an MP's or councillor's website, one could see at the click of a button a list of all the current public consultations to which they felt you might like to contribute? No doubt some might be inclined to be selective. There will always be the possibility that a politician feels strongly that there should be no consultation on a particular subject. But that may be allowable, provided we see a step-change in their willingness to promote consultations in general as a means of being heard.

Some might go further and ask their constituents directly. Our own MP, like others, has regularly canvassed opinions about services of local importance. In *The Art of Consultation* we described his efforts in dealings with the perennial discontent of commuters on the rail route into London. There is no reason why politicians cannot undertake this form of secondary consultation.

'Tell me what you think of the proposals currently being consulted upon, and it will help me formulate my own response.' In principle, this is little different from the chamber of commerce testing the views of local businesspeople on a similar subject

What happens when a politician holds definite views about proposals subject to a consultation? Is it appropriate to encourage participation with a bias towards supporting that viewpoint? In other words, can an MP use the consultation as a campaigning tool? The answer is, sometimes. Politicians promoting a consultation and having such a defined view need to tread very carefully lest they be accused of distorting the debate or otherwise compromising its integrity. It is far better to be cautious and declare a provisional position, adding the rider that a final view will only be adopted when others' opinions have been gathered.

The emphasis should be on the others, reversing the tradition that it is the views of the politician that matters most.

Leverage the power of Parliament

If we want to make our democratic institutions more consultative, we must start with Parliament itself. Attempts to introduce pre-legislative consultation in the British Houses of Parliament were half-hearted and predictably failed. One needs to do more than tinker at the edges. Clearly we need to distinguish between governmental and parliamentary consultations, but members of both Houses have been notably poor at developing their institutions into the listening forums they need to become.

One idea is that for government consultations, there should be a requirement for the relevant ministers to come to the House and table a report on the consultation at its output stage. In effect, a minister would say 'This is what we have heard' and provide fellow parliamentarians with an opportunity to question the statement or to express a view. If it is thought that obliging the whole House to consider every consultation is too onerous, maybe form a special select committee? Such procedural improvements, then, would have many benefits, not least to acknowledge the role of MPs as key stakeholders deserving of such a formal opportunity, and ideally they would be conducted once others' opinions had been obtained and analysed. Contrast this to the current practice where feedback is provided surreptitiously as part of the government's decision on the outcome.

That is if it even bothers to respond. In March 2018 *The Times* conducted a study, examining 1,661 consultations launched by UK ministers since the 2015 general election. It found that two-thirds of them failed to publish feedback within the twelve weeks prescribed in the government's Consultation Principles. A few weeks earlier our attention had been drawn to a consultation launched on 26 October 2015. The government was obviously in a hurry and only allowed thirty-three rather than the customary ninety days to hear people's views. A grand total of thirty-two organisations replied so the task of analysis was not exactly gargantuan. Feedback was finally published on 19 February 2018 – eight hundred and sixteen days after the closing date. And the subject matter? Government policy on 'Late Payments'. So hilarious, we could not possibly have made it up.

Half-completed consultations can lie around Whitehall departments for years. Yet Parliament does nothing to tackle this scandal. In the words of the *Times* editorial that accompanied its story:

> there is nothing wrong with consultation. It is an essential part of the policy-making process. Without it

there would be no guarantee that those likely to be affected by new laws and regulations have a say in their creation. Consultations are useful even if all they do is show that new legislation is not needed. But those that are announced with fanfare only to be shelved, unfinished, are a different matter. They waste money, leave problems to fester and undermine trust in government.*

The general public might be appalled to learn about such failures. With honourable exceptions, journalists who find miscellaneous scandals lurking in parliamentary nooks and crannies have miserably failed to uncover this most obvious flaw in democracy. Even when they get around to it, ministers are too fond of announcing, 'We will do such-and-such, having taken account of the recent consultation.' It makes MPs and others fairly powerless to place their consideration of what people said in their responses under any kind of meaningful scrutiny. A concise, transparent report to Parliament on government consultations of any consequence would assist greatly. We go further. It is time for Parliament to assert itself and demand a greater role in examining the views that have been expressed in government consultations.

There is more. Select committees clearly need funding to conduct their own consultations and we have already described the wholly inadequate attempt to consult on the 800th anniversary of Magna Carta. Parliament should also have a role in the scrutiny of key consultations by executive agencies and regulators, whose activities have a profound impact upon major stakeholders – and of course upon every constituency. It might be possible to devise a form of referral or 'call-in' arrangement that would facilitate

---

* *The Times*, 29 March 2018, associated with research by Paul Morgan Bentley, head of investigations at *The Times*.

355

parliamentary consideration. With or without the suggested Consultation Act or a formal regulator for public engagement, Parliament needs a higher profile in this matter. If it wishes to retain its role as the mouthpiece of the nation, and the fulcrum of debate, important consultations must be considered as part of its routine business.

This means abandoning the cosy 'bubble' in which so many politicians feel comfortable, partly due to being insulated in a cocoon of knowledge which the rest of us do not share. In this context, there are two types of knowledge. Where once parliamentarians' access to *substantive* or issue domain knowledge was a valuable near-monopoly, everyone can now access everything. There is a plethora of information, and too much can be as problematic as too little. The premium is on analysis, and our legislators have far better and routine access to analysis than most of us. The other category of knowledge is *procedural*. This means knowing about political processes and the ways of getting things done. Here those inside the club are still privileged and able to exert influence others can only envy. In a representative democracy that is quite reasonable, but the Open Government movement has rightly blown away the complacency of countries that thought that closed-loop politics can survive.

At the last count seventy-five countries had signed the Open Government Declaration and its four key propositions. The second one is about supporting civic participation and is worth quoting in full:

> We value public participation of all people, equally and without discrimination, in decision-making and policy formulation. Public engagement, including the full participation of women, increases the effectiveness of

governments, which benefit from people's knowledge, ideas and ability to provide oversight. We commit to making policy formulation and decision-making more transparent, creating and using channels to solicit public feedback, and deepening public participation in developing, monitoring and evaluating government activities. We commit to protecting the ability of not-for-profit and civil society organisations to operate in ways consistent with our commitment to freedom of expression, association and opinion. We commit to creating mechanisms to enable greater collaboration between governments and civil society organisations and businesses.

Notice what is missing? Any reference to a parliament. So much of what is fashionable and increasingly popular among civil-society activists can, in theory, bypass a legislature. Parliamentarians who allow this to happen will hasten the day when their role becomes less relevant. To inject themselves into next-generation dialogues on issues of public interest, they have to change their own behaviour and bring Parliament into the debate somehow. In the past, we would have been writing of the need for active citizens to learn how to integrate their activities with the parliamentary timetable and learn the ways of Westminster. Today, it is the other way around. Now it is time for politicians to learn how to integrate their activities into the wider world and the engagement that takes place all around them.

Learn to say 'No'

Yes, we can have too many consultations.

We certainly need more and better stakeholder engagement, but the full-on public consultations along the lines of the models covered in this book are not always necessary. For reasons explored elsewhere, we have burdened the concept with expectations and standards, the enforcement of which poses the challenges we described in the previous chapter. One of the reasons we have so many is that politicians demand them. It is so easy to find reasons to oppose something. Just argue that there should have been consultation, or that such consultation as took place was inadequate.

There are times when politicians should take a step backwards. Recognise that it is unreasonable to require officials to consult where political decisions already taken have made meaningful consultation all but impossible. One of the most frequent complaints we have heard over the years is the lamentation by sincere public servants that the very same ministers as demand consultation were the ones that removed the greater part of their discretion in the first place. No better example can be found than the requirement for local authorities to consult on local council tax benefit schemes, and there is justice as well as irony in the fact that it led to the celebrated Supreme Court judgment that finally endorsed the Gunning Principles.

What we need of politicians is the wisdom to know when stakeholder views will be of some value in influencing their actions, and when they will not. If political parties propose manifesto commitments that are clear and definite, with little scope for amendment if they win, then the case for consultation is weak. Where, however, an integral feature of a proposal needs to accommodate the views of key stakeholders or the general public, then it is strong.

We mentioned earlier the classic case study that is the original introduction of London's congestion charge. Ken Livingstone's manifesto commitment was clear. There would be no consultation on the principle. Everyone knew where they stood. Clarity is all.

Contrast the 2017 general election, in which Theresa May presented a proposal for the funding of social care. It aroused immediate controversy, and within seventy-two hours, her promise to consult on its provisions had to come to her rescue. She announced that a cap on individual contributions would be part of that consultation, and no doubt all eyes will be on that commitment. Sadly for her, the damage had been done. Whatever small print about a post-election consultation may have featured in that original manifesto, the Conservative Party had failed to signal well enough that it wished to be influenced by the public's opinions. It was, therefore, seen as a tactical retreat and clearly damaged her portrayal as a strong and stable leader.

Imagine, however, and admittedly with hindsight, that the proposal had at the outset been couched in more tentative terms. Supposing it had said, 'We are attracted to the idea of x and will hold an extensive consultation before implementing it.' Political opponents might predictably have criticised it as being too vague, but the wider public could have taken a different position. People might have liked being treated as adults, offered a genuine role in determining an important policy. That reaction only happens if consultors are totally and demonstrably honest in their intention. And it must be different from the fudge that amounts to 'We haven't a clue, so we are asking everyone else'.

What politicians seem less capable of doing is offering the public genuinely meaningful choices, and saying 'No' to any consultation if there are no such choices. The sequence of policy-making we described in Chapter 9 demonstrates how ministers' or officials' room for manoeuvre can vary. There is a case for saying 'No' to consultation if it is obvious that it will have little or no impact at that point in the cycle.

This might mean forgoing a consultation when one set of options arises because the public cannot be given the full picture until more work has been done. Imagine a proposal to bypass a small village. All well and good – so proceed to a consultation. But supposing the route would be influenced by decisions yet to be taken about a significant new housing development. Is it best then to wait until the wider picture is clear? Have no doubt that politicians will be under pressure to concede some form of consultation – whether or not under planning laws. If they say 'Yes', the exercise may flounder because of significant uncertainties. If they say 'No', active citizens will complain that they are denied an opportunity to have their say. Politicians cannot win.

Except they could, of course, if our overall planning was better. A piecemeal approach to social and spatial infrastructure has bedevilled our body politic for years. The NHS provides many examples. In 2017 one of the most controversial hospital reconfiguration stories in England was the rearguard action by campaigners to salvage a consultant-led midwifery unit at the Horton Hospital, Banbury, in Oxfordshire. Prominent support from local Conservative MPs failed to persuade Oxfordshire Clinical Commissioning Group to keep this unit open, and the case eventually went to the High Court.* Part of the argument was that the relevant consultation only focused on part of the overall

---

* Cherwell DC *v* Oxfordshire CCG [2017] EWHC 3349 (Admin).

plan for the future of this hospital. NHS managers had already promised a more far-reaching consultation, scheduled for the following year. Lawyers sought to persuade the judge that this would be in breach of the second Gunning Principle. How could local citizens have enough information about the future of their health services, if that wider picture was not available? Mr Justice Mostyn disagreed and found in favour of the NHS, but within weeks, the Independent Reconfiguration Panel was obliged to advise the Secretary of State that splitting the consultation into two had been a mistake.* Politicians should have said 'No'.

Such piecemeal exercises are asking for trouble. A step-by-step approach is attractive to politicians eager to be seen to be doing something, but adds to the confusion if the broader strategy remains obscure. It is surely like attempting a jigsaw puzzle with only a few of the pieces to hand and no access to the overall image. Better leave it in its box.

Take care with referendums

Given all we have said about the case for consultation, it feels almost counter-intuitive to argue against a device that is, at first glance, undoubtedly democratic, undeniably participative and popular among a large part of the population who may have never heard the term 'public consultation'. However, the weaknesses of referendums are not a recent discovery and their limitations have been recognised for a long time. Clement Attlee† is famous for having dismissed them as an alien device because they had been the 'instrument of Nazism and fascism'; in the immediate post-war context, this might not have been unreasonable. The truth is

---

* Independent Reconfiguration Panel, letter to Rt Hon. Jeremy Hunt, 9 February 2018.

† Labour Prime Minister 1945–51.

that referendums have been used for causes good and bad for generations. Our task, however, is not to be side-tracked by the substantive issue but to assess objectively whether a referendum is a satisfactory mode of consultation.

There are, of course, two types of referendums: those that are consultative and those that are decision-making. The first category assumes that the power to take decisions rests firmly in the hands of whatever body has called the referendum, and is a natural choice if legislatures are consciously trying to take account of public opinion in reaching for a solution to intractable problems. The referendum held in Northern Ireland in 1998 is a clear case in point. It was mostly intended to gather support for the Good Friday Agreement, and give it a demonstrable legitimacy. The same applies to the devolution referendums held in Scotland and Wales, first in 1979 and subsequently in 1997. In all these cases, no one pretended that the vote was the end of the matter, though they were obviously intended to have a decisive influence on the debate in Parliament, whose ultimate jurisdiction over the issue was acknowledged.

Traditional enthusiasts for representative democracy still feel queasy about such initiatives. They fear the erosion of its fundamental principle, but grudgingly concede, at least for the regional or national votes, that an all-UK Parliament might not adequately absorb the strength of feelings about their relevant interests. More tellingly, they worry that a single question, at a single point in time, carries risks that public opinion can be captured by brilliant campaigning and media manipulation, with a potentially eccentric result. As Quintin Oliver,* one of Europe's

---

* Quintin Oliver ran the 'Yes' campaign for the referendum on the Good Friday Agreement re Northern Ireland in 1998. He is director of Belfast-based Stratagem International and is also chair of the Consultation Institute.

leading referendum gurus, comments, 'They permit of no shades of grey; "No, unless…" or "Yes, if…" cannot appear on a ballot paper.'

Sometimes a debate can be hijacked, and shift to an unintended or peripheral area of policy. Critics point to the far-reaching technical, socio-economic and political consequences of some of the propositions that people wish to subject to a referendum. If traditionalists object that those who vote may have only the most tenuous grasp of the relevant issue, they are immediately branded as arrogant elites who cannot trust the great British (or Scottish, Welsh or Northern Irish) public to answer a simple question. To which the representative democracy champions will respond that 'there are no simple questions'.

Indeed, the simpler they look, the more complicated the underlying issues might be. The European Commission for Democracy through Law, known as the Venice Commission, acknowledged this in 2006 and produced a Code of Good Practice.* It is a useful, technical manual but cannot hide the political dilemmas inherent in this form of consultation. Who can disagree with its assertion that 'the question put to the vote must be clear; it must not be misleading; it must not suggest an answer'? The same can be said of all consultations.

In practice, and for a great number of parliamentarians, the role of a referendum has become a means of giving them a mandate to proceed in a particular way. Constitutional change is regarded as the kind of issue where this is appropriate. 'Say "Yes" in a referendum, and we will implement the devolution arrangements that we hammered out in Parliament.' In the case of the Scottish

---

* Council of Europe Study No. 371/2006, adopted by the Council for Democratic Elections in December 2006 and March 2007.

devolution referendum of 1979, Parliament had imposed a requirement for a super-majority, by insisting that 40 per cent of the entire electorate should vote 'Yes' for devolution to go ahead. The case for super-majorities is to guard against low turnouts and to minimise disputes about the true level of continuing support for particular policies. For consultative referendums, where the ultimate decisions are made by elected representatives, this seems reasonable enough. It so happened that the first Scottish devolution referendum resulted in a victory for the 'Yes' campaign by 51.6 per cent to 48.4 per cent – numbers that will resonate with many readers* – but only 32 per cent of the total electorate had voted 'Yes'. With a 64 per cent turnout, broadly similar to that achieved in British general elections, the arithmetic was that, to succeed, the pro-devolution campaigners needed to achieve a 63 per cent vote in their favour.

In theory, the UK cannot have a decision-making referendum as we have parliamentary sovereignty, and it is Parliament that wields ultimate power. For the 2011 referendum on the general election voting system in the UK, something different was tried. The minority Liberal Democrat coalition partner needed guarantees that its long-cherished wish for voting reform would be implemented if the referendum gave the green light. The Coalition Agreement even stipulated that both the Conservative and Liberal Democrat front benches would issue a three-line whip to confirm the move to the Alternative Vote system had it been approved in the referendum. In the event the respective whips' offices were not troubled, as the proposition was roundly defeated by a large majority.

---

* They are almost identical to those in the 2016 EU referendum: 51.9 per cent Leave, 48.1 per cent Remain.

In the meantime, the UK has become more familiar with local referendums, notably on neighbourhood planning and whether or not to have mayoral authorities, exciting no-one in particular. For years also, councils have had powers to consult their residents right down to parish polls. Occasionally there is controversy. When the police and crime commissioner for Bedfordshire ran out of any other ideas to address what he felt was the chronic under-funding of the local constabulary, he organised a referendum. Council taxpayers were offered the opportunity to pay more, in order to appoint more police officers. The commissioner duly lost but complained that the question was rigged in favour of the 'No' vote.

The wording of the question in a referendum has always exercised academics and becomes critical to anyone who loses narrowly. The original question, as drafted for the 2016 EU referendum, was phrased 'Should the United Kingdom remain a member of the European Union?', inviting a straightforward 'Yes'/'No' response. This was unacceptable to many who wanted to leave the EU, who argued that it was biased against them. They wanted a different question, using the same words but adding 'or leave the European Union', thereby creating the two options of Remain or Leave. They had polling evidence from ICM* suggesting that the former question led to a 59 per cent Remain vote but that the figure was reduced to 55 per cent when the question was changed. The Electoral Commission agreed with them and the latter formulation was adopted. In the light of the eventual result, we

---

* The polling company ICM is quoted by *The Guardian* in June 2015 as having published a technical paper following tests on alternative referendum questions. This was further referenced by the Electoral Commission in its September 2015 'assessment' of the proposed referendum question.

can appreciate the controversy that still rages over this important but critical detail.

That debate will probably continue, for the case against referendums is that they do not always settle matters and in many cases they make them worse. Far from assisting the development of consensus, fierce campaigns on issues that really concern people tend to expose the divisions in society. The Good Friday Agreement and UK devolution referendums may be exceptions in that they heralded an acceptance of new realities. In general, however, referendums are prone to highlight disagreements and can provoke protagonists to seek to defend their corners more aggressively. They may well be a safety valve to prompt a decision where elected politicians are seen to be vacillating, but catapulting a particular issue to the top of the agenda carries huge risks.

In consultation terms, the biggest risk is *scope drift*. Asking people about one issue leads to it spreading to peripheral topics in an uncontrollable way. What starts out as one precisely defined issue, through a process of dialogue and debate, becomes all things to all people. The result can then be instantly challenged on the grounds that votes were cast on matters well beyond the intended subject matter of the question. A general election is different. Its scope is, by definition, wide enough to cover everything remotely to do with government. The whole point of a referendum is to ask a precise question, so any departure from it will become a matter of controversy. Those who disliked the outcome of the EU referendum in Britain will argue that what began as a question about membership of the European Union became an opportunity to vote for more money for the NHS. One side argues that this is a reasonable extrapolation of the case for saving money by leaving the EU; the other sees it as a monumental digression on the basis of a purely speculative hypothesis.

366

Constant recapitulation of these well-worn arguments advances neither cause with honour but will continue, for few referendums are free of allegations of *scope drift.*

In contrast, public consultations have an in-built safeguard that prevents such changes of agenda from affecting the ultimate decision. With consultation, the eventual decision-makers can conclude that arguments that are *ultra vires** can be set aside in the final decision-making. Veteran pro-European parliamentarians, such as Kenneth Clarke MP, hated the whole idea of an EU referendum, but would probably have been content had Parliament preserved for itself the right to decide, once it had heard the result. It is this that made the legal challenge mounted by Gina Miller† so important, for the Supreme Court confirmed what constitutional experts had asserted, namely that Parliament cannot delegate its authority to change the law under these circumstances.

Britain's problem with the EU referendum is that, in reality, it was a consultative exercise, but was presented to the public as an exercise in collective decision-making. All parties connived at this misrepresentation. They mostly assumed that they were on the winning side and that the best way to maximise the turnout of their supporters was to persuade them that, on this occasion, theirs was the final say. It suited everyone, and created the expectation that, whatever occurred, the government would be bound by the result. There was no super-majority and nothing to prevent a definitive decision by the slenderest of conceivable margins. In many people's eyes, Parliament and politicians

---

* Latin term meaning 'beyond the powers'.

† R (*ex parte* Miller) *v* Secretary of State for Leaving the European Union [2017] UKSC 5, decided by the Supreme Court; a case of constitutional significance in deciding the scope of the royal prerogative in foreign affairs.

connived in the greatest act of constitutional negligence in the country's history. At least the 52 per cent that voted to leave rejoiced in the outcome.

In summary, consultation is overwhelmingly a product of the expectations that are created. To work well it needs to reflect political realities and be designed to engage with those most affected. Unfortunately, politicians are not sufficiently sure-footed. They are ambivalent in their aims, and partisan in their preferences. Their decisions of when and how to consult have frequently been criticised, and nowhere has their judgement been more questioned than on referendums. Excepting local and routine exercises, referendums are best viewed as akin to a nuclear option, held in reserve and used as a deterrent. Because they are capable of unpredictable consequences unless handled with utmost care, wise politicians need to think carefully before using them.

Develop better consultative instincts

At its heart, public consultation is an art, not a science. No amount of statistical analyses or demographic profiling displaces the judgement calls that politicians sometimes have to make about the way they engage the public.

We have heard the phrase 'political nous' used to describe mature instincts that direct a politician towards wise choices. It is not the same as 'political intelligence', for we all know of brilliant people accused of lacking common sense. What matters in politics is the ability to see further ahead, to anticipate the potential for success and the risk of trouble. The best politicians may well be those who instinctively know when a public consultation makes sense, and when it does not. Sometimes it is glaringly obvious, but too late. In early April 2018, the Secretary of State for Wales, Alan Cairns MP, announced with undiluted pride that from the summer the second of the two road bridges that span the Severn Estuary would henceforth be called the Prince of Wales Bridge. What was uncontroversial to the east aroused instant hostility to the west. Plaid Cymru* denounced it as an April Fool joke, albeit five days late! Thirty thousand people signed a petition. Clearly it had not crossed the minds of anyone in London that this gesture should have warranted a public consultation. It reminded us of the failure of ministers to consult as to whether to rebury King Richard III in Leicester rather than York.† In both cases politicians failed to grasp the seriousness with which people view identity and allegiances. It was the same when football clubs abandoned much-loved names for their stadiums to carry the brand of far-flung airlines or overseas footwear manufacturers.

Those with political nous would have seen this coming. They would have realised that in this situation, they are on a hiding to nothing; there will always be those who disapprove. Holding a consultation, however, gives them a form of defence. It would have cost them little to have opened it up for debate. So why not?

We have a theory. Maybe they were influenced by the experience of the National Environment Research Council (NERC) when it consulted on the name for its new Antarctic survey ship? It is now known as the RSS *Sir David Attenborough*, but some readers may fondly remember that most of the consultation responses favoured the name *Boaty McBoatface*.

For all those who have long suspected that politicians take themselves too seriously it is a lovely story from which to

---

* The National Party for Wales.
† See chapter 3

conclude that occasionally it might benefit them to share the public's sense of humour. Australia has its own version of this; a Sydney Harbour ferry proudly displays the name *FerryMcFerryface*. Did not the Italians vote in large numbers for Beppe Grillo, who was a noted comedian?*

True empathy with the mood of the public helps politicians gauge when, how and what to ask. Consultation is frequently a bellwether of public sentiment and those with the most finely developed political antennae can often judge whether the public might feel pleased, enthused, confused or downright appalled by being asked its opinions. That is what makes it an art.

---

* See Chapter 9.

Last words

Since we began this book, there have been momentous events in British politics, including the decision to leave the European Union. In itself, the EU referendum was the largest, most visible exercise in public participation on a meaningful political issue since the Second World War, surpassing any general election in terms of its likely consequences. Those of us who have championed the principle and practice of public consultation winced at some of the abuses and distortions we saw as the debate unfolded. Then after the vote, we worried about the troubling sentiments released as the more uninhibited winners and losers let rip at each other and blamed the other side with vitriol and vehemence. Was it enough, perhaps, to make us think again? Should we maybe reconsider years of advocacy for public consultation?

Well, actually, no! If poor consultations or consultations leading to poor outcomes were going to diminish our enthusiasm, it would have happened years ago. The fundamental mechanism of consultation is sound; the problem has been its implementation. Because it relies upon an assumption that decision-makers who instigate consultation have the moral, legal or political authority to act, it can only be as good as the integrity of its instigators allows. Realistically, it cannot of itself be a tool of revolutionary upheaval. It is therefore unattractive to those who wish to supplant existing power structures in a radical way. What it can do, however, is bring those with decision-making power face-to-face with the views of those whose lives or interests they affect.

A colleague attended a meeting in Scotland, where *co-production* and *participatory budgeting* are all the rage. He heard someone remark that 'consultation is so 1980s', meaning, we think, that the process was now distinctly inferior to more participatory methods. Indeed, those methods all have a place in a world of greater public engagement but they themselves have limitations. When well organised, consultation can engage far more people and reflect more diverse interests than many of the alternative methods.

A decade ago, we were told that consultation was an Anglo-Saxon concept mostly unknown outside the Commonwealth and parts of the USA. Today, it is embraced by the World Bank, the European Bank for Reconstruction and Development, the European Union, the United Nations and most institutions with an interest in strengthening governance and democracy. For many countries, it is alien to their political traditions so the learning curve is steep and challenging. For others, including the UK, the task is to convert what Sherry Arnstein may well have been right to label as tokenistic many years ago into something positive and meaningful today.

Britain has many claims to be the world leader in consultation, but others are catching up fast. Its unique advantage is that English common law, with the status it still enjoys worldwide, has given us a body of jurisprudence that forms an excellent foundation. It supports learning how to apply the rules in so many different spheres of human life. It also helps professionals observe sensible standards and apply them honestly to a wide range of situations. Without knowing this, ultimately one cannot enforce the integrity of a consultation, and citizens and stakeholders can only have limited confidence that their voices will be heard. Our ideas for enhancing *best practice* further with new, more demanding duties for consultors and rights for consultees only work if judicial remedies are there to help change behaviour.

In one sentence, this book claims that consultation is a remarkably powerful idea. When done well, it improves policy-making and decision-taking. Politicians are yet to learn how best to use it, and they need to overcome their temptation to manipulate and misuse it. But the coming years will, no doubt, provide them and all of us with the opportunity to develop and enhance the concept and place it firmly at the heart of democracy.

About the Authors

Rhion H. Jones

Rhion is Founder Director of the Consultation Institute. He studied law for six years but opted for a career in various sectors of industry, which eventually led him to the world of consultation and public engagement. A prolific writer, he has over 350 topic and discussion papers to his name as well as *The Art of Consultation*, published in 2009, jointly authored with Elizabeth Gammell. In 2017 he was the recipient of a Lifetime Achievement Award from the Association of Healthcare Communications Managers. His other interests include travel, music, books... and politics!

Elizabeth A. Gammell

Elizabeth's early career was in teaching, which was overtaken by motherhood. She returned to work in the world of public affairs. This interest made a natural affinity with the aims of the Consultation Institute, of which she has been a Director since its creation in 2003. She was joint author, with Rhion Jones, of *The Art of Consultation*, and she has developed, designed and delivered more than forty training courses on all aspects of consultation and public engagement. Her other interests include singing, conducting, skiing... and knitting for her small grandsons.

Index

38 Degrees, 214

A

Aarhus convention, 32–33, 321–22
academy schools, 144
Acts of Parliament
  Care Act 2014, 164
  Criminal Justice and Courts Act 2015, 323
  Equality Act 2010, 33–34, 37, 45, 54, 55, 146
  Health and Social Care Act 2001, 109
  Health and Social Care Act 2012, 178, 335
  Human Rights Act 1998, 39
  Town and Country Planning Act 1947, 69
  Welfare Reform Bill, 311
Advisory, Conciliation and Arbitration Service (ACAS), 333
Airports
  Edinburgh, 271, 277
  Gatwick, 95, 237
  Heathrow, 27, 85, 95–97, 237
airspace, 96, 271, 277, 281, 337
Amnesty International, 217
appreciative inquiry, 283
Arnstein, Sherry, 60, 372
Art of Consultation, The, xiii, xv, 13, 25, 352
asset-based community development, 222

asymmetry of expertise, 22, 235
Attenborough, Sir David, 169, 369
Audit Commission, 163, 184
Avaaz, 214

B

badger-culling, 254, 255
Bailey, Julie, 107
BBC, 71, 80, 190, 263
Belfast, 9, 70, 130, 349
Best Value, 33, 167–68
Big Conversation, The, 204
Blunders of Our Governments, The, 22, 148, 235, 350
bovine tuberculosis, 253
Brown, Archie, 175
Brussels, 10, 12, 231, 341
Budge, Alan, 159
Bullock, Professor Alan, 248

C

Carnegie, Dale, 309, 312
Change.org, 214
Child Support Agency, 22
Civil Aviation Authority, 235, 337
civil service, 16, 44, 112, 149, 175, 189, 345
Clientelism, 243–44
climate change, 19, 253
Committee for Standards in Public Life, 84
communities of interest, xi, 105, 222, 303, 342
community intelligence, 157

Compact, the, 18–19, 44, 46, 47, 186–87, 189, 218
congestion charge, 20, 359
Consultation duties and rights
consultee right to be heard, 50, 217, 300–309, 312, 318
consultee right to influence, 309–19
consultee right to know, 187, 294–300, 318
consultor duty to define, 275–78, 318
consultor duty to engage, 284–90, 294, 318
continuous engagement, 111–12
co-production, 126, 128, 165, 222, 249, 269, 315, 372
council budgets, 162
council tax, 7, 29, 311, 358
Crewe, Ivor, 22, 27, 32, 148, 149, 199, 350
Cuomo, Mario, 260, 261
customer challenge groups (CCGs), 225–26, 227

D
Davies, Howard, 96
Davis, Evan, 282
decision avoidance, 26
deliberative polling, 158, 264
democracy, xi, 6, 12, 62, 169, 175, 194, 201, 209, 252, 256, 259, 260, 262, 263, 293, 302, 303, 323, 326, 330, 339, 340, 342, 346, 350, 355, 356, 362, 363, 372, 373
Democracy Watch, 340
Democratic Society (Demosoc), 339

devolution, 7, 153–56, 348, 362, 363–64, 366
direct democracy, 214, 255–57
discrimination, 33, 56, 356
due regard, 34, 37, 45, 53–54, 56, 146

E
echo chambers, 266–67, 347
electoral cycle, 199, 202
Environment Agency, the, 88, 99
equality analysis (EA), 34
equality impact assessment (EIA), 34, 54
EU referendum, 158, 161, 202, 255, 265, 340, 347, 365–66, 366, 367–68, 371
European Commission, 261, 341, 363
evidence-based policy-making, 15, 86, 269

F
fake news, 268–69
Farhang, Sean, 327
Fawcett Society, 352
Francis QC, Robert, 107
Fukuyama, Francis, 326

G
Good Friday Agreement, 62, 362, 366
Government Consultation Principles, 46, 186, 354
Government Departments UK
Department for Digital, Culture, Media and Sport, 243

Department of Business, Enterprise and Regulatory Reform, 185–86
Department of Communities and Local Government, 83, 87, 99, 161
Department of Education, 36, 174, 187
Department of Health, 52, 64, 107, 109, 121, 127–28, 133, 134, 241, 296
Department of the Environment, Food and Rural Affairs, 66, 254
Department of Transport, 205–6, 229–30
HM Treasury, 165, 169, 331
Ministry of Defence, 76
Government Guidance on Consultations, 148, 182
Grenfell Tower, 5, 341
Gunning Principles, 39–43, 46–50, 53, 56, 110, 129, 140, 144, 155–56, 189, 274, 278, 280, 284–85, 318, 358, 361

H
Habitats Directive, 296, 341
Healthwatch, 108, 115, 138, 225
housing, 25, 72–77, 79–80, 294, 325, 351

I
infrastructure planning, 84, 90
Ingham, Bernard, 264
Ipsos MORI, 166

J
Judicial Reviews
An Taisce v Secretary of State for Energy, 89

Assisted Reproduction and Gynaecology Centre v Human Fertilisation and Embryology Authority (HFEA), 319
Bracking v Secretary of State for Work & Pensions (Equality), 53, 274
Branwood v Rochdale (Equality), 53, 274
Breckland v Boundary Committee for England, 279–80
British American Tobacco & others v Secretary of State for Health, 238–42
British Dental Association v General Dental Council, 319
Brown v Sec of State for Work & Pensions (Equality), 53, 274
Daws Hill v Wycombe DC, 76–77
Derbyshire County Council v Sheffield Combined Authority, 316–17, 348
Flatley v Hywel Dda Local Health Board (Prince Philip Hospital, Llanelli), 139–40
Friends of the Earth v Welsh Ministers (Newport M4 Relief Road), 322
Greenpeace v Secretary of State for Trade & Industry, 21, 43, 184
Gunning v London Borough of Brent, 39, 284

Harris v (Norfolk and Suffolk) Broads Authority, 322

Hurley and Moore v Secretary of State for Business, Innovation & Skills (Tuition Fees), 146

Kendall v Rochford District Council, 77–79

London Oratory School v Schools Adjudicator, 145

Luton & other Councils v Secretary of State for Education (Building Schools for the Future), 36

Milner v South Central NHS, 329

Moseley v London Borough of Haringey, 8, 311

Nash v London Borough of Barnet, 168, 325

Partingdale Lane Residents Association v London Borough of Barnet, 41–42

Peters v London Borough of Haringey, 325

Plantagenet Alliance v Secretary of State for Justice & Leicester University, 37–38, 323

Royal Brompton Hospital v The Joint Committee of Primary Care Trusts, 128–30

Save our Surgery Ltd v Joint Committee of Primary Care Trusts, 129

W v Birmingham City Council, 44–45

Whitston v Secretary of State for Justice (Asbestosis), 188–89

K

Kagan, Robert, 327–28

King, Anthony, 22, 27, 32, 148, 149, 199, 350

L

legitimate expectation, 35–38, 56, 324

libraries, 156, 164, 198, 314–15

lobbying, 10, 74, 198, 223–25, 341

Local Authority

Bedford Borough Council, 88

Birmingham City Council, 44

Breckland District Council, 279

Buckinghamshire County Council, 76

Central Bedfordshire Council, 88

Cornwall County Council, 151

Derbyshire County Council, 316, 317

Fylde Council, 332

Hampshire County Council, 329

Health and Wellbeing Boards (HWBs), 115–16, 138, 178

Lincolnshire County Council, 198

local authority devolution, 7, 153–55

London Borough of Barnet,
41, 166
London Borough of Brent,
39
London Borough of
Haringey, 8, 311, 325
North-West Norfolk District
Council, 82
Rochford District Council,
78
Sheffield Combined
Authority, 348
Shropshire County Council,
151
Wycombe District Council,
76

N

National School of
Government, the, 147, 196
neighbourhood planning, 61,
74–76, 77, 365
NHS
accountable care
organisations (ACOs), 124
clinical commissioning
groups (CCGs), 103, 116–
17, 118–20, 121, 122–23,
136, 178
commissioning support units
(CSUs), 118–20
General Practitioners (GPs),
103, 120, 121, 122
Independent Reconfiguration
Panel (IRP), 128, 134–35,
220, 361
Joint Strategic Needs
Assessment (JSNA), 115

National Institute for Health
and Care Excellence
(NICE), 329
NHS England, 113, 114–16,
122, 123, 272
NHS Hospitals
Evelina Children's
Hospital, 127, 129
Great Ormond Street
Hospital, 127, 129
Horton Hospital,
Banbury, 360
Kendal Hospital, 131
Leeds Infirmary, 129
Lewisham Hospital, 52–
53, 137–38
Llanelli Hospital, 140
Mid-Staffordshire
Hospital, 5, 107
Royal Brompton Hospital,
127, 128–29
Royal Devon and Exeter
Foundation Trust, 110
Vale of Leven Maternity
Service, 132
Withybush Hospital,
Haverfordwest, 132
**NHS Patient and Public
Involvement**
Commission for Patient
and Public Involvement
in Health (CPPIH),
104, 108, 109
Community Health
Council (CHC), 103–4,
105, 106, 108, 109
expert patients, 125
Friends and Family Test,
300

health overview and scrutiny committees (HOSCs), 104, 135–37

Local Involvement Networks (LINks), 105–7, 108

patient participation groups (PPGs), 121–22

public and patient involvement forums (PPIFs), 103–5, 104–5, 106, 107

Scottish Health Council, 108

NHS Regulators

Care Quality Commission (CQC), 113, 114, 116

Monitor, 113

NHS Improvement, 113, 114, 116

Trust Development Authority, 113

primary care trusts (PCTs), 117–18, 120

Stevens, Simon, 122–24

Sustainability and Transformation Partnerships, 123, 139

P

Parliament UK

House of Commons, 110, 272, 351

House of Commons Health Select Committee, 117, 124

House of Lords, 189

House of Lords Secondary Legislation Scrutiny Committee, 29, 187

Houses of Parliament, 29, 353

Public Accounts Committee, 149

select committees, 18, 94, 154, 176, 177, 303, 304, 355

Parliamentarians

Adebowale (Lord) 147

Allen, Graham, 176

Attlee, Clement, 259, 361

Benn, Tony, 195

Bevan, Aneurin, 71, 102

Bichard (Lord) 187

Birt (Lord) 280

Blair, Tony, 18, 21, 46, 84, 103, 182, 184, 264

Cairns, Alan, 369

Cameron, David, 21, 202, 262, 281

Campbell, Alastair, 264

Carswell, Douglas, 214

Clarke, Kenneth, 367

Clegg, Nick, 21

Corbyn, Jeremy, 6, 195

Farage, Nigel, 6, 261, 263

Findlay, Neil, 271–72, 273

Gove, Michael, 36

Grayling, Chris, 50, 322

Greening, Justine, 27

Harman, Harriet, 352

Hoare, Simon, 272

Hodgson, Dave, 87–88

Hunt, Jeremy, 240, 241

Johnson, Boris, 6, 96, 265

Kelly, Ruth, 213

Lamb, Norman, 272

Lansley, Andrew, 9, 103, 109, 116, 120, 178

Letwin, Oliver, 46, 186, 188, 191
Livingstone, Ken, 20, 359
Redwood, John, 195
Rifkind, Malcolm, 224
Salmond, Alex, 21
Spelman, Caroline, 67, 215
Straw, Jack, 224
Sturgeon, Nicola, 6
Thatcher, Margaret, 4, 73, 103, 264
Whittingdale, John, 190
Wollaston, Dr Sarah, 124

Political Parties
Democratic Unionists, 62
Scottish Nationalist Party (SNP), 65, 161, 202, 277
The Conservative Party, 21, 37, 73, 74, 83, 86, 117, 204, 214, 262, 359
The Green Party, 277
The Labour Party, 36, 203–4, 262
United Kingdom Independence Party (UKIP), 83
pre-determination, 40, 42, 44, 48, 276
protected characteristics, 34–35, 54
Public Consultation Act proposal, 331–32, 335
public consultation hearings, 303–9

Public Consultations
BBC Charter Review Public Consultation 2015, 190, 228–29, 234, 242, 301
Bodelwyddan housing, 80–81

Bristol City Council, 158–59
Building Schools for the Future, 36–37
Edinburgh Airport, 271, 277
EirGrid Transmssion lines, 91
Evelina Children's Hospital, 127–30
Forestry Commission, 66
fracking, 98–99, 236–37
gambling - fixed-odds betting terminals, 242–43
High Speed Two (HS2), 85, 91, 93–95, 232, 282, 301, 314
Hinkley Point Nuclear Power station, 88–90, 282
Horton Hospital, Banbury, 360–61
Incinerators, 82–83, 87–88
Keighley, 159–61
Kendal Hospital, 131
Metropolitan Police (with Mayor of London), 217
parish councils, 212, 293
Royal Borough of Kensington and Chelsea, 342
TATA Steel, 250
Virgin Trains, 229–30
Warwickshire County Council, 314–15
wind farms, 49, 92
Withybush Hospital, Haverfordwest, 132
Public Sector Equality Duty (PSED), 34
purdah, 199–201, 205

Q

quality assurance, 225

R

redundancy / employee
    consultation, 250, 251
regional development agencies
    (RDAs), 74
Royal Society for the Protection
    of Birds (RSPB), 296

S

same-sex marriage, 218, 282
Sciencewise, 252–53, 253
Scottish independence
    referendum, 21, 65, 79
secondary consultation, 292,
    352
Sedley, Sir Stephen, 39–40, 41
Skeffington Report, 70
smoking, 231, 239–42
social media, 11, 82, 105, 157,
    200, 201, 203, 211, 213, 221,
    224, 267–70, 286, 297, 298,
    299, 302, 308, 333, 347
    Facebook, 156, 157, 267,
        286, 299, 302, 304
    Twitter, 157, 267, 269
stakeholder mapping, 179–80,
    235, 286
Starkey, Professor Ken, 147
Statement of Community
    Involvement, 78

sugar tax, 231, 242, 244
SumOfUs, 214
Sunningdale Institute, 147–48

T

Thompson, Mark, 263
tobacco industry, 231, 238–42
Today programme, 24, 242
trades unions, 231, 248, 250
Transparency International, 194
Transport for London (TfL),
    282–83
Trump, Donald, 195, 260–61,
    262, 263, 265

U

utilities, 225–28

V

Venice Commission, 363
voluntary bodies, 105, 134, 159,
    187, 189, 218, 221

W

Water Consumer Council, 225
water industry, 225–27
Welsh Government, 109, 133,
    322
West-Coast Main Line service,
    229–30
Wilcox, David, 60
World Bank, 12, 179, 372